T0214584

Lecture Notes in Computer Science 11174

Commenced Publication in 1973
Founding and Former Series Editors:
Gerhard Goos, Juris Hartmanis, and Jan van Leeuwen

Editorial Board

More information about this series at http://www.springer.com/series/7408

Jonathan P. Bowen · Zhiming Liu
Zili Zhang (Eds.)

Engineering Trustworthy Software Systems

Third International School, SETSS 2017
Chongqing, China, April 17–22, 2017
Tutorial Lectures

Springer

Editors
Jonathan P. Bowen (ID)
London South Bank University
London, UK

Zhiming Liu
Southwest University
Chongqing, China

Zili Zhang
Faculty of Computer and Information
Science
Southwest University
Chongqing, China

ISSN 0302-9743   ISSN 1611-3349   (electronic)
Lecture Notes in Computer Science
ISBN 978-3-030-02927-2   ISBN 978-3-030-02928-9   (eBook)
https://doi.org/10.1007/978-3-030-02928-9

Library of Congress Control Number: 2018958874

LNCS Sublibrary: SL2 – Programming and Software Engineering

This Springer imprint is published by the registered company Springer Nature Switzerland AG
The registered company address is: Gewerbestrasse 11, 6330 Cham, Switzerland

Preface

The Third School on Engineering Trustworthy Software Systems (SETSS 2017) was held during April 17–22, 2017, at Southwest University, Chongqing, China. It was aimed at Ph.D. and Master students, in particular, from around China, and was suitable for university researchers and industry software engineers. This volume contains tutorial papers related to most of the lecture courses delivered at the School.

SETSS 2017 was organized by the School of Computer and Information Science, in particular, the Centre for Research and Innovation in Software Engineering (RISE) at Southwest University, providing lectures on cutting-edge research in methods and tools for use in computer system engineering. The School aimed to enable participants to learn about state-of-the-art software engineering methods and technology advances from experts in the field.

The opening session was chaired by Prof. Zili Zhang. A welcome speech was delivered by the Vice President of Southwest University, Prof. Yanqiang Cui, followed by an introductory briefing for SETSS 2017 by Prof. Zhiming Liu. The session finished with a ceremony for a guest professorship at Southwest University for Prof. Zhou Chaochen and a photograph of participants at the School.

The following lectures courses (four 90-minute lecture sessions each) were delivered during the School:

- Ian Hayes: "Rely/Guarantee Thinking"
- Gary T. Leavens: "Hoare-Style Specification and Verification of Object-Oriented Programs with JML"
- Natarajan Shankar: "Logic, Specification, Verification, and Interactive Proof"
- Andreas Podelski: "Software Model Checking with Automizer"
- Rustan Leino: "Writing Programs and Proofs"
- Xiaoxing Ma: "Engineering Self-adaptive Software-intensive Systems"

  In addition, there were three evening seminars and a meeting on educational issues:

- Maarten de Rijke: "Agents that Get the Right Information to the Right People in the Right Way"
- Dang Van Hung: "A Model for Real-time Concurrent Interaction Protocols in Component Interfaces"
- Zijiang Yang: "Optimizing Symbolic Execution for Software Testing"
- Zhiming Liu (Chair): CCF Formal Methods Division Meeting – "Formal Methods Education"

  These additional presentations and discussions complemented the longer lecture courses.

Courses

Rely/Guarantee Thinking

Lecturer: Prof. Ian Hayes, University of Queensland, Australia

Biography: Ian Hayes is a Professor of Computer Science at the University of Queensland, Australia. His research interests focus on formal methods for the specification and development of software and systems. He has worked on the Z specification notation, and specification and refinement of real-time systems. His most recent research has focused on the specification and refinement of concurrent systems, along with an algebraic approach to defining its semantics with the aim of providing tool support.

Overview: The rely/guarantee approach to reasoning about a concurrent process makes the use of a rely condition to abstractly represent the assumptions the process makes about interference from its environment and a guarantee condition to represent the interference it imposes on its environment. The general view of rely/guarantee thinking appears to apply to a very wide range of applications: it facilitates the development and formal proof of intricate code — at the other extreme, it provides a framework for deriving the specification of control systems that respond to, and actuate, physical systems that interact with the physical world. In the last couple of years, the way of recording rely assumptions and guarantee commitments has been recast into a style similar to the refinement calculus. This results in a much more algebraic feel to reasoning about rely/guarantee thinking and the laws of this calculus were explained and demonstrated on examples.

Hoare-Style Specification and Verification of Object-Oriented Programs with JML

Lecturer: Prof. Gary T. Leavens, University of Central Florida, USA

Biography: Gary T. Leavens is a professor and chair of the department of Computer Science at the University of Central Florida. Previously he was a professor at Iowa State University, where he started in 1989, after receiving his Ph.D. from MIT. Before his graduate studies at MIT, he worked at Bell Telephone Laboratories in Denver, Colorado. Professor Leavens was General Chair for the SPLASH 2012 conference and Research Program Committee chair for the 2009 OOPSLA conference. He was the Research Results Program Committee chair for the Modularity 2015 conference.

Overview: These lectures addressed the problem of specification and verification of sequential object-oriented (OO) programs, which use subtyping and dynamic dispatch. First we described the semantics of class-based object-oriented languages with mutable objects, such as Java. Then we described the problems of applying Hoare-style reasoning to OO programs in a modular way. We look in detail at the key notions of refinement, modular verification, and modular correctness. This leads to a detailed discussion of behavioral subtyping and supertype abstraction. Finally we discussed specification inheritance, its relationship to behavioral subtyping, and how these concepts are embodied in JML.

Logic, Specification, Verification, and Interactive Proof

Lecturer: Prof. Natarajan Shankar, SRI International Computer Science Laboratory, USA

Biography: Prof. Natarajan Shankar is a Distinguished Scientist at the SRI International Computer Science Laboratory. He is the co-developer of a number of cutting-edge tools (http:github.com/SRI-CSL) for automated reasoning and formal verification spanning interactive proof (PVS), model checking (SAL), SMT solving (Yices), and probabilistic inference (PCE). Prof. Shankar is an SRI Fellow and a co-recipient of the 2012 CAV Award.

Overview: Formalization plays a key role in computing in disciplines ranging from hardware and distributed computing to programming languages and hybrid systems. In this course, we explore the use of SRI's Prototype Verification System (PVS, see http://pvs.csl.sri.com) in formal specification and interactive proof construction. PVS and other proof assistants, like ACL2, Coq, HOL, HOL Light, Isabelle, and Nuprl, have been used to formalize significant tracts of mathematics and verify complex hardware and software systems. In the lectures, we explored the formalization of both introductory and advanced concepts from mathematics and computing. We use PVS to interactively construct proofs and to define new proof strategies.

Software Model Checking with Automizer

Lecturer: Prof. Andreas Podelski, University of Freiburg, Germany

Biography: Prof. Andreas Podelski works in the area of programming languages, specifically, on program analysis and verification. He is an associate editor of the journals *ToPLaS, FMSD, JAR,* and *STTT.* He has served as the chair or as a member of the program committee of over 50 conferences and he has been the invited speaker at over 20 conferences. He did his Masters studies in Münster, Germany, his Ph.D. in Paris, France, and postdoctoral research in Berkeley, California, USA. He holds the Chair of Software Engineering at the University of Freiburg since 2006. He has spent sabbaticals for research at Microsoft Redmond, ENS Paris, Microsoft Cambridge, and Stanford Research Institute (SRI).

Overview: We presented a new approach to the verification of programs. The approach was embodied in the tool Automizer. Automizer won this year's gold medal at SV-Comp (the second time in a row). We were able to decompose the set of behaviors of the given program (whose correctness we wanted to prove) according to sets of behaviors for which we already had a proof. We were able to construct a program from the correctness proof of a sequence of statements. A sequence of statements is a simple case of a program (a straight-line program). At the same time, a sequence of statements is a word over a finite alphabet (a word that can be accepted by an automaton). Just as we asked whether a word had an accepting run, we were able to ask whether a sequence of statements had a correctness proof (of a certain form). The automaton accepted exactly the sequences that did. We constructed programs from proofs, repeatedly, until the constructed programs together covered all possible behaviors of the given program (whose correctness we wanted to prove). A crucial step here was the covering check. This step was based on algorithms for automata (inclusion test, minimization, etc.). We explained the approach for a wide range of verification problems: safety, termination, liveness; with (possibly recursive) procedures, multi-threaded, with possibly unboundedly many threads.

Writing Programs and Proofs

Lecturer: Dr. Rustan Leino, Amazon, USA

Biography: Rustan Leino is a senior principal engineer at Amazon Web Services. He was previously a principal researcher in the Research in Software Engineering (RiSE) group at Microsoft Research, Redmond, and has been a visiting professor in the Department of Computing at Imperial College London. He is known for his work on programming methods and program verification tools and is a world leader in building automated program verification tools. One of these tools is the language and verifier Dafny. Leino is an ACM Fellow. Prior to Microsoft Research, Leino worked at DEC/Compaq SRC. He received his Ph.D. from Caltech (1995), but before doing so, he already designed and wrote object-oriented software as a technical lead in the Windows NT group at Microsoft. Leino collects thinking puzzles on a popular web page and hosts the Verification Corner channel on YouTube.

Overview: Reasoning about programs and understanding how to write proofs are important skills for software engineers. In this course, students learned techniques of how to reason about programs, both imperative programs and functional programs. For imperative programs, this included the concepts of assertions, pre- and postconditions, and loop invariants. For functional programs, this additionally included lemmas, proof calculations, and mathematical induction. Throughout the course, the Dafny language and verifier was used.

Engineering Self-adaptive Software-Intensive Systems

Lecturer: Prof. Xiaoxing Ma, Nanjing University, China

Biography: Xiaoxing Ma is a professor and the deputy director of the Institute of Computer Software at Nanjing University. His research interests include self-adaptive software systems, software architectures, and middleware systems. Xiaoxing co-authored more than 60 peer-reviewed papers, some of which were published in major software engineering conferences and journals, such as *FSE, ICSE, ASE* and *IEEE TSE, TC, TPDS*. He has directed and participated in over a dozen research projects funded by the National Natural Science Foundation and the Ministry of Science and Technology of China. He has also served actively in technical program committees of various international conferences and workshops.

Overview: Modern software-intensive systems often need to dynamically adapt to the changes in the environment in which they are embedded and to the requirements they must satisfy. Engineering self-adaptation in software is challenging due to the lack of systematic engineering methods and proper enabling techniques. In this tutorial, we discussed some recent advances in software engineering for self-adaptive systems, with topics covering the sensing and understanding of systems' environmental context, the model-based and control theory-based approaches to adaptation decision making, and the actuation of adaptation decisions through dynamic software updating.

Seminars

Agents that Get the Right Information to the Right People in the Right Way

Lecturer: Prof. Maarten de Rijke, University of Amsterdam, The Netherlands

Biography: Maarten de Rijke, professor at the University of Amsterdam, The Netherlands, leads the prestigious Information Language Processing and System (ILPS) laboratory in the field of information retrieval. He has published more than 670 articles in the top conferences and journals of information retrieval, machine learning, natural language processing and data mining, including *SIGIR (CCF A), WWW (CCF A), KDD (CCF A), ICML (CCF) CCF A), NIPS (CCF A), ACL (CCF A), WSDM (CCF B), CIKM (CCF B), ACM* Transactions on Information Systems *(TOIS, CCF A)* and *IEEE* Transactions on Knowledge and Data Engineering *(TKDE, CCF A)*. Especially in the field of expert finding, online learning, modal logic, and community-based answering. According to the Google Scholar, he has over 20,000 citations and an *h-index* of 65. Professor Maarten de Rijke has served as chairman of the conference or program committee for various meetings in the field of information retrieval, including *SIGIR, WWW, WSDM* and *CIKM*. He is currently the director of the Amsterdam Data Science Center and the director of the Ad de Jonge Intelligence and Safety Center in the Netherlands, as well as the director of the Master of Artificial Intelligence program at the University of Amsterdam. Professor Maarten de Rijke is also the editor-in-chief of several top journals in the field of information retrieval and information systems, including *ACM Transactions on Information Systems (TOIS CCF A)*.

Abstract: Interaction with information is a fundamental activity of the human condition. Interactions with search systems play an important role in the daily activities of many people, so as to inform their decisions and guide their actions. For many years, the field of IR has accepted "the provision of relevant documents" as the goal of its most fundamental algorithms. The focus of the field is shifting towards algorithms that are able to get the right information to the right people in the right way. Artificial intelligence (AI) is entering a new golden age. How can these advances help information retrieval? That is, how can AI help to develop agents that get the right information to the people in the right way? Making search results as useful as possible may be easy for some search tasks, but in many cases it depends on the context, such as a user's background knowledge, age, or location, or their specific search goals. Addressing each optimal combination of search result preferences individually is not feasible. Instead, we need to look for scalable methods that can learn good search results without expensive tuning. In recent years, there has been significant work on developing methods for a range of IR problems that learn directly from natural interactions with their users. In the talk, I sampled from these advances and hinted at future directions.

A Model for Real-time Concurrent Interaction Protocols in Component Interfaces

Lecturer: Dang Van Hung, Vietnam National University, Vietnam

Biography: Dang Van Hung graduated in Mathematics in 1977 at the Department of Mathematics, Hanoi University, Hanoi, Vietnam, and obtained his PhD degree in Computer Science in 1988 at the Computer and Automation Research Institute, Hungarian Academy of Sciences, Budapest, Hungary. He began his career as a research fellow at the Institute of Information Technology, Hanoi, Vietnam. He was a research fellow at the United Nations University, International Institute for Software Technology, located in Macao for more than 12 years. Since 2008, he is a senior lecturer of the University of Engineering and Technology of Vietnam National University in Hanoi. He has been actively involved in many scientific activities such as organising international conferences, editing books and journals. His research interests include formal methods, real-time, parallel and distributed systems, component-based software development.

Abstract: Interaction Protocol specification is an important part for component interface specification. To use a component, the environment must conform to the interaction protocol specified in the interface of the component. We gave a powerful technique to specify protocols which can capture the constraints on temporal order, concurrency, and timing. We also showed that the problem of checking if a timed automaton conforms to a given real-time protocol is decidable and developed a decision procedure for solving the problem.

Optimizing Symbolic Execution for Software Testing

Lecturer: Prof. Zijiang Yang, Western Michigan University, USA

Biography: Zijiang Yang is a professor of Computer Science at Western Michigan University. His research is in the broad areas of software engineering and formal methods. The primary focus is to develop formal method based tools to support the debugging, analysis, and verification of complex systems. He has published over 70 papers, many of which were published in major software engineering conferences and journals such as *FSE, ICSE, ASE, ICST, CAV* and *TSE*. He is also an inventor of ten United States patents. Yang received his Ph.D. from the University of Pennsylvania.

Abstract: Symbolic execution is a powerful technique for systematically exploring the paths of a program and generating the corresponding test inputs. However, its practical usage is often limited by the path explosion problem, that is, the number of explored paths usually grows exponentially with the increase of program size. We proposed new symbolic execution approaches to mitigate the path explosion problem by predicting and eliminating the redundant paths based on symbolic values in the context of software testing.

From the lectures, a record of the School has been distilled in five chapters within this volume as follows:

- Ian J. Hayes and Cliff B. Jones: "A Guide to Rely/Guarantee Thinking"
- Gary T. Leavens and David A. Naumann: "An Illustrated Guide to the Model Theory of Supertype Abstraction and Behavioral Subtyping"
- Natarajan Shankar: "Formalizing Hoare Logic in PVS"
- K. Rustan M. Leino: "Modeling Concurrency in Dafny"
- Xiaoxing Ma, Tianxiao Gu, and Wei Song: "Software Is Not Soft: Challenges and Approaches to Dynamic Software Update"

An additional contribution by Cliff Jones (co-author with Ian Hayes above) was also included. This is a lecture that would have been delivered had Cliff Jones also attended the School. It is a tutorial paper on the formal semantics of programming languages that is co-authored with his PhD student Troy Astarte:

- Cliff B. Jones and Troy K. Astarte: "Challenges for Formal Semantic Description: Responses from the Main Approaches"

For further information on SETSS 2017, including lecture material, see: http://www.swu-rise.net.cn/SETSS2017

Acknowledgments: SETSS 2017 was supported by IFIP Working Group 2.3 on Programming Methodology. The aim of WG 2.3 is to increase a programers' ability to compose programs, which fits very well with SETSS. Several of the lecturers at SETSS 2017 are members of WG 2.3 and they are very pleased to have the opportunity to support the training of researchers and engineers.

We would like to thank the lecturers and their co-authors for their professional commitment and effort, the strong support of Southwest University, and the enthusiastic work of the local organization team, without which SETSS 2017 would not have been possible. Finally, we are grateful for the support of Alfred Hofmann and Anna Kramer of Springer *Lecture Notes in Computer Science* (LNCS) in the publication of this volume.

July 2018   Jonathan P. Bowen
                                                                        Zhiming Liu
                                                                        Zili Zhang

Group photograph at SETSS 2017. Front row, left to right: Zhiming Liu, Yongjun Jin, Dang Van Hung, Gary Leavens, Chaochen Zhou, Yangian Cui, Ian Hayes, Zili Zhang, Guoqiang Xiao, Wu Chen

Selected lecturers and attendees at SETSS 2017. Left to right: Shmuel Tyszberowicz, Ian Hayes, Rustan Leino, Natarajan Shankar, Gary Leavens, Zhiming Liu, Zhibin Yang, Guisen Wu.

Organization

School Chairs

Zhiming Liu   Southwest University, China
Zili Zhang   Southwest University, China

Academic Instructors

Jonathan P. Bowen   RISE, Southwest University, China,
                            and London South Bank University, UK
Zhiming Liu   RISE, Southwest University, China

Local Organization Committee

Huazhen Liang (Chair)   Southwest University, China
Bo Liu (Chair)   Southwest University, China
Xiao Qin   Southwest University, China
Zhisai Shi   Southwest University, China
Qing Wang   Southwest University, China
Tingting Zhang   Southwest University, China
Yukun Zhang   Southwest University, China
Hengjun Zhao   Southwest University, China

School Academic Committee

Michael Butler   University of Southampton, UK
Yixiang Chen   East China Normal University, China
Zhi Jin   Peking University, China
Zhiming Liu   Southwest University, China
Cong Tian   Xi'Dian University, China
Ji Wang   National University of Defence Science
                            and Technology, China
Yi Wang   Uppsala University, Sweden,
                            and Northeast University, China
Jim Woodcock   University of York, UK
Jianhua Zhao   Nanjing University, China

Reviewers

Jonathan P. Bowen   RISE, Southwest University, China,
                            and London South Bank University, UK
Ian J. Hayes   University of Queensland, Australia

Cliff B. Jones   Newcastle University, UK
K. Rustan M. Leino   Amazon, USA
Zhiming Liu   RISE, Southwest University, China
Natarajan Shankar   SRI International Computer Science Laboratory, USA
Shmuel Tyszberowicz   RISE, Southwest University, China,
                              and Tel Aviv University, Israel
Mark Utting   University of the Sunshine Coast, Australia

Contents

A Guide to Rely/Guarantee Thinking

Ian J. Hayes[1]([✉])ⓘ and Cliff B. Jones[2]ⓘ

[1] School of Information Technology and Electrical Engineering,
The University of Queensland, Brisbane, Australia
Ian.Hayes@uq.edu.au
[2] School of Computing Science, Newcastle University, Newcastle upon Tyne, UK

Abstract. Designing concurrent shared-variable programs is difficult. The Rely-Guarantee concept provides a compositional approach to the challenge. This paper reviews some recent developments in the approach, offers worked examples and relates the approach to other research.

1 Introduction

This paper provides a guide to one of the approaches to reasoning about the design of concurrent programs. The focus is on the interference that occurs when concurrent threads access and update shared variables. The so-called "Rely/Guarantee" (R/G) approach records such interference in specifications and provides rules for reasoning about the coherence of different levels of abstraction thus making the ideas useful in formally justifying program designs. In a sense that is made precise below, such development steps can be made "compositional".

The sense in which this paper provides a "guide" is that the origins and recent developments of the approach are set out together with a number of illustrative examples. This section outlines the general R/G idea; Sect. 2 presents a number of general laws; Sects. 3 and 4 present worked examples. The concluding Sect. 5 of the paper relates R/G to other approaches.

1.1 Interference

Sequential (or non-concurrent) programs begin execution in some starting state and make changes to that state. Crucially, the designer of such a program can assume that no changes to the state are made by an external agent during execution of the sequential code.

It is precisely *interference* with the state that makes it difficult to construct and reason about *concurrent* programs. When thinking about the development of concurrent programs, it is useful to distinguish one component and its (entire)

This work was supported by Australian Research Council (ARC) Discovery Project DP130102901 and the UK EPSRC "Taming Concurrency" and "Strata" research grants.

J. P. Bowen et al. (Eds.): SETSS 2017, LNCS 11174, pp. 1–38, 2018.
https://doi.org/10.1007/978-3-030-02928-9_1

environment but this initial motivation can be made clearer by assuming that there are only two processes that can interact. Assume that P and Q share one variable x and:

- Process Q may do atomic steps that either
  - do not change x, i.e. $x' = x$, where x stands for the initial value of the variable x and x' its final value, or
  - increment x by one, i.e. $x' = x + 1$
- Before or after each atomic step of process P, P may observe
  - no steps of Q, i.e. $x' = x$
  - one step of Q, i.e. $x' = x \lor x' = x + 1$
  - many steps of Q, i.e. $x \leq x'$
- Observe that both $x' = x$ and $x' = x + 1$ imply $x \leq x'$
- Hence we can use $x \leq x'$ to represent the possible interference from Q on P

This abstract view of the interference can be recorded with rely and guarantee conditions:

- a *rely* condition of P
- a *guarantee* condition of Q

The assumption that P and Q share only one variable can be recorded as part of the specification of each thread.

Specifications of sequential code are normally given using pre and post conditions. Few programs will achieve a useful effect in arbitrary starting states and a pre condition is a record of assumptions that the designer of a program can make about the states in which the program will begin execution. In the same way, almost no concurrent program could achieve a useful effect in the presence of arbitrary state changes during its execution and the rely condition invites the designer to assume limitations on the potential interference. With both pre and rely conditions, it is the obligation of the designer of the context to check that the assumptions hold. In contrast, a post condition relation expresses the expected behaviour of a program and is thus an obligation on the behaviour of the code to be created. The same applies to guarantee conditions.

To be useful in a design and development process, an important property of a formal system is that it is *compositional*. This idea is first explained in terms of sequential program constructs. The advantage of abstracting a specification as a post condition is that the relation expresses all that the code to be developed is required to achieve; no details of the internal execution are dictated; any implementation that always achieves the required relation is deemed to be acceptable. Furthermore, if a design decision is made to achieve some given post condition q by using the sequential composition of two sub-programs $s_1; s_2$, the correctness of such a step can be argued solely in terms of the specifications of s_1 and s_2 (and subsequent development of each sub component can ignore both the specification of its sibling and that of its parent q).

The possibility of interference is precisely what makes it difficult to achieve useful compositional methods for concurrent programs. Willem-Paul de Roever's extensive study of compositional and non-compositional methods [dR01] reviews how early approaches such as Susan Owicki's [Owi75] fall short because of the need for a final global check on the combined threads. A key claim for R/G approaches is that, for a large class of shared-variable concurrent programs, using rely and guarantee conditions offers a compositional approach. Thus a design that satisfies a specification given as pre/rely/guarantee/post conditions will not be rejected as a result of a *post facto* check.

1.2   The Basis of Rely/Guarantee Thinking

As indicated above, the rely/guarantee approach explicitly addresses interference both in the specification and design processes. Executions of concurrent programs can be pictured as traces of the sequence of states that arise. An execution trace starts in an initial state σ_0 (that satisfies $pre(\sigma_0)$) and ends in σ_f (that paired with the starting state should satisfy the postcondition $post(\sigma_0, \sigma_f)$).

$$\overbrace{\sigma_0}^{pre} \quad \cdots \quad \overbrace{\epsilon(\sigma_i\ \sigma_{i+1})}^{rely} \quad \cdots \quad \underbrace{\pi(\sigma_j\ \sigma_{j+1})}_{guar} \quad \cdots \quad \sigma_f$$

$$\underbrace{\phantom{\sigma_0 \cdots \epsilon(\sigma_i\ \sigma_{i+1}) \cdots \pi(\sigma_j\ \sigma_{j+1}) \cdots \sigma_f}}_{post}$$

For concurrent threads, it is necessary to distinguish environment steps $\epsilon(\sigma_i\ \sigma_{i+1})$ from program steps $\pi(\sigma_i\ \sigma_{i+1})$. The designer of a thread can assume that:

- the initial state satisfies the precondition *pre*
- any environment step satisfies the rely condition *rely*

Under those assumptions, the commitment is that the code created must:

- terminate in a final state that is related to its initial state by *post*
- every program step satisfies the guarantee condition *guar*

A *rely* condition is an abstraction of the interference to be tolerated. Note that the use of *relations* is key to the rely/guarantee approach.

Given that there are four predicates and the *frame* of variables that can be accessed/changed to be specified, it is necessary to adopt a format for R/G specifications. It is worth emphasising that there are various layouts (concrete syntax) for the same underlying concepts. Early papers [Jon81, Jon83a, Jon83b] followed the VDM keyword style. To take the example from Sect. 3, the task of removing all of the composite numbers (abbreviated C) from a set might be presented as follows:

$$Sieve(n : \mathbb{N})$$

ext wr $s : \mathbb{F}\,\mathbb{N}$

pre $s \subseteq 0 \mathbin{..} n$

rely $s' \subseteq s$

guar $s' \subseteq s \wedge s - s' \subseteq C$

post $s' \cap C = \emptyset$

Comparison with a specification for a sequential version of *Sieve* is instructive. If there were no interference, the post condition could be given as an equality $s' = s - C$. In the presence of interference, the post condition provides a lower bound on the removal $s' \cap C = \emptyset$; the upper bound of the elements that can be removed goes into the guarantee condition $s - s' \subseteq C$. The rely condition (which is also the other conjunct of the guarantee condition) is essential in the subsequent development.

In order to present proof rules for R/G specifications, it proved to be convenient to adopt a more compact concrete syntax than the keyword style; this can be done by extending Floyd/Hoare [Flo67, Hoa69] triples to write:

$$\{p, r\}\; s\; \{g, q\} \tag{1}$$

The key proof obligation about concurrent threads can then be written:

$$
\begin{array}{c}
\{p, r_l\}\; s_l\; \{g_l, q_l\} \\
\{p, r_r\}\; s_r\; \{g_r, q_r\} \\
r \vee g_r \Rrightarrow r_l \\
r \vee g_l \Rrightarrow r_r \\
g_l \vee g_r \Rrightarrow g \\
p \wedge q_l \wedge q_r \wedge (r \vee g_l \vee g_r)^* \Rrightarrow q
\end{array}
$$

$$\boxed{\text{Par-I}} \rule{5cm}{0.4pt}$$

$$\{p, r\}\; s_l \parallel s_r\; \{g, q\}$$

As pointed out, the underlying idea ("rely/guarantee thinking") is the important concept; the specific concrete syntax to be used should be a matter of convenience. Section 1.4 offers a markedly different style but, despite this new format, the keyword presentation is in fact useful for long specifications and is used in several publications.

1.3   Data Abstraction

The use of abstract objects is important for the specification of any non-trivial computer system. Fortunately, the proof steps for data reification are compositional in the same way as (and work together with) those that deal with decomposition using programming constructs.

Data abstraction has a particularly strong role in the specification and design of concurrent programs. As is illustrated below in the examples considered in Sects. 3 and 4, an abstraction can yield a clear description of a problem that can only yield an efficient implementation by choosing a clever representation. In the *Sieve* example (Sect. 3), the specification in terms of sets of natural numbers is brief and intuitive and the choice to reify this to a vector of bits affords a natural way of ensuring the monotonic reduction of the set. The fact that a machine is likely to read and write multiple bits in a single operation presents an interesting challenge that is resolved in Sect. 3.5 using a compare-and-swap instruction.

A further important use of abstraction manifests itself in the development of "Simpson's four slot" implementation of an "asynchronous communication mechanism": a shared data structure is used in [JH16]; because the reader and writer processes both access it, this abstract object appears to be subject to data races but the development can partition which sub-parts of the shared object are being used by the two processes at any point in time. The final data-race-freedom property on the individual "slots" –that is the clever part of Hugo Simpson's design– is thus justified at a level of abstraction where the argument is clearest.

Data abstraction and reification sit perfectly with rely/guarantee thinking. A further interesting link to Separation Logic [O'H07] is made in [JY15]—this point is explored in Sect. 5.

1.4 Pulling Apart the Old R/G Notation

Much research has been built on the original R/G ideas: over 20 PhDs more or less directly contribute extensions; the ideas are also often used in conjunction with other approaches including Separation Logic (e.g. [BA10, BA13]).

Recently, new presentations of R/G specifications have been proposed. It is shown in [HJC14, JH16] how a refinement calculus [BvW98, Mor90] specification can be qualified by rely or guarantee clauses of the form (**rely** $r \bullet c$) and (**guar** $g \bullet c$), where c is an arbitrary command. The specification of *Sieve* in Sect. 1.2 becomes:

$$(\textbf{guar } s' \subseteq s \land s - s' \subseteq C \bullet$$
$$(\textbf{rely } s' \subseteq s \bullet$$
$$s : \left[s \subseteq 0 \mathbin{..} n, \ s' \cap C = \emptyset \right]))$$

Although this can be viewed as an alternative concrete syntax for the original specification, this style lends itself to exploring algebraic properties of the operators such as distribution of guarantee conditions over sequential and parallel constructs (see Sect. 2). The algebraic ideas are taken further in [HCM+16] where relies and guarantees are represented as separate commands (**rely** r) and (**guar** g) which are combined with other constructs using a new weak conjunction operator "⋓".[1] That facilitates proofs of some properties at a significantly more abstract level. In the new form the specification of *Sieve* becomes:

$$(\textbf{rely } s' \subseteq s) \Cap (\textbf{guar } s' \subseteq s \land s - s' \subseteq C) \Cap \{s \subseteq 0 \mathbin{..} n\} ; s : \left[s' \cap C = \emptyset \right]$$

A crucial advantage of the newer presentations of rely and guarantee conditions is that they expose the algebraic properties of the components of specifications. In particular, it makes it possible to express properties of each construct as well as their combinations.

---

[1] This operator was originally devised by us to allow guarantees to be expressed as a separate command, which is then combined with the rest of the specification using weak conjunction. Weak conjunction has since found wider use as a general composition operator.

2 Laws

This section presents an overview of the laws used in the examples; the reader is expected to refer back to these laws when trying to comprehend the examples in Sects. 3 or 4. Any reader who is unfamiliar with R/G might benefit from scanning one of the examples in Sects. 3 or 4 before digesting the laws in this section.

As a notational convention throughout this section, p is used for a predicate characterising a set of states, g, q and r are used for predicates characterising relations between states, and c and d are used for commands. Subscripted versions of these names follow the same convention.

2.1   Refinement

The approach presented here is based on the refinement calculus [BvW98, Mor90] in which the fact that command c is refined (or implemented) by d is written $c \sqsubseteq d$. An operator is *monotonic with respect to refinement* if refining one operand of the operator refines the whole. The operators sequential composition $(\,;\,)$, parallel composition $(\|)$, and weak conjunction $(\Cap)$, explained below, are all monotonic in both arguments.

Law 1 (monotonicity). *If $c_0 \sqsubseteq c_1 \wedge d_0 \sqsubseteq d_1$ all the following hold.*

$$c_0 \,;\, d_0 \;\sqsubseteq\; c_1 \,;\, d_1 \tag{2}$$

$$c_0 \parallel d_0 \;\sqsubseteq\; c_1 \parallel d_1 \tag{3}$$

$$c_0 \Cap d_0 \;\sqsubseteq\; c_1 \Cap d_1 \tag{4}$$

Note that as refinement is reflexive, i.e. $c \sqsubseteq c$ for any c; the above law can be applied when just the first (or just the second) operand is refined.

2.2   Pre Conditions and Post Conditions

The sequential refinement calculus [BvW98, Mor90] makes use of an assertion (or pre condition) command $\{p\}$ and a specification (or post condition) command $\lceil q \rfloor$ to express a pre-post specification as the sequential composition $\{p\} \,;\, \lceil q \rfloor$, in which p is a predicate characterising a set of states and q is a predicate characterising a relation between a pair of (before and after) states. The pre condition $\{p\}$ represents an assumption that the initial state satisfies p. If p holds in the initial state, $\{p\}$ acts as the **nil** command and hence has no effect; but, if p does not hold in the initial state, any behaviour at all is allowed; thus $\{p\}$ behaves like **abort**, the command that allows any behaviour whatsoever and is strict in the sense that **abort** ; $c = $ **abort** for any command c and hence one cannot recover from aborting.

The basic laws regarding pre condition and post condition specifications from the sequential refinement calculus are still valid in the concurrent refinement calculus. It is a refinement to assume less about the initial state, i.e. weaken the pre condition, and the ultimate weakening is to {true}, which is equivalent to **nil** and hence corresponds to removing the pre condition.

Law 2 (weaken-pre). *If $p_1 \Rrightarrow p_2$, then $\{p_1\} \sqsubseteq \{p_2\}$.*

Law 3 (remove-pre). $\{p\} ; c \sqsubseteq c$.

It is a refinement to produce a subset of the behaviours of a specification command, which corresponds to strengthening the post condition, but in doing so one can assume the pre condition holds initially.

Law 4 (strengthen-post-pre). *If $p \wedge q_2 \Rrightarrow q_1$, then $\{p\} ; \left[q_1 \right] \sqsubseteq \{p\} ; \left[q_2 \right]$.*

A post condition specification that takes the form of the relational composition $q_1 \,\fatsemi\, q_2$ of two relations can be decomposed into a sequential composition of two specifications, the first satisfying q_1 and the second q_2. In addition, if the first establishes p_1 in the final state, represented here by p_1', the second may assume p_1 as a pre condition.

Law 5 (sequential). $\left[q_1 \,\fatsemi\, q_2 \right] \sqsubseteq \left[q_1 \wedge p_1' \right] ; \{p_1\} ; \left[q_2 \right]$.

2.3   Concurrent Specifications

To express concurrent specifications, two additional commands, **rely** r and **guar** g, are used, in which both r and g are predicates characterising a relation between a pair of states. A concurrent specification can then be written in the form

$$(\textbf{rely } r) \Cap (\textbf{guar } g) \Cap \{p\} ; \left[q \right]$$

in which $\Cap$ is the weak conjunction operator defined so that behaviours of $c \Cap d$ are the common behaviours of c and d unless either c or d aborts, in which case $c \Cap d$ aborts. Weak conjunction is associative, commutative and idempotent; it has identity **chaos**, the command that allows any non-aborting behaviour.

2.4   Rely Conditions

A rely command **rely** r represents an assumption that all environment steps satisfy r. It aborts if any atomic environment step does not satisfy r in the same way that a pre condition $\{p\}$ aborts if the state does not satisfy p. A rely combined with a command, i.e. $(\textbf{rely } r) \Cap c$, behaves as c unless its environment makes a step that does not satisfy r, in which case the rely command aborts and hence the whole command $(\textbf{rely } r) \Cap c$ aborts. A weak (rather than strong) conjunction is essential here to allow the aborting behaviour of the rely to be promoted to aborting behaviour of the whole command. Note that a strong conjunction would mask the aborting behaviour of the rely if c by itself was non-aborting.

The basic laws for relies mimic those for pre conditions: one can assume less about the environment (i.e. a rely can be weakened) and the ultimate weakening is to remove the rely altogether because (**rely** true) = **chaos**, which is the identity of ⋒.

Law 6 (weaken-rely). *If $r_1 \Rrightarrow r_2$, then* (**rely** r_1) $\sqsubseteq$ (**rely** r_2).

Law 7 (remove-rely). (**rely** r) ⋒ $c \sqsubseteq c$.

A rely applied to a sequential composition effectively applies the rely to each statement in the composition, and hence if one, c_2, is refined to d in a rely context of r, the whole is refined by replacing c_2 by d. Taking either c_1 or c_3 as **nil** gives the special cases of refining the first or last commands in a sequence.

Law 8 (refine-within-rely). *If* (**rely** r) ⋒ $c_2 \sqsubseteq$ (**rely** r) ⋒ d,

$$(\textbf{rely } r) ⋒ c_1 ; c_2 ; c_3 \sqsubseteq (\textbf{rely } r) ⋒ c_1 ; d ; c_3.$$

2.5   Guarantee Conditions

A guarantee command (**guar** g) allows any non-aborting behaviour in which all atomic program steps satisfy g between their before and after states. A guarantee combined with a command, i.e. (**guar** g) ⋒ c, only allows behaviours of c in which all program steps satisfy g unless c aborts in which case (**guar** g) ⋒ c aborts. Again a weak (rather than strong) conjunction is essential to ensure that the guarantee command, which never aborts, does not mask any aborting behaviour of c, for example, c may contain a failing pre or rely condition.

In the same way that strengthening a post condition restricts the allowed behaviours and hence is a refinement, strengthening a guarantee is also a refinement. It is also a refinement to introduce a guarantee because the weakest guarantee, (**guar** true), equals **chaos**, the identity of ⋒.

Law 9 (strengthen-guar). *If $g_2 \Rrightarrow g_1$, then* (**guar** g_1) $\sqsubseteq$ (**guar** g_2).

Law 10 (introduce-guar). $c \sqsubseteq$ (**guar** g) ⋒ c.

Conjoining two guarantees requires every program step to satisfy both guarantees and hence the guarantees can be merged to give a guarantee satisfying both guarantees.

Law 11 (merge-guars). (**guar** g_1) ⋒ (**guar** g_2) = (**guar** $g_1 \wedge g_2$).

A guarantee distributes into a sequential composition or parallel composition, regardless of whether the latter is a binary parallel or a multiway parallel.

Law 12 (distrib-guar-sequential).
(**guar** g) ⋒ $(c ; d) \sqsubseteq$ ((**guar** g) ⋒ c); ((**guar** g) ⋒ d).

Law 13 (distrib-guar-parallel).
(**guar** g) ⋒ $(c \parallel d) \sqsubseteq$ ((**guar** g) ⋒ c) $\parallel$ ((**guar** g) ⋒ d).

Law 14 (distrib-guar-multi-parallel). (**guar** g) ⋒ $\parallel_i c_i \sqsubseteq \parallel_i$((**guar** g) ⋒ c_i).

2.6 Frames

The sequential refinement calculus makes use of a frame, a set of variables x that are allowed to be modified; all other variables must remain unchanged. In a sequential setting, the implied post condition that the final value of such variables is the same as their initial values would not preclude them being changed providing their initial values were reestablished. In the context of concurrency, a frame of x forbids any atomic program step to modify any variables other than x. If we let $id(y)$ stand for the relation constraining all variables in y to be unchanged, and $\overline{x}$ to stand for the set of all variables other than x, then $id(\overline{x})$ represents the relation constraining all variables other than x to be unchanged. To impose that constraint on all program steps one can use a guarantee of the form $(\mathbf{guar}\, id(\overline{x}))$ and hence to constrain any command c to not modify variables other than x, one can use $(\mathbf{guar}\, id(\overline{x})) \Cap c$. We introduce the abbreviation $x : c$ for this.

$$x : c \mathrel{\widehat{=}} (\mathbf{guar}\, id(\overline{x})) \Cap c \tag{5}$$

For example, a specification command $\left[q\right]$ with a frame of x is expressed as $x{:}\left[q\right]$, in the syntax of Morgan's sequential refinement calculus [Mor90]. Note that a specification with an empty frame is written $\emptyset{:}\left[q\right]$ and hence corresponds to $(\mathbf{guar}\, id) \Cap \left[q\right]$, which constrains all program steps to not modify any program variables, i.e. all program steps are stuttering or idle steps. Restricting a frame is a refinement because it strengthens the implicit guarantee of the frame.

Law 15 (restrict-frame). *For sets of variables X and Y, if $Y \subseteq X$, then $X : c \sqsubseteq Y : c$.*

Laws for a command c can be promoted to laws for a command with a frame $x : c$ by expanding $x : c$ to $(\mathbf{guar}\, id(\overline{x})) \Cap c$, applying the law (assuming it does not affect the guarantee) to give $\mathbf{guar}\, id(\overline{x})) \Cap c_1$ and then abbreviating that to $x : c_1$. In particular, laws for specifications of the form $\left[q\right]$ can be promoted to laws for framed specifications $x{:}\left[q\right]$ in this manner. This paper does not give the promoted laws explicitly but we assume all laws are promoted in this fashion and implicitly make use of the promoted versions while quoting the un-promoted law.

2.7 Introducing a Parallel Composition

The *raison d'être* for rely and guarantee conditions is to provide a law that allows a specification that is the conjunction of two post conditions to be decomposed into a parallel composition with each branch achieving one of the post conditions. The first branch relies on the interference from the second branch being bounded by r_1 and hence the second branch needs to guarantee its program steps guarantee r_1. Symmetrically, the second branch assumes interference from the first is bounded by r_2 and hence the first branch needs to guarantee its program steps guarantee r_2. Both branches also need to allow interference from the environment of the whole, which is bounded by r.

Law 16 (introduce-parallel)

$$(\textbf{rely } r) \Cap \left[q_1 \wedge q_2\right] \sqsubseteq ((\textbf{rely } r \vee r_1) \Cap (\textbf{guar } r_2) \Cap \left[q_1\right]) \parallel$$
$$((\textbf{rely } r \vee r_2) \Cap (\textbf{guar } r_1) \Cap \left[q_2\right])$$

While the binary version of parallel introduction (above) allows asymmetric relies and guarantees, the multiway version (below) is normally used where the guarantees of all the component processes are the same. The interference on each component process is either from the environment of the whole and satisfies r, or from some other process in the set and satisfies r_1.

Law 17 (introduce-multi-parallel). *For a finite index set I,*

$$(\textbf{rely } r) \Cap \left[\textstyle\bigwedge_{i \in I} q_i\right] \sqsubseteq \parallel_{i \in I} (\textbf{guar } r_1) \Cap (\textbf{rely } r \vee r_1) \Cap \left[q_i\right].$$

2.8   Trading Law

If every program step made by a command satisfies g and every environment step is assumed to satisfy r, then every step satisfies $r \vee g$, and hence if the command terminates after a finite number of steps, end-to-end it will satisfy the reflexive, transitive closure of $r \vee g$, i.e. $(r \vee g)^*$. Hence a specification command with a post condition of q in the context of a rely of r and a guarantee g is equivalent to a specification command with a post condition of $(r \vee g)^* \wedge q$.

Law 18 (trading).

$$(\textbf{rely } r) \Cap (\textbf{guar } g) \Cap \left[q\right] = (\textbf{rely } r) \Cap (\textbf{guar } g) \Cap \left[(r \vee g)^* \wedge q\right].$$

2.9   Interference on Predicates and Expressions

A pre condition p may hold initially but, before a command has a chance to do any program steps, the environment may execute some steps which may invalidate p. To avoid such issues one needs to use predicates that are stable under interference satisfying the rely condition r.

Definition 1 (stable). *A predicate p characterising a set of states is stable under r iff $r \Rightarrow (p \Rightarrow p')$.*

When dealing with post conditions of two states, it is advantageous to use a post condition q that is unaffected by interference occurring before the initial state or after the final state. Further, if the initial state satisfies a pre condition p, it can be taken into account.

Definition 2 (tolerates). *A predicate q characterising a relation between a pair of states* tolerates *interference r from p iff p is stable under r and both*

$$p \wedge (r \,\fatsemi\, q) \Rrightarrow q$$
$$p \wedge (q \,\fatsemi\, r) \Rrightarrow q.$$

If these conditions hold, $p \wedge (r^* \,\fatsemi\, q \,\fatsemi\, r^*) \Rrightarrow q$.

If an expression is evaluated under interference from its environment, the values of the variables in the expression may change between accesses to those variables. To handle this, two restricted forms of expressions are used: constant expressions and single-reference expressions. An expression that is constant under interference r evaluates to the same value before and after the interference.

Definition 3 (constant-expression). *An expression e is constant under interference r iff $r \Rrightarrow (e = e')$, where e' stands for the evaluation of e in the final state.*

For example, both $x + x$ and $2 * x$ are constant under interference satisfying $x' = x$, and $x - x$ is constant under any interference. A less obvious example is that $x \bmod N$ is constant under interference that adds multiples of N to x.

Note that the definition of a constant expression only considers evaluating the whole of the expression in a single state, either the initial or final state; however, an expression like $x - x$ may evaluate to a non-zero value if the two accesses to x take place in states in which x is different. The other special class of expression is a single-reference expression, which means that the evaluation of the expression corresponds to its value in one single state during the expression's evaluation. For example, $2 * x$ is single reference but $x + x$ is not and neither is $x - x$.

Definition 4 (single-reference-expression). *An expression e is single reference under interference r iff e is*

- *a constant,*
- *a variable and access to the variable is atomic,*
- *a unary expression $\ominus e$ and e is single reference, or*
- *a binary expression $e_1 \oplus e_2$ and both e_1 and e_2 are single reference under r and either e_1 and e_2 is constant under r.*

Below, accesses to variables are assumed to be atomic, unless they are vectors. If an expression is both constant and single reference then its evaluation under interference corresponds to its value in any of the states during its evaluation. That means there is no interference on its evaluation.

2.10 Introducing an Atomic Step

An atomic step command $\langle p, q \rangle$ represents a command that performs a single atomic step satisfying q from a state satisfying p and aborts from states not satisfying p. The atomic step may be preceded or followed by a finite number of stuttering steps that do not change the state. Note that $\langle p, q \rangle$ is not the same as $\{p\};\langle \text{true}, q \rangle$ because in the latter p is evaluated in the initial state σ_0 whereas in the former p is evaluated in a state σ just before the atomic step satisfying q and there may be environment steps in between that change σ_0 to σ. An atomic step command is used to define a compare-and-swap primitive used in the example in Sect. 3. A specification can be refined to an atomic step that satisfies both the guarantee and the postcondition. The guarantee must be reflexive to allow for any stuttering steps made by $\langle p, g \wedge q \rangle$.

Law 19 (introduce-atomic). *If p is stable under r, g is reflexive and q tolerates r from p,*

$$(\mathbf{guar}\ g) \Cap (\mathbf{rely}\ r) \Cap \{p\}\,;\,\big[q\big] \sqsubseteq (\mathbf{rely}\ r) \Cap \langle p, g \wedge q \rangle\,.$$

2.11   Introducing an Assignment

An assignment, $x := e$, is subject to interference on both the expression e and the assigned variable x. The simple case is if the rely condition implies there is no interference at all, in which case the law is quite similar to the sequential refinement law except that the assignment also has to satisfy any guarantee. The guarantee is required to be reflexive to allow for stuttering steps in the evaluation of the expression.

Law 20 (local-assignment). *If e is an expression that is both single-reference and constant under r, p is stable under r, q tolerates r from p, g is reflexive and $p \wedge \mathrm{id}(\overline{x}) \Rrightarrow (g \wedge q)[x'\backslash e]$,*

$$(\mathbf{rely}\ r) \Cap (\mathbf{guar}\ g) \Cap \{p\}\,;\,x\!:\!\big[q\big] \sqsubseteq x := e\,.$$

The following law is useful for refining a specification to an updated specification followed by assignment. The law assumes that there is no interference on e.

Law 21 (post-assignment). *If e is an expression that is both single-reference and constant under r, p_0 and p_1 are stable under r, q tolerates r from p, g is reflexive and $p_1 \wedge \mathrm{id}(\overline{x}) \Rrightarrow g[x'\backslash e]$,*

$$(\mathbf{rely}\ r) \Cap (\mathbf{guar}\ g) \Cap \{p_0\}\,;\,x\!:\!\big[q\big] \sqsubseteq$$
$$((\mathbf{rely}\ r) \Cap (\mathbf{guar}\ g) \Cap \{p_0\}\,;\,\big[q[x'\backslash e'] \wedge p_1'\big])\,;\,x := e\,.$$

A special case of an assignment is if there is interference on a single-reference expression e whereby the interference implies that the before and after values of e are related by a reflexive, transitive relation "$\succcurlyeq$". In that case, the value assigned to x is between the initial and final values of e.

Law 22 (rely-assignment). *Let p be stable under r, x be a variable that is constant under r, e be an expression that is single-reference under r and "$\succcurlyeq$" a reflexive, transitive binary relation, such that $\mathrm{id}(\overline{x}) \vee r \Rightarrow e \succcurlyeq e'$, and $p \wedge \mathrm{id}(\overline{x}) \Rightarrow g[x' \backslash e]$, then*

$$(\textbf{rely}\, r) \cap (\textbf{guar}\, g) \cap \{p\}; x : \left[e \succcurlyeq x' \succcurlyeq e' \right] \sqsubseteq x := e.$$

2.12   Introducing a Local Variable

If before introducing a local variable called x, a pre condition p refers to a more global variable also called x, then there are two separate variables both named x and within the local variable block references within its pre condition are to the local x. To address this issue, any information about x within p is removed by existentially quantifying x within the pre condition within the local block to give a pre condition $(\exists x \cdot p)$. A common case is where x is a fresh variable and hence there are no references to x within p and $(\exists x \cdot p) \equiv p$.

A similar situation applies to references to x within the initial rely condition. Such references are existentially quantified in the rely condition within the local block to give a local rely of $(\exists x, x' \cdot r)$. Further, local variable x is private to the block and thus not subject to any interference. Hence any rely condition within the block is strengthened by $x' = x$ within the local variable's scope.

If within the local block there is a guarantee of g, any references to x within g are to the local variable and hence the guarantee outside the block has to be weakened to $(\exists x, x' \cdot g)$. Further, because all references to x within the local block are to the local occurrence of x, the more global x cannot be modified within the local block and hence the guarantee outside the local block can be strengthened with $x' = x$.

A similar situation applies to the post condition, in that any references to x within the post condition within the local block refer to the local x and must be existentially quantified in the outer post condition. Note that the outer post condition cannot be strengthened with $x' = x$ (as for the outer guarantee) because although the local block does not change the more global x, its environment may. Again, if x is fresh and not referred to in q we have $(\exists x, x' \cdot q) \equiv q$.

Finally, the local x is added to the frame of the specification within the block.

Law 23 (introduce-var). *For a variable x and set of variables Y, if p is stable under r, and q tolerates r from p,*

$$(\textbf{rely}\, r) \cap (\textbf{guar}\, x' = x \wedge (\exists x, x' \cdot g)) \cap \{p\}; Y : \left[\exists x, x' \cdot q \right] \sqsubseteq$$

$$\textbf{var}\, x \cdot (\textbf{rely}\, x' = x \wedge (\exists x, x' \cdot r)) \cap (\textbf{guar}\, g) \cap \{\exists x \cdot p\}; x, Y : \left[q \right].$$

A useful combination is to introduce a local variable and initialise it to satisfy the pre condition of the residual specification. This rule assumes there is no interference on the expression e assigned as the initial value of x.

Law 24 (introduce-var-init). *For a variable x and set of variables Y, if p_1 is stable under r, q tolerates r from p_1, e is both single reference and constant under r and $(\exists x \cdot p_1) \Rrightarrow p_2[x \backslash e]$,*

$$(\mathbf{rely}\ r) \Cap (\mathbf{guar}\ x' = x \wedge (\exists x, x' \cdot g)) \Cap \{p_1\}; Y : \big[\exists x, x' \cdot q\big] \sqsubseteq$$
$$\mathbf{var}\ x \cdot x := e;$$
$$((\mathbf{rely}\ x' = x \wedge (\exists x, x' \cdot r)) \Cap (\mathbf{guar}\ g) \Cap \{p_2\}; x, Y : \big[q\big]).$$

2.13   Introducing a Conditional

The law for introducing a conditional needs to handle interference that may affect the evaluation of the loop guard. To simplify the handling of such interference, the loop guard b is required to be single reference under r, which means that its evaluation corresponds to its value in some single state during its evaluation, let us call that the evaluation state. If b is not stable under r, its value in the evaluation state may not correspond to its value when the "then" or "else" components start. To handle this, use is made of additional predicates b_0 and b_1. If b evaluates to true, the "then" branch will be executed. To handle the possibility that b may no longer hold when the "then" branch begins executing, a weaker predicate b_0 that is stable under r is used. Because b_0 also holds in the evaluation state and it is stable under r, it holds (stably) at the beginning of the "then" branch. In a similar fashion, if b evaluates to false, $\neg\, b$ may no longer hold at the start of the "else" branch. In this case, a weaker predicate b_1 that is stable under r and implied by $\neg\, b$ is used.

Law 25 (rely-conditional). *For a boolean expression b, predicates p, b_0 and b_1 and relation q, if b is single reference under r, p is stable under r, q tolerates r from p, $p \wedge b \Rrightarrow b_0$, $b_0 \wedge p \wedge r \Rrightarrow b_0'$, $\neg\, b \wedge p \Rrightarrow b_1$ and $b_1 \wedge p \wedge r \Rrightarrow b_1'$,*

$$(\mathbf{rely}\ r) \Cap \{p\}; [q] \sqsubseteq$$
$$\mathbf{if}\ b\ \mathbf{then}\ ((\mathbf{rely}\ r) \Cap \{b_0 \wedge p\}; [q]\,)\ \mathbf{else}\ ((\mathbf{rely}\ r) \Cap \{b_1 \wedge p\}; [q]).$$

Note that if b is stable under r, b_0 can be chosen to be b and if $\neg\, b$ is stable under r, b_1 can be chosen to be $\neg\, b$.

2.14   Introducing a While Loop

The law for introducing a while loop is complicated by the possibility that interference from the environment may affect the evaluation of the loop guard. The approach to handling this interference is similar to that used for interference on the guard of a conditional in Law 25 (rely-conditional). To simplify handling of such interference, the loop guard b in the following law is required to be single reference under the interference represented by the rely condition r, which means that on each iteration, the value of the loop guard is equivalent to its value in one single state during its evaluation; let us call this the evaluation state. If b evaluates to false, the loop will terminate but if $\neg\, b$ is not stable under r, one cannot conclude that $\neg\, b$ holds on termination. To handle this a weaker predicate b_1 that is stable under r and is implied by $\neg\, b$ is introduced. Because b_1 holds in the evaluation state and is stable under r, it will still hold at loop termination.

If the loop guard b evaluates to true, unless b is stable under r, one cannot assume b holds at the start of the loop body. To handle this a weaker predicate b_0 that is stable under r and implied by b is used. If b evaluates to true then b_0 will also hold in the evaluation state and as it is stable under r, it will still hold at the start of the loop body.

A variant expression is used to show termination. The variant expression is assumed to be decreased according to a well-founded relation $(\_ \prec \_)$ on each iteration. If the interference were allowed to increase v, that would invalidate the termination argument, so the interference is assumed to imply the variant does not increase.

The loop rule below also handles "early termination", in which the loop body does not have to decrease the loop variant if it establishes a condition that ensures the loop terminates. To handle this, a third predicate b_2 is introduced that is stable under r and implies $\neg\, b$ holds. Because b_2 is stable under r, if it is established at the end of the loop body it will still hold in the next guard evaluation state and hence the guard will evaluate to false and the loop will terminate. If the early termination version is not needed, b_2 can be chosen to be false, as that satisfies the required properties vacuously.

Law 26 (rely-loop). *Given a loop invariant p that is a state predicate, a rely condition r that is a reflexive, transitive relation on states, a variant function v of type T and a binary relation $\_ \prec \_$ on T, a boolean expression b and predicates b_0, b_1 and b_2, if g is reflexive, p is stable under r, i.e. $r \Rrightarrow (p \Rightarrow p')$, $\_ \prec \_$ is well-founded on p, i.e. $p \lhd (\_ \prec \_)$ is well-founded, v is non-increasing under r, i.e. $r \Rrightarrow v' \preceq v$, b is single reference under r, $p \wedge b \Rightarrow b_0$ and $p \wedge r \Rrightarrow (b_0 \Rightarrow b_0')$, $p \wedge \neg\, b \Rightarrow b_1$ and $p \wedge r \Rrightarrow (b_1 \Rightarrow b_1')$ and $p \wedge b_2 \Rightarrow \neg\, b$ and $p \wedge r \Rrightarrow (b_2 \Rightarrow b_2')$ then,*

$$(\mathbf{guar}\ g) \cap (\mathbf{rely}\ r) \cap \{p\}\,;\left[p' \wedge b_1' \wedge v' \preceq v \right]$$
$$\sqsubseteq \mathbf{while}\ b\ \mathbf{do\ invariant}\ p\ \mathbf{variant}\ v$$
$$((\mathbf{guar}\ g) \cap (\mathbf{rely}\ r) \cap \{p \wedge b_0\}\,;\left[p' \wedge (v' \prec v \vee b_2') \right])$$

The annotations for the invariant p and variant v of the while loop are included so that they are documented in the final code; the annotations are not part of the semantics of the while loop.

2.15   Developing Laws

More complex laws may be developed from the above laws, for example, a law the same as Par-I in Sect. 1.2 but expressed in a refinement calculus style can be developed as follows.

Law 27 (Par-I). *If (a) $g_l \vee g_r \Rrightarrow g$, (b) $p \wedge q_l \wedge q_r \wedge (r \vee g_l \vee g_r)^* \Rrightarrow q$, (c) $r \vee g_r \Rrightarrow r_l$ and (d) $r \vee g_l \Rrightarrow r_r$,*

$$(\mathbf{guar}\, g) \pitchfork (\mathbf{rely}\, r) \pitchfork \{p\} \, ; \left[q\right] \sqsubseteq (\mathbf{guar}\, g_l) \pitchfork (\mathbf{rely}\, r_l) \pitchfork \{p\} \, ; \left[q_l\right] \;\|$$
$$(\mathbf{guar}\, g_r) \pitchfork (\mathbf{rely}\, r_r) \pitchfork \{p\} \, ; \left[q_r\right].$$

Proof.

$\quad (\mathbf{guar}\, g) \pitchfork (\mathbf{rely}\, r) \pitchfork \{p\} \, ; \left[q\right]$

$\sqsubseteq \quad$ by Law 9 (strengthen-guar) to $g_l \vee g_r$ using (a)

$\quad (\mathbf{guar}\, g_l \vee g_r) \pitchfork (\mathbf{rely}\, r) \pitchfork \{p\} \, ; \left[q\right]$

$\sqsubseteq \quad$ by Law 4 (strengthen-post-pre) using (b)

$\quad (\mathbf{guar}\, g_l \vee g_r) \pitchfork (\mathbf{rely}\, r) \pitchfork \{p\} \, ; \left[q_l \wedge q_r \wedge (r \vee g_l \vee g_r)^*\right]$

$= \quad$ by Law 18 (trading)

$\quad (\mathbf{guar}\, g_l \vee g_r) \pitchfork (\mathbf{rely}\, r) \pitchfork \{p\} \, ; \left[q_l \wedge q_r\right]$

$\sqsubseteq \quad$ by Law 16 (introduce-parallel)

$\quad (\mathbf{guar}\, g_l \vee g_r) \pitchfork \left(\begin{array}{l} (\mathbf{guar}\, g_l) \pitchfork (\mathbf{rely}\, r \vee g_r) \pitchfork \{p\} \, ; \left[q_l\right] \;\| \\ (\mathbf{guar}\, g_r) \pitchfork (\mathbf{rely}\, r \vee g_l) \pitchfork \{p\} \, ; \left[q_r\right] \end{array} \right)$

$\sqsubseteq \quad$ by Law 13 (distrib-guar-parallel) and Law 11 (merge-guars)

$\quad ((\mathbf{guar}\, g_l) \pitchfork (\mathbf{rely}\, r \vee g_r) \pitchfork \{p\} \, ; \left[q_l\right]) \;\| \; ((\mathbf{guar}\, g_r) \pitchfork (\mathbf{rely}\, r \vee g_l) \pitchfork \{p\} \, ; \left[q_r\right])$

$\sqsubseteq \quad$ by Law 6 (weaken-rely) twice using (c) and (d)

$\quad ((\mathbf{guar}\, g_l) \pitchfork (\mathbf{rely}\, r_l) \pitchfork \{p\} \, ; \left[q_l\right]) \;\| \; ((\mathbf{guar}\, g_r) \pitchfork (\mathbf{rely}\, r_r) \pitchfork \{p\} \, ; \left[q_r\right])$

Note how aspects of the more complex laws, for example the use of the reflexive transitive closure of the disjunction of rely and guarantee to strengthen the postcondition, are treated as separate simpler laws, e.g. Law 18 (trading). The availability of simpler laws that each deal with one concept allows a wide variety of new laws to be developed by combining them in a fashion similar to that used for the proof of Law 27 (Par-I).

3   A First Example: Parallel SIEVE of Eratosthenes

The task is to determine the prime numbers up to some given n. This example illustrates:

- starting the development with abstract types
- need to document interference (relies)
- interplay between guarantees and the postcondition
- development to code (using a compare-and-swap)
- symmetric processes (identical relies and guarantees)

3.1   Intuition

The overall specification is for a program that determines all of the prime numbers up to some specified value n. The idea attributed to Eratosthenes is to start with a set of all of the numbers from 2 up to n and then successively remove the multiples (2 and above) of $2, 3, \cdots$ up to the square root of n. The initialisation phase is trivial but there is a subtlety in choosing the right specification for the second phase that sieves out the composites. There is a temptation to have a pre condition that says that the set must contain all of the numbers up to n—this temptation should be resisted. The specification of $Sieve(n)$ in Sect. 1.2 has the advantage that it separates this phase from the specific context: it defines an appropriate result whatever starting set is present when $Sieve$ begins execution.

Sequential code for $Sieve$ would be as follows.

$$\textbf{for } i \leftarrow 2 \cdots RemMultsSeq(i, n)$$

where for the sequential version the specification of $RemMultsSeq(i)$ is simple: it only changes s and removes the set of all multiples of i that are no greater than n, $C(i, n)$, from s.

$$RemMultsSeq \mathrel{\widehat{=}} \lambda\, i \in \mathbb{N}_1, n \in \mathbb{N} \cdot \{s \subseteq 0 \mathinner{.\,.} n\};\ s : [s' = s - C(i, n)]$$

The idea behind the concurrent implementation is pictured in Fig. 1. For the parallel implementation

$$Sieve \mathrel{\widehat{=}} \big\|_i\ RemMults(i, n),$$

the interference between the processes means that the specification of $RemMults(i)$ needs:

– a rely condition $s' \subseteq s$
– to relax the equality in the postcondition to $s' \cap C(i, n) = \emptyset$
– to avoid removing too much with a guarantee of $s - s' \subseteq C(i, n)$
– because processes are identical, add a guarantee of no reinsertion: $s' \subseteq s$.

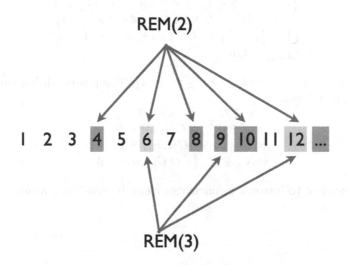

Fig. 1. Two concurrent threads deleting elements

3.2   Initial Refinement Calculus Style Development of Sieve

The set s initially contains the natural numbers from 2 up to some n. The set of all composite numbers is defined as follows, where the notation $\{x \in T \mid P(x) \cdot E(x)\}$ is the set of all values of $E(x)$ for x ranging over all elements of T that satisfy $P(x)$.

$$C \mathrel{\widehat{=}} \{i, j \in \mathbb{N} \mid 2 \le i \wedge 2 \le j \cdot j * i\}$$

In this section the top-level specification is refined to a multiway parallel. Each refinement step is accompanied by a reason (in blue) and the part of the line before it that is being refined is highlighted via an under-brace, while the part it refines to is highlighted by an over-brace. The first steps of the refinement transform the postcondition so that part of it, $s' \subseteq s \wedge s - s' \subseteq C$, is a reflexive, transitive relation that can "traded" to be used as a guarantee that is maintained by every program step and hence, in the context of a rely that no elements are added to s, holds overall as a postcondition.

$$(\textbf{rely } s' = s) \Cap \{s \subseteq 0 \mathinner{..} n\}; s: \Big[\underbrace{s' = s - C} \Big]$$

$=$ by Law 4 (strengthen-post-pre) using set theory

$$(\textbf{rely } s' = s) \Cap \{s \subseteq 0 \mathinner{..} n\}; s: \Big[\overbrace{s' \subseteq s \wedge s - s' \subseteq C \wedge s' \cap C \cap (0 \mathinner{..} n) = \emptyset} \Big]$$

$\sqsubseteq$ by Law 18 (trading) and Law 3 (remove-pre)

$$\overbrace{(\textbf{guar } s' \subseteq s \wedge s - s' \subseteq C)} \Cap (\textbf{rely } s' = s) \Cap s: \big[s' \cap C \cap (0 \mathinner{..} n) = \emptyset \big]$$

Using set theory and a bit of number theory one can derive the following, which uses the abbreviation $R \mathrel{\widehat{=}} 2 \mathinner{..} \lfloor \sqrt{n} \rfloor$.

$$\begin{aligned}
& C \cap (0 \mathinner{..} n) \\
&= \{i, j \in \mathbb{N} \mid 2 \le i \wedge 2 \le j \wedge j * i \le n \cdot j * i\} \\
&= \{i, j \in \mathbb{N} \mid i \in R \wedge 2 * i \le j * i \le n \cdot j * i\} \\
&= \textstyle\bigcup_{i \in R} \{j \in \mathbb{N} \mid 2 * i \le j * i \le n \cdot j * i\} \\
&= \textstyle\bigcup_{i \in R} C(i, n)
\end{aligned}$$

where $C(i, n) \mathrel{\widehat{=}} \{j \in \mathbb{N} \mid 2 * i \le j * i \le n \cdot j * i\}$. The postcondition can now be transformed as follows.

$$\begin{aligned}
& s' \cap C \cap (0 \mathinner{..} n) = \emptyset \\
&\Leftrightarrow s' \cap (\textstyle\bigcup_{i \in R} C(i, n)) = \emptyset \\
&\Leftrightarrow \textstyle\bigcup_{i \in R} (s' \cap C(i, n)) = \emptyset \\
&\Leftrightarrow \forall i \in R \cdot (s' \cap C(i, n)) = \emptyset
\end{aligned}$$

The refinement to introduce concurrency can be continued as follows.

$$(\textbf{guar}\ s' \subseteq s \wedge s - s' \subseteq C) \between (\textbf{rely}\ s' = s) \between s\colon \left[\underbrace{s' \cap C \cap (0\mathbin{..}n) = \emptyset}\right]$$

$=$ by Law 4 (strengthen-post-pre) using the above reasoning

$$(\textbf{guar}\ s' \subseteq s \wedge s - s' \subseteq C) \between (\textbf{rely}\ s' = s) \between s\colon \left[\underbrace{\forall i \in R \cdot s' \cap C(i,n) = \emptyset}\right]$$

$\sqsubseteq$ by Law 17 (introduce-multi-parallel) as $s' = s \vee s' \subseteq s \equiv s' \subseteq s$

$$\underbrace{(\textbf{guar}\ s' \subseteq s \wedge s - s' \subseteq C) \between}$$
$$(\,\|_{i \in R}\ (\textbf{guar}\ s' \subseteq s) \between (\textbf{rely}\ s' \subseteq s) \between s\colon [s' \cap C(i,n) = \emptyset]\,)$$

$\sqsubseteq$ by Law 13 (distrib-guar-parallel) and Law 11 (merge-guars)

$$\|_{i \in R}(\textbf{guar}\ s' \subseteq s \wedge \underbrace{s - s' \subseteq C}) \between (\textbf{rely}\ s' \subseteq s) \between s\colon [s' \cap C(i,n) = \emptyset]$$

$\sqsubseteq$ by Law 9 (strengthen-guar) as $C(i,n) \subseteq C$

$$\|_{i \in R}(\textbf{guar}\ s' \subseteq s \wedge \overbrace{s - s' \subseteq C(i,n)}) \between (\textbf{rely}\ s' \subseteq s) \between s\colon [s' \cap C(i,n) = \emptyset]$$

$=$ introducing $RemMults$ (see below)

$$\|_{i \in R}\ RemMults(i, n)$$

A specification of a single parameterised process that removes the multiples of i up to n is introduced. Note that the parameter i is assumed to be a non-zero natural number (i.e. $i \in \mathbb{N}_1$) to avoid the anomalous case where i is zero and hence $C(i, n) = \{0\}$.

$$RemMults \mathrel{\widehat{=}} \lambda\, i : \mathbb{N}_1, n \in \mathbb{N} \cdot$$
$$(\textbf{guar}\ s' \subseteq s \wedge s - s' \subseteq C(i,n)) \between (\textbf{rely}\ s' \subseteq s) \between s\colon [s' \cap C(i,n) = \emptyset] \quad (6)$$

The parameters i and n are treated as constants within the body of $RemMults$ and hence are not subject to interference and always refer to the values of the actual parameters at the start of the call. For the use of $RemMults$ in the parallel above, $i \in R = 2\mathbin{..} \lfloor\sqrt{n}\rfloor$ and hence i is of the correct type $\mathbb{N}_1$.

3.3   Removing Multiples of a Natural Number

The derivation of the code for $RemMults$ largely follows that for a sequential implementation, the main difference being that the implementation of removing a single element from the set needs to be done atomically (see Sect. 3.5). The derivation includes a data reification to introduce a more concrete representation of the set as a vector (see Sect. 3.4), which enables the removal of a single element from the set to be atomic.

$RemMults$ may be implemented by a loop that successively removes each multiple of i. A local variable k is used to keep track of the multiple of i reached so far. The loop has an invariant that all multiples of i less than k have been removed from s, that is, $s \cap C(i, (k - 1) * i) = \emptyset$, which can be established by setting k to 2, because the multiples start at 2. The loop has a strictly increasing variant $k * i$, which is bounded above by $n + i$ whenever the loop guard holds. For the moment we leave the guarantee as part of the context and refine the remainder of (6). When a local variable is introduced, it is not subject to interference from the environment and is added to the frame. In this case k is initialised to establish the loop invariant $s \cap C(i, (k-1)*i) = \emptyset$. The loop invariant is stable under the rely condition because k is not modified and s is never increased by the environment. The invariant is established by setting k to 2 because $s' \cap C(i,i) = \emptyset$ holds vacuously. The guarantee in the context, i.e. $s' \subseteq s \wedge s - s' \subseteq C(i,n)$, does not refer to k and hence it is satisfied by this assignment.

$(6) \sqsubseteq$ by Law 24 (introduce-var-init) k

$\quad$ **var** $k : \mathbb{N} \cdot k := 2$;

$\qquad (\textbf{rely } s' \subseteq s \wedge k' = k) \, \pitchfork$

$$\{s \cap C(i,(k-1)*i) = \emptyset\}; k, s : \left[s' \cap C(i,n) = \emptyset \right] \quad (7)$$

At this point the postcondition of (7) is strengthened so that it is in the form of the loop invariant conjoined with the negation of the loop guard.

$(7) \sqsubseteq$ by Law 4 (strengthen-post-pre)

$\quad (\textbf{rely } s' \subseteq s \wedge k' = k) \, \pitchfork$

$\quad \{s \cap C(i,(k-1)*i) = \emptyset\}; k, s : \left[s' \cap C(i,(k'-1)*i) = \emptyset \wedge n < k' * i \right]$

$$\tag{8}$$

As k is constant under the rely and i and n are constants within *RemMults*, the guard $k*i \leq n$ is stable under the rely, as is the invariant $s \cap C(i,(k-1)*i) = \emptyset$ because s is never increased. For natural number valued variables, the variant $k*i$ gives a well-founded relation $k*i < k'*i \leq n+i$. For this application of Law 26 (rely-loop), b_0 is taken to be $k*i \leq n$, b_1 is $k*i > n$ and b_2 is taken to be false because we do not need the early termination variant of the law.

$(8) \sqsubseteq$ by Law 26 (rely-loop)

$\quad$ **while** $k*i \leq n$ **do**

$\qquad (\textbf{rely } s' \subseteq s \wedge k' = k) \, \pitchfork$

$\qquad \{k*i \leq n \wedge s \cap C(i,(k-1)*i) = \emptyset\};$

$\qquad k, s : \left[s' \cap C(i,(k'-1)*i) = \emptyset \wedge k*i < k'*i \leq n+i \right] \quad (9)$

The loop body establishes the invariant for k one larger and then increases k by one.

$(9) \sqsubseteq$ by Law 21 (post-assignment)

$\quad ((\textbf{rely } s' \subseteq s \wedge k' = k) \, \pitchfork$

$\quad \{k*i \leq n \wedge s \cap C(i,(k-1)*i) = \emptyset\}; s : \left[s' \cap C(i, k*i) = \emptyset \right]); \quad (10)$

$\quad k := k+1$

Bringing back the guarantee from the context and strengthening the guarantee gives the following.

$$(10) \sqsubseteq \quad \text{by Law 4 (strengthen-post-pre) and Law 2 (weaken-pre)}$$

$$(\textbf{guar } s' \subseteq s \wedge s - s' \subseteq \{k * i\}) \cap (\textbf{rely } s' \subseteq s \wedge k' = k) \cap$$

$$\{k * i \leq n\}; s : \big[k * i \notin s'\big] \tag{11}$$

At this point we introduce a procedure to represent the removal of a single element from s. The specification of $Rem(m)$ allows interference that removes elements from s. It guarantees to remove element m only.

$$Rem \,\widehat{=}\, \lambda\, m : \mathbb{N} \,\cdot$$
$$(\textbf{guar } s' \subseteq s \wedge s - s' \subseteq \{m\}) \cap (\textbf{rely } s' \subseteq s) \cap \{m \leq n\}; s : \big[m \notin s'\big]$$

Hence

$$(11) \sqsubseteq Rem(k * i)$$

The collected code for the body of *RemMults* follows.

var $k : \mathbb{N} \cdot k := 2;$
    while $k * i \leq n$ **invariant** $s \cap C(i, (k-1) * i) = \emptyset$ **variant** $k * i$ **do**
      $(Rem(k * i); k := k + 1)$

The loop control only uses local variables and constants hence is not subject to interference. The interesting part is $Rem(k * i)$ which removes element $k * i$ from s and is subject to interference from other processes removing elements from s, perhaps even the same element.

3.4 Change of Data Representation

The obvious representation for the set is a bitmap, where s is represented as a vector v of words each representing part of the set. At this stage, an intermediate representation is used in which s is represented by a vector v of (small) sets, each of which can later be represented as a bitmap in a single word. The importance of splitting the set into a vector of subsets, each of which can be represented as a word, is that operations on a word can be performed atomically. Each word contains ws bits and hence can represent any subset of $0 \,..\, ws - 1$.

$$v : \textbf{array } 0..\left\lfloor \tfrac{n}{ws} \right\rfloor \textbf{ of } \mathbb{F}(0 \,..\, ws - 1)$$

The set s can be retrieved from v using the function $retr$, where $s = retr(v)$.

$$retr(v) \,\triangleq\, \{j \in 0 \,..\, n \mid j \bmod ws \in v(\lfloor \tfrac{j}{ws} \rfloor)\}$$

Note that for all $j \in 0 \,..n$, $\left\lfloor \tfrac{j}{ws} \right\rfloor \in 0 \,..\, \left\lfloor \tfrac{n}{ws} \right\rfloor$ and of course $j \bmod ws \in 0 \,..ws{-}1$. The operation Rem on s is data refined by the operation $RemI$ on v.

$$RemI \,\widehat{=}\, \lambda\, m : \mathbb{N} \,\cdot$$
$$(\textbf{guar } retr(v') \subseteq retr(v) \wedge retr(v) - retr(v') \subseteq \{m\}) \cap \tag{12}$$
$$(\textbf{rely } retr(v') \subseteq retr(v)) \cap \{m \leq n\}; v : \big[m \notin retr(v')\big]$$

By restricting the frame of the specification to a single element $v(\lfloor \frac{m}{ws} \rfloor)$, the body of $RemI$ can be refined to the following. A frame consisting of an element of a vector $v(i)$ corresponds to a guarantee that no variables other than v are modified and no element of v other than $v(i)$ is modified. The index i is taken to be its value in the initial state.

$$(12) \sqsubseteq (\mathbf{guar}\; v'(\lfloor \frac{m}{ws} \rfloor) \subseteq v(\lfloor \frac{m}{ws} \rfloor) \wedge v(\lfloor \frac{m}{ws} \rfloor) - v'(\lfloor \frac{m}{ws} \rfloor) \subseteq \{m \bmod ws\}) \Cap$$

$$(\mathbf{rely}\; v'(\lfloor \frac{m}{ws} \rfloor) \subseteq v(\lfloor \frac{m}{ws} \rfloor)) \Cap$$

$$\{m \bmod ws < ws\}; v(\lfloor \tfrac{m}{ws} \rfloor): \left[(m \bmod ws) \notin v'(\lfloor \tfrac{m}{ws} \rfloor)\right]$$

The implementation of $RemI$ then uses $RemW$ which removes an element from the set (as a word).

$$RemI(m) \sqsubseteq RemW(m \bmod ws, v(\lfloor \tfrac{m}{ws} \rfloor))$$

The specification of $RemW$ matches that of Rem except for the assumptions about the size of the set. The qualifier **ref** on the parameter indicates it is a call-by-reference parameter, i.e. any reference or update to the formal parameter is applied to the actual parameter. There must be no aliasing via reference parameters which is straightforward in this case because there is only one reference parameter and there are no references to global variables.

$$RemW \mathrel{\widehat{=}} \lambda\, i: 0..ws - 1, \mathbf{ref}\; w: \mathbb{F}(0..ws - 1) \cdot$$

$$(\mathbf{guar}\; w' \subseteq w \wedge w - w' \subseteq \{i\}) \Cap (\mathbf{rely}\; w' \subseteq w) \Cap w: \left[i \notin w'\right] \quad (13)$$

3.5 Removing an Element from a (Small) Set Atomically

The implementation avoids the use of locks and, instead, makes use of a compare-and-swap (CAS) operation, which is provided as an instruction on many machine architectures. CAS has the following specification.

$$CAS \mathrel{\widehat{=}} \lambda\, \mathbf{ref}\; w \in \mathbb{F}(0..ws - 1), lw, nw \in \mathbb{F}(0..ws - 1), \mathbf{ref}\; done \in \mathbb{B} \cdot$$

$$(\mathbf{rely}\; lw' = lw \wedge nw' = nw \wedge done' = done) \Cap$$

$$w, done: \left\langle \begin{array}{l} (w = lw \Rightarrow w' = nw \wedge done') \wedge \\ (w \neq lw \Rightarrow w' = w \wedge \neg\, done') \end{array} \right\rangle \quad (14)$$

Introduce Loop. Using CAS to remove i from w may either succeed, or fail and leave w unchanged. Hence to ensure i is removed, a loop is needed that repeatedly tries to remove i from w until it succeeds. It has a loop variant that the set w gets strictly smaller either by the CAS succeeding in removing i or the interference removing some element from w. For this application of Law 26 (rely-loop), b_0 is taken to be true because the loop guard is not stable under the rely, b_1 is $i \notin w$ because the negation of the loop guard is stable, and b_2 is also $i \notin w$ because we need to use the early termination form of the law.

(13) $\sqsubseteq$ by Law 26 (rely-loop) with variant w under the strict subset ordering

while $i \in w$ **invariant** true **variant** w **do**

$(\textbf{guar } w' \subseteq w \wedge w - w' \subseteq \{i\}) \cap (\textbf{rely } w' \subseteq w) \cap$

$w : \left[w' \subset w \vee i \notin w' \right]$ (15)

Refine Loop Body. To refine the body of the loop, a local variable lw, representing the last value of w, is introduced and the body is refined by a sequential composition that sets lw to a possible value of w (remember w may be changed by the environment) and then either succeeds in removing i from w or the interference removes a value from w and hence w is a strict subset of lw, thus ensuring the variant is decreased.

(15) $\sqsubseteq$ by Law 23 (introduce-var); Law 9 (strengthen-guar); Law 5 (sequential)

var $lw \cdot$

$(\textbf{guar } w' = w \vee w' = w - \{i\}) \cap (\textbf{rely } w' \subseteq w \wedge lw' = lw) \cap$

$lw : \left[w' \subseteq lw' \subseteq w \right] ;$ (16)

$\{w \subseteq lw\}; \; w : [w' \subset lw \vee i \notin w']$ (17)

The first specification is refined by an assignment, assuming accesses to w are atomic (which is why the vector of words was introduced). Because the environment may remove elements from w either before or after it is read, the value of lw is between the final and initial values of w. The guarantee is trivially satisfied as it does not mention lw.

(16) $\sqsubseteq$ by Law 22 (rely-assignment)

$lw := w$

Refining the second specification makes use of the CAS. First a local variable nw is introduced to contain the new value for w with i removed from lw.

(17) $\sqsubseteq$ by Law 24 (introduce-var-init) for nw to contain the updated value

var $nw \cdot nw := lw - \{i\};$

$(\textbf{guar } w' = w \vee w' = w - \{i\}) \cap$

$(\textbf{rely } w' \subseteq w \wedge lw' = lw \wedge nw' = nw) \cap$

$\{w \subseteq lw \wedge nw = lw - \{i\}\}; w : \left[w' \subset lw \vee i \notin w' \right]$ (18)

The specification is transformed so that it can be refined by the CAS. The variables lw and nw are local so the rely in the specification of *CAS* is satisfied; *done* is not used, as represented here by an underscore for the actual parameter.

$(18) \sqsubseteq$ by Law 4 (strengthen-post-pre)

$(\textbf{guar } w' = w \lor w' = w - \{i\}) \Cap$

$(\textbf{rely } w' \subseteq w \land lw' = lw \land nw' = nw) \Cap$

$w : \big[(w = lw \Rightarrow w' = nw) \land (w \neq lw \Rightarrow w' = w) \big]$

$\sqsubseteq$ by Law 19 (introduce-atomic) and (14)

$CAS(w, lw, nw, \_)$

The following code is collected from the above refinement.

while $i \in w$ **invariant** true **variant** w **do**
  var $lw := w$;
  var $nw := lw - \{i\}$;   – stable because variables local
  $CAS(w, lw, nw, \_)$;   – refines $w : \left\langle \begin{array}{l} w \subseteq lw \land nw = lw - \{i\}, \\ (w = lw \Rightarrow w' \subseteq w - \{i\}) \land \\ (w \neq lw \Rightarrow w' \subset lw) \end{array} \right\rangle$

The loop terminates because on each iteration either

– the CAS succeeds, and hence i is removed from w and the loop terminates, or
– the CAS fails because of interference that removes some element from w and hence the loop variant w decreases.

Note that it is possible for another process to remove i from w. In this case the guard may initially be true, i.e. $i \in w$, and there are two cases to consider:

– when lw samples w, i has already been removed (thus decreasing the variant) and no matter whether the CAS succeeds or fails, it has no effect on w, or
– when lw samples w, i has not been removed but then i is removed by the interference before the CAS executes, in which case the CAS then fails but the variant w has been decreased.

  The final refinement to use a bitmap representation and operators is straightforward and left as an exercise.

3.6   Conclusions

– Rely/guarantee provides a simple but effective abstraction of concurrency
– Importance of data abstraction
– New algebraic style makes proving new laws simpler
– New style allows new forms of specifications

4   Find Least First Element of an Array that Satisfies P

This section presents a development of a well-known concurrent algorithm. The choice of example facilitates comparison with other publications: it is taken from

Susan Owicki's thesis [Owi75] (and is also used by [Jon81] and, importantly, [dR01] employs it to contrast the compositional rely/guarantee approach with the "Owicki/Gries" method with its final *Einmischungsfrei* (interference free) global proof obligation).

The task is, given an array v with indices in the range $0 .. N-1$, to find the least index t for which a predicate $Pr(v(t))$ holds,[2] or if Pr does not hold for any element of v, to set t to N, where it is given that $0 \leq N$. It is assumed Pr is a function of just its argument (and hence does not refer to any other program variables directly). To simplify the development, the predicate P is defined as follows.

$$P \,\widehat{=}\, \lambda\, i \in \mathbb{N} \cdot i < N \Rightarrow Pr(v(i))$$

The task is then to find the minimum i such that $P(i)$ holds; given the form of P the minimum is less than or equal to N. The specification of *findP* includes a rely condition that both t and v are not modified. The frame of t guarantees no variables other than t are modified.

$$findp \,\widehat{=}\, (\textbf{rely } t' = t \wedge v' = v) \cap t : \big[t' = min\{i \in \mathbb{N} \mid P(i)\} \big] \qquad (19)$$

The abbreviation,

$$minP \,\widehat{=}\, \lambda\, S \in \mathbb{PN} \cdot min\{i \in S \mid P(i)\}$$

allows the postcondition of (19) to be re-written as $t' = minP(\mathbb{N})$.

4.1   Decomposition into Parallel Searches of Even and Odd Indices

Concurrency can be utilised by partitioning the task into parallel searches of the even and odd indices.[3] One danger that is to be avoided is to end up with a design that needs to "lock" the variable t during updates but there is a better approach followed here. One can finesse the penalties of sharing t by having a separate index for each of the concurrent processes and representing t by $min\{ot, et\}$.[4] Hence the first development step is to introduce local variables et and ot, which satisfy the following invariants.

$$et \neq N \Rightarrow et = minP(even) \qquad (20)$$
$$ot \neq N \Rightarrow ot = minP(odd) \qquad (21)$$

---

[2] For brevity, it is assumed here that $Pr(x)$ is always defined—undefinedness is considered in [CJ07] but it has little bearing on the concurrency aspects of the application.

[3] Generalising to an arbitrary number of threads presents no conceptual difficulties but also offers no further insight.

[4] As observed in Sect. 1.3, achieving rely and/or guarantee conditions is often linked with data reification, for instance, viewing $min\{ot, et\}$ as a representation of the abstract variable t.

These invariants can be established by setting both et and ot to N. The abbreviation,

$$inv \mathrel{\widehat{=}} \lambda \, st \in \mathbb{N}, S \in \mathbb{P}\mathbb{N} \cdot st \neq N \Rightarrow st = minP(S)$$

allows (20) and (21) to be re-written as $inv(et, even)$ and $inv(ot, odd)$, respectively.

For a sequential program, a loop invariant must be established before the loop and re-established at the end of each iteration but within the loop body it may be broken temporarily. For invariants on shared variables used for communication the requirement is stronger: the invariant must be maintained by every atomic step. To assist with that, a (stronger) guarantee invariant is used that is a guarantee that a predicate p is stable.

$$\textbf{guar-inv } p \mathrel{\widehat{=}} (\textbf{guar } p \Rightarrow p')$$

Note that for such an invariant to always hold, it must also be stable under the rely condition. A guarantee invariant can be used to handle the invariants on et (20) and ot (21), which can be established by assigning N to both et and ot.

$$(19) \sqsubseteq \quad \text{by Law 24 (introduce-var-init) twice; Law 10 (introduce-guar)}$$

$\textbf{var } et, ot : 0 \mathinner{\ldotp\ldotp} N \cdot et := N \, ; ot := N \, ;$

$(\textbf{guar-inv } inv(et, even) \wedge inv(ot, odd)) \pitchfork$

$\quad (\textbf{rely } v' = v \wedge t' = t \wedge et' = et \wedge ot' = ot) \pitchfork$

$\quad \{inv(et, even) \wedge inv(ot, odd)\} \, ; et, ot, t : \left[t' = minP(\mathbb{N}) \right]$ (22)

At this stage, the postcondition of (22) needs to be transformed to utilise et and ot. The transformation depends on the rely and guarantee conditions and hence requires the following refinement laws.

Law 28 (strengthen-under-rely-guar). *If* $p \wedge (r \vee g)^* \wedge q_2 \Rightarrow q_1$,

$$(\textbf{rely } r) \pitchfork (\textbf{guar } g) \pitchfork \{p\} \, ; \left[q_1 \right] \sqsubseteq (\textbf{rely } r) \pitchfork (\textbf{guar } g) \pitchfork \{p\} \, ; \left[q_2 \right].$$

Proof.

$\quad (\textbf{rely } r) \pitchfork (\textbf{guar } g) \pitchfork \{p\} \, ; \left[q_1 \right]$

$\sqsubseteq \quad$ by Law 4 (strengthen-post-pre) using assumption

$\quad (\textbf{rely } r) \pitchfork (\textbf{guar } g) \pitchfork \{p\} \, ; \left[(r \vee g)^* \wedge q_2 \right]$

$= \quad$ by Law 18 (trading)

$\quad (\textbf{rely } r) \pitchfork (\textbf{guar } g) \pitchfork \{p\} \, ; \left[q_2 \right]$

$\hfill \square$

Law 29 (strengthen-under-invariant). *If* $r \Rightarrow (p \Rightarrow p')$ *and* $g \Rightarrow (p \Rightarrow p')$, *and* $p \wedge p' \wedge q_2 \Rightarrow q_1$,

$$(\textbf{rely } r) \pitchfork (\textbf{guar } g) \pitchfork \{p\} \, ; \left[q_1 \right] \sqsubseteq (\textbf{rely } r) \pitchfork (\textbf{guar } g) \pitchfork \{p\} \, ; \left[q_2 \right].$$

Proof. The proof follows directly from Law 28 (strengthen-under-rely-guar) provided $p \wedge (r \vee g)^* \wedge q_2 \Rrightarrow q_1$, which follows from assumption $p \wedge p' \wedge q_2 \Rrightarrow q_1$:

$$p \wedge (r \vee g)^* \wedge q_2 \Rrightarrow p \wedge (p \Rightarrow p')^* \wedge q_2 \equiv p \wedge p' \wedge q_2 \Rrightarrow q_1.$$

A poor solution would then use disjoint parallelism based on the postcondition,

$$t' = min\{et', ot'\} \wedge et' = minP(even) \wedge ot' = minP(odd),$$

where the two processes ignore each other's progress. The aim here is an algorithm in which the processes "interfere" to achieve better performance. To facilitate this, note that if $minP(even) \geq ot$ then, given (21), it is not necessary to calculate et precisely because the minimum index satisfying P will be the final value of ot. By symmetry, if $minP(odd) \geq et$, it is not necessary to calculate ot precisely. Hence the postcondition of (22) can be relaxed.

(22) $\sqsubseteq$ by Law 29 (strengthen-under-invariant)

$\quad$ (**guar-inv** $inv(et, even) \wedge inv(ot, odd)$) $\pitchfork$

$\qquad$ (**rely** $v' = v \wedge t' = t \wedge et' = et \wedge ot' = ot$) $\pitchfork$

$\qquad$ $\{inv(et, even) \wedge inv(ot, odd)\}$;

$$et, ot, t : \begin{bmatrix} (minP(even) \geq ot' \vee et' = minP(even)) \wedge \\ (minP(odd) \geq et' \vee ot' = minP(odd)) \wedge \\ t' = min\{et', ot'\} \end{bmatrix} \quad (23)$$

It is straightforward to prove that the postcondition of (23) implies the postcondition of (22), by considering the four cases based on whether or not $et' = minP(even)$ and whether or not $ot' = minP(odd)$.

The final assignment to t can be split off from the specification (23). Because all of the variables involved are constant in the rely condition, the assignment does not suffer any interference. Note that reducing a frame corresponds to strengthening the corresponding guarantee and hence is always a refinement. The assignment trivially maintains guarantee invariants (20) and (21) because it does not modify either et or ot.

(23) $\sqsubseteq$ by Law 21 (post-assignment)

$\quad$ (**guar-inv** $inv(et, even) \wedge inv(ot, odd)$) $\pitchfork$

$\qquad$ (**rely** $t' = t \wedge v' = v \wedge ot' = ot \wedge et' = et$) $\pitchfork$

$\qquad$ $\{inv(et, even) \wedge inv(ot, odd)\}$;

$$et, ot : \begin{bmatrix} (minP(even) \geq ot' \vee et' = minP(even)) \wedge \\ (minP(odd) \geq et' \vee ot' = minP(odd)) \end{bmatrix}; \quad (24)$$

$\qquad$ $t := min\{ot, et\}$

4.2   Introducing Concurrency

The next step is the epitome of rely-guarantee refinement: splitting the specification command. To simplify the presentation, the guarantee invariant is elided for the next few steps and brought back in when it needs to be discharged.

(24) $\sqsubseteq$ by Law 16 (introduce-parallel)

$(\textbf{guar } ot' = ot \land et' \leq et) \Cap (\textbf{rely } et' = et \land ot' \leq ot \land v' = v) \Cap$

$\{inv(et, even) \land inv(ot, odd)\};$

$et, ot: \left[minP(even) \geq ot' \lor et' = minP(even) \right]$ (25)

$\parallel$

$(\textbf{guar } et' = et \land ot' \leq ot) \Cap (\textbf{rely } ot' = ot \land et' \leq et \land v' = v) \Cap$

$\{inv(et, even) \land inv(ot, odd)\};$

$et, ot: \left[minP(odd) \geq et' \lor ot' = minP(odd) \right]$

The above is all in the context of the guarantee invariants (20) and (21) above. The guarantee invariant eventually needs to be discharged for each atomic step but it is only possible to do that when the final code has been developed. However, during the development one needs to be aware of this requirement to avoid making design decisions that result in code that is inconsistent with the guarantee invariants.

4.3   Refining the Branches to Code

We focus on the first (evens) branch (25); the other (odds) branch follows an almost identical development and is not detailed here. For (25), the guarantee $ot' = ot$ is equivalent to removing ot from the frame of the branch.

(25) $\sqsubseteq$ by Law 15 (restrict-frame)

$(\textbf{guar } et' \leq et) \Cap (\textbf{rely } et' = et \land ot' \leq ot \land v' = v) \Cap$

$\{inv(et, even) \land inv(ot, odd)\};$

$et: \left[minP(even) \geq ot' \lor et' = minP(even) \right]$ (26)

The body of this can be refined to sequential code, however, because the specification refers to ot', it is subject to interference from the parallel (odds) process which may update ot. That interference is however bounded by the rely condition which assumes that the parallel process never increases ot.

The next task is to introduce a loop to search for the least even index satisfying P. For that a local variable ec with an invariant

$inv\_loop \,\widehat{=}\, \lambda\, ec, et \in \mathbb{N}, even \in \mathbb{PN} \cdot$ (27)
$ec \leq minP(even) \land ec \in even \land ec \leq et + 1$

is introduced, where the bound $et + 1$ on ec allows for the fact that ec only takes on even values. This invariant is established by setting ec to zero. (The odds branch similarly introduces a variable oc but it is initialised to one.)

$(26) \sqsubseteq$ by Law 24 (introduce-var-init) for ec

$\textbf{var } ec : 0 \mathinner{.\,.} N + 1 \cdot ec := 0;$

$(\textbf{rely } ot' \le ot \land ec' = ec \land et' = et \land v' = v) \cap (\textbf{guar } et' \le et) \cap$

$\{inv\_loop(ec, et, even) \land inv(et, even) \land inv(ot, odd)\};$

$$ec, et : \begin{bmatrix} inv\_loop(ec', et', even) \land \\ (minP(even) \ge ot' \lor et' = minP(even)) \end{bmatrix} \qquad (28)$$

Next the second part of the postcondition of (28) needs to be strengthened in the context of the invariant. Given the invariant $ec \le minP(even)$, the first disjunct can be strengthened to $ec' \ge ot'$. The second disjunct can be replaced by $ec' \ge et'$. This conjunct does not imply $et' = minP(even)$ but if $et' \ne minP(even)$ then by the invariant, $et' = N$ and hence $minP(even) \ge ec' \ge et' = N$, and so $minP(even) \ge ot'$ and the first disjunct holds.

$(28) \sqsubseteq$ by Law 29 (strengthen-under-invariant)

$(\textbf{rely } ot' \le ot \land ec' = ec \land et' = et \land v' = v) \cap (\textbf{guar } et' \le et) \cap$

$\{inv\_loop(ec, et, even) \land inv(et, even) \land inv(ot, odd)\};$

$$ec, et : \begin{bmatrix} inv\_loop(ec', et', even) \land (ec' \ge ot' \lor ec' \ge et') \end{bmatrix} \qquad (29)$$

Specification (29) is refined using Law 26 (rely-loop). The first part of the postcondition of (29) becomes the loop invariant and negation of the second part becomes the loop guard $ec < ot \land ec < et$. Because ec and et are constant under the rely condition, the invariant $inv\_loop(ec, et, even)$ and guarantee invariant $inv(et, even)$ are stable under the rely condition. Only the second conjunct of the loop guard $ec < ot \land ec < et$ is preserved by the rely condition because ot may be decreased. Hence the boolean expression b_0 for this application of the law is $ec < et$. The loop termination condition, $ec \ge ot \lor ec \ge et$, is preserved by the rely condition as decreasing ot will not falsify it. Hence b_1 for Law 26 (rely-loop) is $ec \ge ot \lor ec \ge et$. For this application b_2 is false because we do not need the early termination variant. For loop termination, a well-founded relation reducing the variant $et - ec$ is used.

$(29) \sqsubseteq$ by Law 26 (rely-loop)

$\textbf{while } ec < ot \land ec < et \textbf{ do}$

$(\textbf{rely } ot' \le ot \land ec' = ec \land et' = et \land v' = v) \cap (\textbf{guar } et' \le et) \cap$

$\{ec < et \land inv\_loop(ec, et, even) \land inv(et, even)\};$

$$ec, et : \begin{bmatrix} inv\_loop(ec', et', even) \land (-1 \le et' - ec' < et - ec) \end{bmatrix} \quad (30)$$

The specification of the loop body only involves variables which are stable under interference.

(30) $\sqsubseteq$ by Law 6 (weaken-rely)

$\quad$ (**rely** $ec' = ec \wedge et' = et \wedge v' = v$) $\Cap$ (**guar** $et' \leq et$) $\Cap$

$\qquad \{ec < et \wedge inv\_loop(ec, et, even) \wedge inv(et, even)\};$

$\qquad ec, et : \big[inv\_loop(ec', et', even) \wedge (-1 \leq et' - ec' < et - ec)\big]$ $\quad$ (31)

The precondition $ec < et$ along with $et \leq N$ ensures $Pr(v(ec))$ is well defined (i.e. the index ec is not out of range) allowing a refinement using Law 25 (rely-conditional) and, for this application, the guard $Pr(v(ec))$ is constant under r and hence b_0 can be chosen to be the guard $Pr(v(ec))$ and b_1 can be chosen to be the negation of the guard $\neg\, Pr(v(ec))$.

(31) $\sqsubseteq$

$\quad$ **if** $Pr(v(ec))$ **then**

$\qquad$ (**rely** $ec' = ec \wedge et' = et \wedge v' = v$) $\Cap$ (**guar** $et' \leq et$) $\Cap$

$\qquad\quad \{Pr(v(ec)) \wedge ec < et \wedge inv\_loop(ec, et, even) \wedge inv(et, even)\};$

$\qquad\qquad ec, et : \big[inv\_loop(ec', et', even) \wedge (-1 \leq et' - ec' < et - ec)\big]$ $\quad$ (32)

$\quad$ **else**

$\qquad$ (**rely** $ec' = ec \wedge et' = et \wedge v' = v$) $\Cap$ (**guar** $et' \leq et$) $\Cap$

$\qquad\quad \{\neg\, Pr(v(ec)) \wedge ec < et \wedge inv\_loop(ec, et, even) \wedge inv(et, even)\};$

$\qquad\qquad ec, et : \big[inv\_loop(ec', et', even) \wedge (-1 \leq et' - ec' < et - ec)\big]$ $\quad$ (33)

Each of the branches of the conditional is refined by an assignment but each assignment must ensure the guarantee $et' \leq et$ is satisfied and the guarantee invariant, i.e.

$$et \neq N \Rightarrow et = minP(even) \qquad (34)$$

is maintained. For (32), $Pr(v(ec)) \wedge ec < et \wedge ec \leq minP(even) \wedge ec \in even$ implies $ec = minP(even)$, and hence (34) is maintained by assigning ec to et, which also reestablishes the invariant as $ec = et \leq et + 1$. Because $ec < et$ initially, the assignment satisfies the guarantee $et' \leq et$ and decreases the variant $et - ec$.

(32) $\sqsubseteq$ by Law 20 (local-assignment)

$\qquad et := ec$

For the second branch, $\neg\, Pr(v(ec)) \wedge ec < et \wedge ec \leq minP(even) \wedge ec \in even$ implies $ec + 2 \leq minP(even) \wedge ec + 2 \in even \wedge ec + 2 \leq et + 1$ and hence the invariant is reestablished by assigning $ec + 2$ to ec, which also maintains (34) because et is not modified. The guarantee $et' \leq et$ is satisfied because et is not modified. The assignment decreases the invariant $et - ec$ because ec is increased and et is unchanged.

$$(33) \sqsubseteq \quad \text{by Law 20 (local-assignment)}$$
$$ec := ec + 2$$

4.4 Collected Code

As mentioned above, the development of the "odds" branch of the parallel composition follows the same pattern as that of the "evens" branch given above but oc starts at one. The collected code follows.

```
var et, ot · et, ot := N, N ;
⎛ var ec ·                          ‖  var oc ·                          ⎞
  ec := 0;                          ‖  oc := 1;
  while ec < ot ∧ ec < et do        ‖  while oc < et ∧ oc < ot do        ;
    if Pr(v(ec)) then et := ec      ‖    if Pr(v(oc)) then ot := oc
    else ec := ec + 2               ‖    else oc := oc + 2
⎝
t := min{ot, et}
```

The two branches (*evens*/*odds*) step through their respective subsets of the indices of v looking for the first element that satisfies P. The efficiency gain over a sequential implementation comes from parallelism between the two searches and allowing one of the processes to exit its loop early if the other has found an index i such that $Pr(v(i))$ that is lower than the remaining indexes that the first process has yet to consider. The extra complication for reasoning about this interprocess communication manifests itself particularly in the steps that introduce concurrency and the while loop because the interference affects variables mentioned in the test of the loop.

This implementation is guaranteed to satisfy the original specification due to its use at every step of the refinement laws. In many ways, this mirrors the development in [CJ07]. In particular, the use of Law 16 (introduce-parallel) in Sect. 4.2 mirrors the main thrust of "traditional" rely/guarantee thinking. What is novel in the new development is both the use of a guarantee invariant and the fact that there are rules for every construct used. Moreover, because all of the results are derived from a small number of basic lemmas, it is possible to add new styles of development without needing to go back to the semantics.

Although weak memory models [LV16] are not explicitly considered in this paper, note that the only interference on the evens process is on ot. If the memory delayed writing to ot, the only effect would be that the evens search loop may execute more iterations, but that will not change the correctness of the algorithm. In fact, if the evens process never sees the update of ot, the program is still correct, although it may be less efficient.

5   Further Material

5.1   Other Examples

The examples in Sects. 3 and 4 both exhibit symmetric concurrency where all of the threads have the same specification; some of the more interesting applications of R/G are where the concurrent processes perform different tasks.[5] Such examples include:

- parallel "cleanup" operations for the *Fisher/Galler* Algorithm for the *union/find* problem are developed in [CJ00]
- Simpson's "four-slot" implementation of *Asynchronous Communication Mechanisms* is tackled in [JP11] but a far clearer specification is given in [JH16].
- concurrent garbage collection [JVY17] (this paper explores a possible expressive weakness of R/G).

Other examples of symmetric parallelism include:

- Mergesort in [JY15]
- The Treiber stack was presented at the SETSS event.

5.2   Semantics

The laws used in this paper are proven in terms of a theory of concurrent programming built as a hierarchy of algebraic theories, including a general concurrent program algebra [Hay16], an algebra of synchronous atomic steps [HCM+16, HMWC18] and a theory of tests similar to that of Kozen [Koz97]. The core language contains recursion, a handful of operators—lattice infimum ($\sqcap$) and supremum ($\sqcup$), sequential (;), parallel ($\parallel$), weak conjunction ($\Cap$), and an un-restriction operator ($\backslash$) to handle local variables—and three primitive commands—$\tau(p)$, representing a test; $\pi(r)$, representing a single atomic program step and $\epsilon(r)$, representing a single atomic environment step. All other commands are defined in terms of these three primitives and the operators of the language. For example, a guarantee command **guar** g is defined in terms of an iteration of a nondeterministic choice of atomic steps:

$$\textbf{guar } g \mathrel{\widehat{=}} (\pi(g) \sqcap \epsilon)^{\omega}$$

where $\pi(g)$ performs a single atomic step satisfying g, ϵ allows any single atomic environment step and c^{ω} stands for the iteration of a command c zero or more times, including the possibility of infinite iteration. The iteration c^{ω} is defined in terms of a fixed point. The proofs of some of the laws in this paper are given in [HMWC18], which extends the work in [Hay16, HCM+16].

The core algebraic theories each make use of a small set of axioms from which all the other properties are derived. To show that the axioms of these theories are consistent, a trace semantics for the core language has been developed [CHM16].

---

[5] Compare Law 17 (introduce-multi-parallel) and Law 16 (introduce-parallel) in Sect. 2.7.

5.3 Further R/G Publications

The literature on R/G is now extensive enough that the authors of the current paper no longer attempt to maintain a full list. However, it serves the purpose of this paper being a guide to R/G to point to some publications.

There have been a significant number of theses published on R/G approaches including:

- both [Hen04, Pie09] apply R/G to Simpson's "four-slot" algorithm;
- two theses that justify the soundness of the original R/G parallel introduction rule are:
  - [Pre01] which provides an Isabelle-checked soundness proof with some restrictions on the parallel statement;
  - [Col08] tackles a more general language allowing nested parallel constructs and avoiding fixing atomicity at the assignment statement level—this proof is, however, not machine checked;
- [Mid90][6] combines the rely and guarantee conditions into a single temporal logic expression;
- Both [Stø90] and [Xu92] offer extensions to R/G to address progress arguments;
- [Col94] looks at "assumption-commitment" extensions to Unity [CM88];
- [Din00] covers message-passing as well as shared-variable concurrency;
- [Wic13] investigates the notion of predicate stability in R/G (and also proposes "ribbon proofs");
- [Lia14] introduces RGSim that covers refinement;
- [Bue00] proposes a compositional symmetric sharing mechanism based on R/G;
- [Vaf07] present a way of combining R/G and Separation Logic;[7]
- Mechanisation of algebraic-style R/G reasoning is addressed in [Arm16, Dia17].

A specific extension to R/G that has increased the expressiveness is the notation for "possible values"—see [HBDJ13, JHC15, JH16].

A number of Separation Logic (see Sect. 5.4) papers actually employ R/G reasoning (e.g. [BA10, BA13]). Another contribution from Separation Logic authors that relates strongly to R/G is "Deny-Guarantee Logic" [DFPV09, DYDG+10].

Other related research includes:

- RGITL [STER11, STE+14] offers a combination of Interval Temporal Logic [Mos86] with rely-guarantee reasoning;
- CSimpl [SZH+17];
- Concurrent Kleene Algebra [HvSM+16] extends Kleene algebra with a parallel operator and can encode a rely/guarantee quintuple similar to (1), although the approach only supports partial correctness and the treatment of guarantees requires them to hold for all program steps, even after an environment step that does not satisfy the rely condition.

---

[6] Published as a book [Mid93].
[7] SAGL [FFS07] has a similar scope.

5.4   Related Work

Separation Logic was first introduced by John Reynolds as a way of reasoning about programs that manipulate heap variables [Rey02]. Notice that this was initially intended for sequential programs. The step to Concurrent Separation Logic was a joint effort but first widely available in [O'H07].

Comparisons are sometimes made between R/G and *Separation Logic*. In fact, Peter O'Hearn suggests in [O'H07] that there is a rough characterisation of the applicability of the two methods:

- Separation Logic should be used to reason about race freedom
- R/G is applicable to "racy"[8] programs

This is not the place to make an extensive comparison (nor would the current authors be considered to be fair adjudicators) but it is worth commenting that [JY15] indicates that some cases of separation can be handled via levels of abstraction.

5.5   Conclusions

It is clear that interference between processes vastly complicates reasoning: in addition to the enormous number of paths through a non-trivial sequential program, one has to consider state changes that can be made by the environment of the process under review. Once this observation is accepted, it is reasonable to look for ways of documenting (in specifications) constraints that can be assumed about interference. Just as recording assumptions in a pre condition about the starting state of a component forces a proof obligation on anyone using said component to establish that the pre condition will hold in the deployed context, there are proof obligations to be discharged when introducing a parallel decomposition.

One possibility for recording the environment of a process is to have the code of everything that comprises its context. This is impractical for several reasons: it means that proof obligations can only be discharged finally when all of the code has been developed; such documentation is extremely brittle in the sense that the slightest change requires extensive re-evaluation of delicate proof work.

R/G offers one level of abstraction in terms of which interference can be recorded and reasoned about—the approach is practical and has proved to be influential. Furthermore, the recent presentation of R/G thinking in a more algebraic setting has revitalised the research. In particular, it has made it look more feasible to provide mechanical support for R/G developments.

Although it is not the main topic of the current paper, it is worth pointing to an avenue of related research that uses R/G ideas in the design of fault-tolerant cyber-physical systems [JHJ07, Jon10].

---

[8] The negative flavour of this adjective was probably intentional.

Acknowledgements. This research was supported by Australian Research Council (ARC) Discovery Grant DP130102901 "Understanding concurrent programs using rely-guarantee thinking" and the UK EPSRC "Taming Concurrency" and "Strata" research grants. Thanks are due to Robert Colvin, Diego Machado Dias, Larissa Meinicke, Patrick Meiring, Andrius Velykis, Kirsten Winter and Nisansala Yatapanage for feedback on ideas presented in this paper. The authors are particularly grateful to the anonymous reviewers for detailed and constructive comments.

References

[Arm16] Armstrong, A.: Formal analysis of concurrent programs. Ph.D. thesis, University of Sheffield (2016)

[BA10] Bornat, R., Amjad, H.: Inter-process buffers in separation logic with rely-guarantee. Formal Aspects Comput. **22**(6), 735–772 (2010)

[BA13] Bornat, R., Amjad, H.: Explanation of two non-blocking shared-variable communication algorithms. Formal Aspects Comput. **25**(6), 893–931 (2013)

[Bue00] Buechi, M.: Safe language mechanisms for modularization and concurrency. Ph.D. thesis, Turku (2000)

[BvW98] Back, R.-J.R., von Wright, J.: Refinement Calculus: A Systematic Introduction. Springer, New York (1998). https://doi.org/10.1007/978-1-4612-1674-2

[CHM16] Colvin, R.J., Hayes, I.J., Meinicke, L.A.: Designing a semantic model for a wide-spectrum language with concurrency. Formal Aspects Comput. **29**, 853–875 (2016)

[CJ00] Collette, P., Jones, C.B.: Enhancing the tractability of rely/guarantee specifications in the development of interfering operations (Chap. 10). In: Plotkin, G., Stirling, C., Tofte, M. (eds.) Proof, Language and Interaction, pp. 277–307. MIT Press (2000)

[CJ07] Coleman, J.W., Jones, C.B.: A structural proof of the soundness of rely/guarantee rules. J. Logic Comput. **17**(4), 807–841 (2007)

[CM88] Chandy, K.M., Misra, J.: Parallel Program Design: A Foundation. Addison-Wesley, Boston (1988)

[Col94] Collette, P.: Design of compositional proof systems based on assumption-commitment specifications - application to UNITY. Ph.D. thesis, Louvain-la-Neuve, June 1994

[Col08] Coleman, J.W.: Constructing a tractable reasoning framework upon a fine-grained structural operational semantics. Ph.D. thesis, Newcastle University, January 2008

[DFPV09] Dodds, M., Feng, X., Parkinson, M., Vafeiadis, V.: Deny-guarantee reasoning. In: Castagna, G. (ed.) ESOP 2009. LNCS, vol. 5502, pp. 363–377. Springer, Heidelberg (2009). https://doi.org/10.1007/978-3-642-00590-9_26

[Dia17] Dias, D.M.: Mechanising an algebraic rely-guarantee refinement calculus. Ph.D. thesis, School of Computing, Newcastle University (2017)

[Din00] Dingel, J.: Systematic parallel programming. Ph.D. thesis, Carnegie Mellon University (2000). CMU-CS-99-172

[dR01] de Roever, W.-P.: Concurrency Verification: Introduction to Compositional and Noncompositional Methods. Cambridge University Press, Cambridge (2001)

[DYDG+10] Dinsdale-Young, T., Dodds, M., Gardner, P., Parkinson, M.J., Vafeiadis, V.: Concurrent abstract predicates. In: D'Hondt, T. (ed.) ECOOP 2010. LNCS, vol. 6183, pp. 504–528. Springer, Heidelberg (2010). https://doi. org/10.1007/978-3-642-14107-2_24

[FFS07] Feng, X., Ferreira, R., Shao, Z.: On the relationship between concurrent separation logic and assume-guarantee reasoning. In: De Nicola, R. (ed.) ESOP 2007. LNCS, vol. 4421, pp. 173–188. Springer, Heidelberg (2007). https://doi.org/10.1007/978-3-540-71316-6_13

[Flo67] Floyd, R.W.: Assigning meanings to programs. In: Proceedings of Symposia in Applied Mathematics: Mathematical Aspects of Computer Science, vol. 19, pp. 19–32 (1967)

[Hay16] Hayes, I.J.: Generalised rely-guarantee concurrency: an algebraic foundation. Formal Aspects Comput. 28(6), 1057–1078 (2016)

[HBDJ13] Hayes, I.J., Burns, A., Dongol, B., Jones, C.B.: Comparing degrees of non-determinism in expression evaluation. Comput. J. 56(6), 741–755 (2013)

[HCM+16] Hayes, I.J., Colvin, R.J., Meinicke, L.A., Winter, K., Velykis, A.: An algebra of synchronous atomic steps. In: Fitzgerald, J., Heitmeyer, C., Gnesi, S., Philippou, A. (eds.) FM 2016. LNCS, vol. 9995, pp. 352–369. Springer, Cham (2016). https://doi.org/10.1007/978-3-319-48989-6_22

[Hen04] Henderson, N.: Formal modelling and analysis of an asynchronous communication mechanism. Ph.D. thesis, University of Newcastle upon Tyne (2004)

[HJC14] Hayes, I.J., Jones, C.B., Colvin, R.J.: Laws and semantics for rely-guarantee refinement. Technical report CS-TR-1425, Newcastle University, July 2014

[HMWC18] Hayes, I.J., Meinicke, L.A., Winter, K., Colvin, R.J.: A synchronous program algebra: a basis for reasoning about shared-memory and event-based concurrency (2018). Formal Aspects of Computing. Online 6 August 2018

[Hoa69] Hoare, C.A.R.: An axiomatic basis for computer programming. Commun. ACM, 12(10), 576–580, 583 (1969)

[HvSM+16] Hoare, T., van Staden, S., Möller, B., Struth, G., Zhu, H.: Developments in concurrent Kleene algebra. J. Log. Algebraic Methods Program. 85(4), 617–636 (2016)

[JH16] Jones, C.B., Hayes, I.J.: Possible values: exploring a concept for concurrency. J. Log. Algebraic Methods Program. 85(5, Part 2), 972–984 (2016). Articles dedicated to Prof. J. N. Oliveira on the occasion of his 60th birthday

[JHC15] Jones, C.B., Hayes, I.J., Colvin, R.J.: Balancing expressiveness in formal approaches to concurrency. Formal Aspects Comput. 27(3), 475–497 (2015)

[JHJ07] Jones, C.B., Hayes, I.J., Jackson, M.A.: Deriving specifications for systems that are connected to the physical world. In: Jones, C.B., Liu, Z., Woodcock, J. (eds.) Formal Methods and Hybrid Real-Time Systems. LNCS, vol. 4700, pp. 364–390. Springer, Heidelberg (2007). https://doi. org/10.1007/978-3-540-75221-9_16

[Jon81] Jones, C.B.: Development methods for computer programs including a notion of interference. Ph.D. thesis, Oxford University, June 1981. Available as: Oxford University Computing Laboratory (now Computer Science) Technical Monograph PRG-25

[Jon83a] Jones, C.B.: Specification and design of (parallel) programs. In: Proceedings of IFIP 1983, pp. 321–332. North-Holland (1983)

[Jon83b] Jones, C.B.: Tentative steps toward a development method for interfering programs. ACM ToPLaS **5**(4), 596–619 (1983)

[Jon10] Jones, C.B.: From problem frames to HJJ (and its known unknowns) (Chap. 16). In: Nuseibeh, B., Zave, P. (eds.) Software Requirements and Design: The Work of Michael Jackson, pp. 357–372. Good Friends Publishing Company (2010)

[JP11] Jones, C.B., Pierce, K.G.: Elucidating concurrent algorithms via layers of abstraction and reification. Formal Aspects Comput. **23**(3), 289–306 (2011)

[JVY17] Jones, C.B., Velykis, A., Yatapanage, N.: General lessons from a rely/guarantee development. In: Larsen, K.G., Sokolsky, O., Wang, J. (eds.) SETTA 2017. LNCS, vol. 10606, pp. 3–22. Springer, Cham (2017). https://doi.org/10.1007/978-3-319-69483-2_1

[JY15] Jones, C.B., Yatapanage, N.: Reasoning about separation using abstraction and reification. In: Calinescu, R., Rumpe, B. (eds.) SEFM 2015. LNCS, vol. 9276, pp. 3–19. Springer, Cham (2015). https://doi.org/10.1007/978-3-319-22969-0_1

[Koz97] Kozen, D.: Kleene algebra with tests. ACM Trans. Prog. Lang. Syst. **19**(3), 427–443 (1997)

[Lia14] Liang, H.: Refinement verification of concurrent programs and its applications. Ph.D. thesis, USTC, China (2014)

[LV16] Lahav, O., Vafeiadis, V.: Explaining relaxed memory models with program transformations. In: Fitzgerald, J., Heitmeyer, C., Gnesi, S., Philippou, A. (eds.) FM 2016. LNCS, vol. 9995, pp. 479–495. Springer, Cham (2016). https://doi.org/10.1007/978-3-319-48989-6_29

[Mid90] Middelburg, C.A.: Syntax and semantics of VVSL: a language for structured VDM specifications. Ph.D. thesis, PTT Research, Leidschendam, Department of Applied Computer Science, September 1990

[Mid93] Middelburg, C.A.: Logic and Specification: Extending VDM-SL for Advanced Formal Specification. Chapman and Hall, Boca Raton (1993)

[Mor90] Morgan, C.: Programming from Specifications. Prentice-Hall, Upper Saddle River (1990)

[Mos86] Moszkowski, B.C.: Executing Temporal Logic Programs. Cambridge University Press, Cambridge (1986)

[O'H07] O'Hearn, P.W.: Resources, concurrency and local reasoning. Theor. Comput. Sci. **375**(1–3), 271–307 (2007)

[Owi75] Owicki, S.: Axiomatic proof techniques for parallel programs. Ph.D. thesis, Department of Computer Science, Cornell University (1975)

[Pie09] Pierce, K.: Enhancing the useability of rely-guaranteee conditions for atomicity refinement. Ph.D. thesis, Newcastle University (2009)

[Pre01] Prensa Nieto, L.: Verification of parallel programs with the Owicki-Gries and rely-guarantee methods in Isabelle/HOL. Ph.D. thesis, Institut für Informatic der Technischen Universitaet München (2001)

[Rey02] Reynolds, J.C.: Separation logic: a logic for shared mutable data structures. In: IEEE Symposium on Logic in Computer Science (LICS), pp. 55–74. IEEE Computer Society (2002)

[STE+14] Schellhorn, G., Tofan, B., Ernst, G., Pfähler, J., Reif, W.: RGITL: a temporal logic framework for compositional reasoning about interleaved programs. Ann. Math. Artif. Intell. **71**(1–3), 131–174 (2014)

[STER11] Schellhorn, G., Tofan, B., Ernst, G., Reif, W.: Interleaved programs and rely-guarantee reasoning with ITL. In: TIME, pp. 99–106 (2011)

[Stø90] Stølen, K.: Development of parallel programs on shared data-structures. Ph.D. thesis, Manchester University (1990). Available as UMCS-91-1-1

[SZH+17] Sanán, D., Zhao, Y., Hou, Z., Zhang, F., Tiu, A., Liu, Y.: CSimpl: a rely-guarantee-based framework for verifying concurrent programs. In: Legay, A., Margaria, T. (eds.) TACAS 2017. LNCS, vol. 10205, pp. 481–498. Springer, Heidelberg (2017). https://doi.org/10.1007/978-3-662-54577-5_28

[Vaf07] Vafeiadis, V.: Modular fine-grained concurrency verification. Ph.D. thesis, University of Cambridge (2007)

[Wic13] Wickerson, J.: Concurrent verification for sequential programs. Ph.D. thesis, Cambridge (2013)

[Xu92] Xu, Q.: A theory of state-based parallel programming. Ph.D. thesis, Oxford University (1992)

An Illustrated Guide to the Model Theory of Supertype Abstraction and Behavioral Subtyping

Gary T. Leavens[1]([⊠]) and David A. Naumann[2]

[1] University of Central Florida, Orlando, FL 32816, USA
leavens@cs.ucf.edu
[2] Stevens Institute of Technology, Hoboken, NJ 07030, USA
naumann@cs.stevens.edu
http://www.cs.ucf.edu/~leavens,
https://www.cs.stevens.edu/~naumann/

Abstract. Object-oriented (OO) programs, which use subtyping and dynamic dispatch, make specification and verification difficult because the code executed by a method call may dynamically be dispatched to an overriding method in any subtype, even ones that did not exist at the time the program was specified. Modular reasoning for such programs means allowing one to add new subtypes to a program without re-specifying and re-verifying it. In a 2015 *ACM TOPLAS* paper we presented a model-theoretic characterization of a Hoare-style modular verification technique for sequential OO programs called "supertype abstraction," defined behavioral subtyping, and proved that behavioral subtyping is both necessary and sufficient for the validity of supertype abstraction. The present paper is aimed at graduate students and other researchers interested in formal methods and gives a comprehensive overview of our prior work, along with the motivation and intuition for that work, with examples.

Keywords: Object-oriented programming · Hoare-style verification
JML specification language · Behavioral subtyping
Supertype abstraction · Specification inheritance

1 Introduction

The goal of our prior work [17] and the 2017 SETSS lectures, was to explain how to modularly reason about sequential object-oriented (OO) programs that use subtyping and dynamic dispatch. The key modular verification technique is "supertype abstraction" [16, 20, 21]. In supertype abstraction, one verifies a call to a method by using the specification of the receiver's static type. The validity of this reasoning technique depends on two conditions:

Leavens's work was supported in part by the US National Science Foundation under grants CNS 08-08913 and CCF 1518789 and Naumann's work was supported in part by the US NSF under grant CNS 1718713.

J. P. Bowen et al. (Eds.): SETSS 2017, LNCS 11174, pp. 39–88, 2018.
https://doi.org/10.1007/978-3-030-02928-9_2

1. in each method call, $E.m()$, the dynamic type of the actual receiver object (the value of E) must be a subtype of the static type of the receiver expression, E, and
2. every override of the method named m must correctly implement each of the specifications (given in its supertypes) for that method.

Together, these two conditions allow the specification of the method m in E's static type to be used in verification of the call $E.m()$, since any subtype of that static type will correctly implement that specification. The first condition can be enforced by a static type system, such as the one in Java, in which the static type of an expression is an upper bound on the dynamic types of all objects it may denote (in the sense that the expression's static type must be a supertype of the runtime classes of those objects). The second condition is the essence of behavioral subtyping [1–3, 17, 20–23]. To a first approximation, behavioral subtyping is necessary for valid use of supertype abstraction, because the supertype's specification is used in reasoning, so the subtypes must all correctly implement that specification.

1.1 JML

This paper illustrates (with examples, not pictures) the idea of supertype abstraction using sequential Java, with specifications written in the Java Modeling Language (JML) [16, 19]. As a behavioral interface specification language, JML specifies the functional behavior of Java methods, classes, and interfaces. Functional behavior involves the values of data; thus a JML method specification describes the allowed values of variables (e.g., method formals) and object fields before the method starts running (its precondition) and the relationship between such values and the method's result after the method finishes (its postcondition and frame condition).

JML and the work reported here only deal with sequential Java programs, so we henceforth assume that there is no multi-threading or parallelism in the programs discussed.

1.2 OO Programs and Dynamic Dispatch

As the start of a JML example that illustrates how OO programs use dynamic dispatch, consider the type IntSet, which is shown in Fig. 1 on the next page.

JML specifications are written as comments that start with an at-sign (@); these are processed by the JML compiler (but would be ignored by a standard Java compiler). Figure 1 on the next page shows the specification of an interface, which specifies five methods. The contains method is only specified as being pure, which means that it has no write effects (i.e., **assignable \nothing**). It has no precondition (the default in JML is **requires true**), which means it can be called in any state. It also has no postcondition; the default (**ensures true**) imposes no obligations on an

```
//@ model import org.jmlspecs.lang.JMLDataGroup;

public interface IntSet {
    //@ public instance model JMLDataGroup state;

    public /*@ pure @*/ boolean contains(int i);

    //@ requires size() > 0;
    //@ assignable state;
    //@ ensures contains(\result);
    public int pick();

    //@ assignable state;
    //@ ensures contains(i);
    //@ ensures size() >= \old(size());
    public void add(int i);

    //@ assignable state;
    //@ ensures !contains(i) && size() <= \old(size());
    public void remove(int i);

    //@ ensures \result >= 0;
    public /*@ pure @*/ long size();
}
```

Fig. 1. A JML specification of the interface IntSet.

implementation. The last method, size, is also specified as being pure. However, size has a specified postcondition, which is that the result of the method
is always non-negative. (As can be seen in this example, the specification for
each method is written before the method's header.) The contains and size
methods are used to specify the behavior of the other methods. This specification technique is similar to that used in equational algebraic specifications [10]
and in Meyer's Eiffel examples [24].

The other methods in Fig. 1 have more extensive specifications. The pick
method exhibits the three standard clauses used in a JML method specification.
The pick method's precondition, given by its **requires** clause, is that the
result of calling size() must be strictly greater than zero; that is, the method
should only be called when the object contains some elements. The frame condition for pick is given by its **assignable** clause, which says that it may assign
to the locations in the data group named state; this datagroup is declared in
the interface. The state datagroup will be populated with fields in the types
that implement the IntSet interface (as we will see below). The postcondition,
given in the **ensures** clause, says that the result will be an element of the set,
since the value returned will satisfy the assertion **this**.contains(**\result**).
The add method has a default precondition of **true**, can assign to the locations
in the datagroup state, and has a postcondition that says that its argument

(i) will be in the set at the end of the operation, and that the size of the set will not decrease. The notation \old(E), which is borrowed from Eiffel [24], denotes the value of the expression E in the method's pre-state. (The *pre-state* of a method m is the state of the program after passing parameters to m, but before running any of its code.) Similarly, the remove method's postcondition says that after the method executes, its argument (i) will no longer be in the set and the size will not increase.[1]

1.3   Verifying Method Calls with Supertype Abstraction

The basic technique for verifying a method call is to:

1. check (assert) the method's precondition before the call,
2. "havoc" all locations that are assignable by the method, and
3. assume that the method's postcondition holds after the call.

Locations that are assignable by the called method are imagined to be set by the method to an arbitrary, unknown value; this is what "havoc" does. However, such locations will usually be constrained by the method's postcondition to values that satisfy that postcondition. On the other hand, locations that are not assignable in the method are preserved by the method's execution. Thus the frame in the method's specification can be used to prove that properties that hold before the call (in the call's pre-state) also hold after the call (in the call's post-state). Properties are automatically preserved by the call if they do not depend on locations that may be assigned by the method called (i.e., if they are independent of the method's frame).

This technique for method call verification is modular because it avoids checking the correctness of the method's implementation each time the method is called. The verification technique is independent of the method's implementation, as verification relies only on its specification (its precondition, frame, and postcondition). Therefore a method's specification plays the key role in verifying calls to that method.

With supertype abstraction, once we know the specification of IntSet, we can verify client code written for it, even though we do not know any of the details of the classes that implement IntSet. Two simple examples of some client code are shown in Fig. 2.

We demonstrate the above technique by verifying the testPick method; the verification is recorded with intermediate assertions in Fig. 3 on the next page. At the beginning of the method testPick, its precondition is assumed. To verify the call to pick, following supertype abstraction we use the specification of pick from the static type of the call's receiver (iset), which is IntSet. So the method's specification is taken from Fig. 1. Its precondition is the same as the assumption (with the receiver substituted for the implicit receiver (**this**) in the

---

[1] The size is not specified to decrease, since it can stay the same if the element being removed was not in the set in the pre-state.

```
public class IntSetClient {
    //@ requires iset.size() > 0;
    public static void testPick(IntSet iset) {
        int k = iset.pick();
        //@ assert iset.contains(k);
    }

    //@ requires iv.size() == 3;
    //@ assignable iv.state;
    public static void testAddRemove(IntSet iv) {
        iv.add(1);
        //@ assert iv.contains(1);
        long s = iv.size();
        //@ assert s >= 3;
        iv.remove(1);
        //@ assert !(iv.contains(1)) && iv.size() <= s;
    }
}
```

Fig. 2. Client code that uses `IntSet`.

specification[2]). Since we are assuming that `iset.size()>0`, that follows, and so we can assume the postcondition of the `pick` method. Again, in the assumed postcondition the actual receiver (`iset`) is substituted for the implicit receiver (**this**) in the specification. With this assumption, the assertion to prove at the end of the method follows immediately.

```
//@ requires iset.size() > 0;
public static void testPick(IntSet iset) {
    //@ assume iset.size() > 0;
    //@ assert iset.size() > 0;    // checking method precondition
    int k = iset.pick();
    //@ assume iset.contains(k);   // assumed method postcondition
    //@ assert iset.contains(k);
}
```

Fig. 3. Client code that uses `IntSet` with intermediate assertions.

For the `testAddRemove` method, the assertions can also be verified using just the specifications given for `IntSet`'s methods (see Fig. 4 on the next page). Again this is independent of the implementation of the argument `iv`. Note that only the specifications given in `IntSet` can be used, so one cannot conclude that the value of `s`, the size of `iv` after adding 1 to `iv`, will be 4, only that `s` will be no less than the original size (3).

---

[2] Recall that a call such as `size()` is shorthand for **this**.`size()` in Java, thus substituting `iset` for **this** in `size()>0` turns it into `iset.size() > 0`.

```
//@ requires iv.size() == 3;
//@ assignable iv.state;
public static void testAddRemove(IntSet iv) {
    //@ assume iv.size() == 3;
    //@ assert true;            // add's precondition
    addcall: iv.add(1);
    //@ assume iv.contains(1); // add's postcondition
    //@ assume iv.size() >= \old(iv.size(),addcall); // continued
    //@ assume iv.size() >= 3; // meaning of \old(,addcall) (*)
    //@ assert iv.contains(1);
    //@ assume true;        // size's precondition
    long s = iv.size();
    //@ assume s == iv.size(); // meaning of assignment (**)
    //@ assume s >= 0;      // size's postcondition
    //@ assume s >= 3;       // size is pure so (*) is preserved (***)
    //@ assert s >= 3;
    rmc: iv.remove(1);
    //@ assume !iv.contains(1) && iv.size() <= \old(iv.size(), rmc);
    //@ assume !iv.contains(1) && iv.size() <= s; // by (**) & (***)
    //@ assert !(iv.contains(1)) && iv.size() <= s;
}
```

Fig. 4. Client code that uses `IntSet`'s add and remove methods, with a verification recorded using assertions. The assertions use labelled statements and the operator **\old**(,) with a label argument, to reference the prestate of the statement with the given label.

These examples illustrate the modularity properties of supertype abstraction. There are two important points to make. First, the specification is modular in the sense that it is given independently of any subtypes of `IntSet`, and does not need to be changed if new subtypes implementing `IntSet` are added to the program. Second, the verification of the client code is similarly modular in the sense that it does not depend on the possible subtypes of `IntSet`, and thus does not need to be redone when new subtypes are added to the program.

1.4   Subtypes for the IntSet Example

To make some of these ideas more concrete, we will consider several subtypes of `IntSet`.

One family of simple implementations for `IntSet` are closed intervals of integers, represented by objects that track a lower and upper bound in the fields `lb` and `ub`. The **in** declaration adds these fields to the datagroup `state`. This design's common parts are described in the abstract class `AbsInterval` (see Fig. 5 on the next page). The objects of subtypes of this class represent closed intervals of integers, which we can think of as containing all integers between the instance field values `lb` and `ub`, inclusive, i.e., $[lb, ub]$. An interval such as $[3, 2]$ represents the empty set.

The abstract class `AbsInterval` represents `lb` and `ub` as **long** (64-bit) integers. These fields have **protected** visibility in Java, but are also declared to be **spec_public** in the first JML annotation. One can think of **spec_public** fields as being declared to be public for purposes of specification, but having the declared visibility (protected in this case) for use in Java code. Declaring the fields to be public for specification purposes allows them to be used in specifications intended to be seen by all clients. There is a public invariant; invariants state properties that must hold whenever a method call is not in progress [19, Sect. 8.2]. The invariant states that lb must be in the range of **int** values (between Integer.MIN_VALUE and Integer.MAX_VALUE). It also says that ub cannot be greater than the largest **int** value and that it can only be one smaller than the smallest int value. The type **long** is used for the fields lb and ub in order to (a) avoid integer overflow, and (b) to allow representation of extreme cases of empty intervals. An empty interval is one in which the value of ub is less than the value of lb; indeed the invariant lb <= ub+1 implies that this only happens when lb-1 == ub. (Note that conjunct of the invariant would not make sense if both these fields had type **int** and if lb held the smallest **int** value.)

The constructor for AbsInterval has a requirement that its arguments, l and u, must be such that l is not greater than u+1, so that the invariant will hold when l is assigned to lb and u is assigned to ub. The constructor of AbsInterval has a "heavyweight" specification [19, Sect. 2.3], which says that when called in a state that satisfies its precondition, it must terminate normally (without throwing an exception), as it is a **normal_behavior** specification.

The specification of the contains method starts with the keyword **also**, to indicate that the specification adds to the specification inherited from the supertype IntSet. Since both specifications have the same precondition (**true**), effectively this adds an additional postcondition to the method's specification for all subtypes of AbsInterval. This specification thus allows a verifier to equate contains(i) with (lb <= i && i <= ub) in proofs, as **<==>** means "if and only if" in JML.

The specification of the method size (at the end of the figure) is similar. It says that the size of the set is the value of the expression ub - lb + 1. The reader can check that this expression is the number of integers i such that contains(i) is true.

The add method in AbsInterval inherits the specification from IntSet unchanged. Thus, if iv is an object of type AbsInterval, then when iv.add(i) returns, it must be that iv.contains(i) holds. The implementation may add more elements to the set, in addition to the argument (i), as the implementation can only represent closed intervals. Indeed the implementation will set either the lower bound (lb) or the upper bound (ub) to i. This may not seem like the expected behavior for sets, but it satisfies the specification given in IntSet.

The remove method similarly inherits its specification from IntSet. The implementation will set either the lower or the upper bound to just past the element to be removed. The assert statements used in the method are designed to help the prover in the JML tools conclude that the method is implemented

```
public abstract class AbsInterval implements IntSet {
    /*@ spec_public @*/ protected long lb, ub; //@ in state;
    /*@ public invariant Integer.MIN_VALUE <= lb
      @                  && lb <= Integer.MAX_VALUE
      @                  && lb <= ub+1 && Integer.MIN_VALUE <= ub+1
      @                  && ub <= Integer.MAX_VALUE; @*/

    //@ public normal_behavior
    //@   requires Integer.MIN_VALUE <= l && l <= Integer.MAX_VALUE;
    //@   requires Integer.MIN_VALUE <= u+1 && u <= Integer.MAX_VALUE;
    //@   requires l <= ((long)u)+1;
    //@   assignable state;
    //@   ensures lb == (long)l && ub == (long)u;
    public AbsInterval(int l, int u) {
        lb = l; ub = u;
    }
    //@ also ensures \result <==> (lb <= i && i <= ub);
    public /*@ pure @*/ boolean contains(int i) {
        return lb <= i && i <= ub;
    }
    public void add(int i) {
        if (!contains(i)) {
            //@ assert (i < lb || i > ub);
            if (i < lb) { //@ assume i < ub && i <= ub;
                lb = i;
                //@ assert contains(i) && lb < \old(lb);
            } else { //@ assert i > ub && lb <= i;
                ub = i;
                //@ assert contains(i) && ub > \old(ub);
            }
            /*@ assert this.contains(i)
              @        && this.size() > \old(this.size()); @*/
        }
        //@ assert this.contains(i) && this.size() >= \old(this.size());
    }
    public void remove(int i) {
        long il = (long)i;
        if (!contains(i)) { return; }
        //@ assert lb <= il && il <= ub;
        if (lb == ub) {
            lb = 0; ub = -1;
            //@ assert !contains(i) && lb <= ub+1;
        } else if (il-lb < ub-il && il != Integer.MAX_VALUE) {
            lb = il+1;
            //@ assert !contains(i) && lb <= ub+1;
        } else { //@ assert (il-lb >= ub-il) || il == Integer.MAX_VALUE;
            ub = il-1;
            //@ assert !contains(i) && lb <= ub+1;
        } }
    //@ also ensures \result == ub - lb + 1;
    public /*@ pure @*/ long size() {
        return ub - lb + 1;
    } }
```

Fig. 5. The abstract class `AbsInterval`, which is a subtype of `IntSet`.

correctly. In each case the method must ensure that the argument is no longer in the set and that the second invariant (lb <= ub+1) holds. The reader is urged to verify these assertions, recalling that both the lower and upper bound fields are of type **long**.

As an example of supertype abstraction, the verification of the client code in figure Fig. 4 still holds, even if the argument is a subtype of AbsInterval.

To understand these modularity properties better, it will be useful to consider some concrete subtypes of IntSet, which implement the pick method.

The first of these concrete subtypes of AbsInterval is the class Interval shown in Fig. 6. This class's implementation of pick always returns the lower bound of the interval. The specification of pick in Fig. 6 says that, in addition to the inherited specification, it returns the value of lb, when lb <= ub, i.e., when the interval is not empty. Since that precondition is equivalent (by the specification of contains) to the precondition of pick given in IntSet (see Fig. 1), this added specification case effectively adds an additional postcondition to pick, when the receiver's type is a subtype of Interval. The implementation satisfies both the inherited postcondition and the postconditions in this additional specification when the interval is not empty.

```
public class Interval extends AbsInterval {
    //@ requires l <= ((long)u)+1;
    //@ ensures lb == l && ub == u;
    public Interval(int l, int u) {
        super(l,u);
    }

    //@ also
    //@     requires lb <= ub;
    //@     assignable state;
    //@     ensures lb == \old(lb) && ub == \old(ub);
    //@     ensures \result == (int)lb;
    public int pick() {
        //@ assert lb <= (int)lb && (int)lb <= ub;
        return (int)lb;
    }
}
```

Fig. 6. A subtype of IntSet, the concrete class Interval.

The second of these concrete subtypes of AbsInterval is the class Interval2 shown in Fig. 7 on the next page. This class's implementation of pick returns the value of the field next_pick, which is constrained by its invariants to be an element of the interval and to have a value that can be represented by an **int**. The added specification for pick in Fig. 7 describes this behavior. Again, the implementation is correct if the interval is not empty.

```
public class Interval2 extends AbsInterval {
    /*@ spec_public @*/ protected long next_pick; //@ in state;
    //@ public invariant Integer.MIN_VALUE <= next_pick;
    //@ public invariant next_pick <= Integer.MAX_VALUE;
    //@ public invariant lb <= ub ==> contains((int)next_pick);

    //@ requires l <= ((long)u)+1;
    //@ assignable state;
    //@ ensures lb == l && ub == u;
    //@ ensures next_pick == lb;
    public Interval2(int l, int u) {
        super(l,u);
        next_pick = lb;
    }

    //@ also
    //@    requires lb <= ub;
    //@    assignable next_pick;
    //@    ensures lb == \old(lb) && ub == \old(ub);
    //@    ensures \result == (int)next_pick;
    public int pick() {
        //@ assume lb <= ub;
        if (next_pick < ub) {
            next_pick++;
            if (next_pick > ub) { next_pick = lb; }
            //@ assert (lb <= next_pick && next_pick <= ub);
        } else {
            next_pick = lb;
            //@ assert (lb <= next_pick && next_pick <= ub);
        }
        //@ assert contains((int)next_pick);
        return (int)next_pick;
    }
}
```

Fig. 7. A subtype of IntSet, the class Interval2.

Consider now the code in Fig. 8 on page 10. The final assertion in that figure verifies because iv has type Interval, and the added specification case for pick in Interval's specification (see Fig. 6) says it returns the lower bound of the interval. In JML, a method that is specified with several specification cases (some of which may be inherited) must obey all of them, so a client can either pick one specification case and use that to verify a call to the method, as is done in Fig. 8, or use the combined meaning of the specification cases.

However, suppose that the type of iv in Fig. 8 were changed to IntSet, and the initialization for that variable called the constructor of Interval2. In that case, the value of iv would be an object of the class Interval2. And in that case the last assertion in Fig. 8 would not always be valid, since Interval2's method pick need not always return the lower bound of the interval. Supertype

```
public void testPickConcrete() {
    Interval iv = new Interval(5,7);
    //@ assume iv.lb == 5 && iv.ub == 7;
    int p;
    //@ assert iv.lb <= iv.ub;
    pck: p = iv.pick();
    //@ assume p == iv.lb;
    //@ assert p == 5;
}
```

Fig. 8. A test of the pick method for a concrete subtype of IntSet.

abstraction safely avoids drawing such invalid conclusions, because it only allows using the specification of the supertype (e.g., IntSet) in such cases.

2 Background and Motivation

Ideally, one could characterize supertype abstraction in a way that does not depend on the details of a specification language and the details of a particular verification logic. This is what was done in our earlier *TOPLAS* paper [17]. Instead of repeating that formal development, in what follows we will try to adapt those more general results (from the *TOPLAS* paper [17]) to Java and JML. In the process we will skim over some of the formal details, which may not match Java and JML exactly.

2.1 Background: Denotational and Axiomatic Semantics

A verification logic that is sound must, by definition, only draw conclusions that are valid in all possible executions. This requires a model of both the meaning of a specification and of how a program executes: the semantics of the specification language and the semantics of the programming language.

There are three broad families of programming language semantics, developed in the 1960s:

- Denotational semantics, developed by Strachey and Scott [28–31]. A standard summary is found in Schmidt's book [27]. A denotational semantics describes the meaning of a program as a mathematical function.
- Operational semantics, developed by Landin [14,15]. A modern treatment is given in Hennessy's book [11]. An operational semantics describes the meaning of a program as a rewrite machine.
- Axiomatic semantics, developed by Floyd and (Tony) Hoare [9,12]. An axiomatic semantics describes the meaning of a program as a proof system. A modern treatment is given in Apt and Olderog's book [4].

For example, in the denotational semantics of a simple imperative language, one may use states, σ, that are finite functions from variable names to values.

Thus the denotational semantics of an assignment statement such as k = k+1; would be given by a meaning function, such as $\mathcal{C}$, that maps commands (statements) and states to states; for example

$$\mathcal{C}[\![k \ = \ k{+}1;]\!](\sigma) = [\sigma \mid k : \sigma(k) + 1]$$

where the notation $[\sigma \mid k : (\sigma(k) + 1)]$ means a mapping that is the same as σ except that for the argument k the result is the value $\sigma(k) + 1$:

$$[f \mid x : v] = \lambda y \cdot \textbf{if } y \equiv x \textbf{ then } v \textbf{ else } f(y).$$

An axiomatic semantics describes states using predicates; one can think of a predicate as representing the set of all states that satisfy it. For example, the predicate k > 0 describes all states in which the value of the variable k (presumably an integer) is strictly greater than zero. A Hoare logic for a programming language gives axioms and rules for drawing conclusions about program states. Hoare logic uses "Hoare triples" of the form $\{P\}\ C\ \{Q\}$ which mean that if the command C is executed starting in a state satisfying the predicate P (the precondition), and if C terminates normally, then the predicate Q (the postcondition) will hold. For example, the following is a valid Hoare triple (ignoring integer overflow):

$$\{k \ > \ 0\} \ k \ = \ k{+}1; \ \{k \ > \ 1\}.$$

We will sometimes write Hoare triples using assume and assert in JML; thus the example above would be written in JML as follows.

```
//@ assume k > 0;
k = k+1;
//@ assert k > 1;
```

To define a programming language's meaning, one must generalize from specific examples, such as those above. In a Hoare Logic, this is done by giving

ASSIGN
$\vdash \{P[E/x]\}\ x{=}E;\ \{P\}$

SKIP
$\vdash \{P\}\ ;\ \{P\}$

SIMPLESEQ
$$\frac{\vdash \{P\}\ C_1\ \{Q\}, \qquad \vdash \{Q\}\ C_2\ \{R\}}{\vdash \{P\}\ C_1\ C_2\ \{R\}}$$

CONSEQ
$$\frac{\vdash \{P'\}\ C\ \{Q'\}}{\vdash \{P\}\ C\ \{Q\}} \text{ if } P \Rightarrow P' \text{ and } Q' \Rightarrow Q$$

WHILE
$$\frac{\vdash \{I\ \&\&\ x\}\ C\ \{I\}}{\vdash \{I\}\ \textbf{while } (x)\ \{\ C\}\ \{I\ \&\&\ !x\}}$$

IF
$$\frac{\vdash \{P\ \&\&\ x\}\ C_1\ \{Q\}, \qquad \vdash \{P\ \&\&\ !x\}\ C_2\ \{Q\}}{\vdash \{P\}\ \textbf{if } (x)\ \{\ C_1\ \}\ \textbf{else }\{\ C_2\ \}\ \{Q\}}$$

Fig. 9. Some simple Hoare Logic rules. These rules assume that test expressions in while and if statements are variables, since those have no side effects, and that the expressions in assignment statements have no side effects.

axiom schemes for simple statements and proof rules for compound statements. Some simple axioms and inference rules in a Hoare Logic are presented in Fig. 9. The "turnstile", ⊢, can be read as "one can prove that." The rules SEQ, CONSEQ, WHILE, and IF are inference rules, with hypotheses above the horizontal line and a conclusion below it. The CONSEQ rule has a side condition, starting with **if**, which tells when the rule can be used.

Example 1. A proof in Hoare logic can be written as a tree. For example to prove the Hoare triple in the conclusion below, one uses the SEQ rule, with two sub-derivations (sub-trees, growing upwards), named (A1) and (I1), corresponding to the two hypotheses of the SEQ rule. So overall the tree looks as follows, where the subderivations (A1) and (I1) will be explained below.

$$
\cfrac{(A1), \qquad \cfrac{(C1), \qquad (C2)}{(I1)} \; \text{IF}}{\vdash \{\texttt{true}\} \; \texttt{xGty = x>y; if (xGty) \{m=x;\} else \{m=y;\} } \{\texttt{m>=x\&\&m>=y}\}} \; \text{SEQ}
$$

Derivation (A1) uses the CONSEQ rule and has a hypothesis that is an instance of the ASSIGN axiom scheme. The conclusion of (A1) is the first hypothesis needed by the SEQ rule above.

$$
(A1) \; \cfrac{\vdash \{\texttt{(x>y) == (x>y)}\} \; \texttt{xGty=x>y; } \{\texttt{(xGty)==(x>y)}\} \; \text{ASSIGN}}{\vdash \{\texttt{true}\} \; \texttt{xGty=x>y; } \{\texttt{(xGty)==(x>y)}\}} \; \text{CONSEQ}
$$

The derivation (I1) uses the IF rule. Since the IF rule has two hypotheses, there are two more sub-derivations, named (C1), and (C2) as required by the IF rule.

$$
(I1) \; \cfrac{(C1), \qquad (C2)}{\vdash \{\texttt{(xGty)==(x>y)}\} \; \texttt{if (xGty) \{m=x;\} else \{m=y;\} } \{\texttt{m>=x\&\&m>=y}\}} \; \text{IF}
$$

The derivation (C1) is as follows. Note that the conclusion is the formula needed for the first hypothesis of the IF rule. The implications can be proven using the theory of integer arithmetic.

$$
(C1) \; \cfrac{\vdash \{\texttt{x>=x\&\&x>y}\} \; \texttt{m=x; } \{\texttt{m>=x\&\&m>y}\}}{\vdash \{\texttt{((xGty)==(x>y))\&\&xGty}\} \; \texttt{m=x; } \{\texttt{m>=x\&\&m>=y}\}} \; \text{CONSEQ}
$$

The derivation (C2) is similar. Its conclusion is the formula needed for the second hypothesis of the IF rule.

$$
(C2) \; \cfrac{\vdash \{\texttt{y>=x\&\&(y>=y)}\} \; \texttt{m=y; } \{\texttt{y>=x\&\&m>=y}\}}{\vdash \{\texttt{((xGty)==(x>y))\&\&!xGty}\} \; \texttt{m=y; } \{\texttt{m>=x\&\&m>=y}\}} \; \text{CONSEQ}
$$

■

Another way to display this proof is to use intermediate assertions, as shown in Fig. 10 below. In the figure preconditions of Hoare triples follow the keyword **assume** and postconditions follow **assert**. Two such conditions written next to each other indicate a use of the CONSEQ rule. Overall the first assume and the last assert are the formulas in the main derivation given above, with the assertion (xGty) == (x>y) being the assertion that is between the two statements as demanded by the SEQ rule. The proof of the first statement (lines 1–5) corresponds to the derivation (A1) above. The proof of the if-statement is given in the rest of the lines, with the five lines around each assignment statement corresponding to derivations (C1) and (C2) above. Comments to the right of each assume or assert indicate which rule these preconditions and postconditions correspond to.

```
//@ assume true;                        // Seq
//@ assume (x>y) == (x>y);              // Assign (A1)
xGty = x>y;
//@ assert (xGty) == (x>y);             // Assign (A1)
//@ assume (xGty) == (x>y);             // If
if (xGty) {
    //@ assume ((xGty) == (x>y)) && xGty; // Conseq (C1)
    //@ assume x>=x && x>y;             // Assign
    m = x;
    //@ assert m>=x && m>y;             // Assign
    //@ assert m>=x && m>=y;            // Conseq (C1)
} else {
    //@ assume ((xGty) == (x>y)) && !xGty; // Conseq (C2)
    //@ assume y>=x && y>=y;            // Assign
    m = y;
    //@ assert m>=x && m>=y;            // Assign
    //@ assert m>=x && m>=y;            // Conseq (C2)
}
//@ assert m >= x && m >= y;            // If
//@ assert m >= x && m >= y;            // Seq
```

Fig. 10. Code for computing the maximum value of x and y with intermediate assertions.

In sum, Hoare Logic uses predicates to represent sets of states. Statements transform preconditions into postconditions. And intermediate assertions can stand for a Hoare Logic proof.

The challenge is to extend this verification technique in a modular way to the verification of method calls in Java.

2.2   Specification Language Semantics

A fundamental step towards modular verification of method calls is to specify the state transformation that a method call achieves. Declaring method speci-

```
//@ requires true;
//@ ensures \result >= x && \result >= y;
public int max(int x, int y);
```

Fig. 11. Specification of a max function in JML.

fications avoids having to inline method bodies to verify method calls. It also allows the verification of recursive and mutually-recursive methods.

In JML method specifications are written with **requires** and **ensures** clauses (and possibly with **assignable** clauses). For example, a specification for a max method on two **int** arguments is shown in Fig. 11.

To deal with Java's **return** statement, some extension to Hoare Logic is needed, as this statement does not terminate normally, but abruptly stops execution of the surrounding method [13]. Instead of investigating such extensions here, we will content ourselves with proving that the value returned satisfies the appropriate condition, just before the return statement.

In this way one can show that the code given in Example 1, when put in sequence with **return** m; correctly implements the specification of Fig. 11.[3]

To abstract a bit from the syntax of specifications we define some terms, following the *TOPLAS* paper [17]. (A table of notations appears in Fig. 18 on page 42 at the end of this paper.)

A pair of a precondition and a postcondition, (P, Q), is called a *simple specification* [17].

Validity of specifications is defined with respect to the denotational semantics of the language. If C is the meaning function for commands, then a Hoare formula $\{P\} \, C \, \{Q\}$ is *valid in state* σ, written $\sigma \models \{P\} \, C \, \{Q\}$ if and only if: whenever P holds in state σ and the meaning of C starting in state σ is a state σ', then Q holds in state σ'. As a mathematical formula, we write this as follows

$$\sigma \models \{P\} \, C \, \{Q\} \stackrel{\text{def}}{=} (\sigma \in P \wedge \mathcal{C}[\![C]\!](\sigma) = \sigma') \Rightarrow (\sigma' \in Q) \tag{1}$$

thinking of predicates as sets of states, so that $\sigma \in P$ means that P holds in state σ and using $\mathcal{C}[\![C]\!](\sigma) = \sigma'$ to mean that the meaning of command C started in state σ is state σ'. This is partial correctness; since if the command C does not terminate normally (does not produce a state σ'), then the implication holds trivially.

A Hoare triple $\{P\} \, C \, \{Q\}$ is *valid*, written $\models \{P\} \, C \, \{Q\}$, if and only if it is valid for all states.

Definition 1 (Validity of Simple Specifications). *A* command *C correctly* implements *a simple specification* (P, Q) *if and only if* $\models \{P\} \, C \, \{Q\}$.

The concept of refinement of specifications is of great importance in what follows. To define refinement, it is useful to define the set

---

[3] There still are some other details omitted, such as how declarations (e.g., of the variable xGty) are handled.

of commands that correctly implement a specification. We notate this
$Impls(P, Q) \overset{\text{def}}{=} \{C \mid \models \{P\}\ C\ \{Q\}\}$.

Definition 2 (Refinement). *Let* (P, Q) *and* (P', Q') *be simple specifications. Then* (P', Q') *refines* (P, Q), *written* $(P', Q') \sqsupseteq (P, Q)$, *if and only if* $Impls(P', Q') \subseteq Impls(P, Q)$.

It is an easy corollary that if $(P', Q') \sqsupseteq (P, Q)$, then for all commands C, if $\models \{P'\}\ C\ \{Q'\}$, then $\models \{P\}\ C\ \{Q\}$.

2.3   Programming Language Semantics

An *object* in an OO language is data with an identity (its address on the heap) and several named fields (also called instance variables). In most OO languages objects have infinite lifetimes and live on the heap. Objects are referred to indirectly by their addresses and their fields are mutable (can hold different values over time). In addition, in a class-based OO language, like Java, objects refer to their class, so it is possible to determine their class dynamically.

A *class* is a code module that describes objects. Classes are a built-in feature of Java and other OO languages, such as Smalltalk-80, C++, and C#. Classes contain declarations for the fields of objects of that class, methods, which are procedures that operate on objects, and constructors, which initialize objects. Examples of classes in Java are given in Figs. 6 and 7. A method declaration in a class may be *abstract* if it does not have an implementation. In Java an abstract method is either declared with a semicolon (;) instead of a method body or is inherited from a supertype but not implemented.

An *interface* is like a class, but with no method implementations; that is, all the methods it declares are abstract. Interfaces can be used as types in Java.

In Java, subtype relationships are declared. A class may declare that it implements one or more interfaces, making it a *subtype* of all of those interfaces, and those interfaces are its *supertypes*. For example, the examples in the introduction directly declare the following subtype relationships.

```
AbsInterval ≤ IntSet
Interval    ≤ AbsInterval
Interval2   ≤ AbsInterval
```

In addition, subtyping is reflexively and transitively closed, so `Interval` $\leq$ `IntSet`.

Types are upper bounds in an OO language. Thus, if S is a subtype of T, which we write as $S \leq T$, then one can assign an object of type S to a variable declared to have type T and one can pass an actual parameter of type S to a formal parameter of type T.

To have indefinite lifetimes, objects are stored in the heap, as shown in Fig. 12. Local variables, such as `ivl`, are stored in the runtime stack. When a variable's type is a reference type its contents consist of a reference (i.e., a pointer) to an

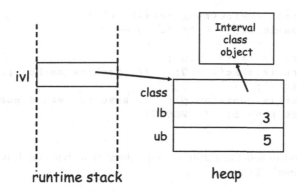

Fig. 12. Picture of the stack and heap after executing the statement
ivl = new Interval(3,5);.

object, in this case an object of class `Interval`. Objects are typically represented as records that can be mathematically modeled as mappings from field names to values. There is a distinguished field named `class` that contains a reference to the class object, which is a run-time representation of the class declaration.

Class objects themselves contain their name, a reference to their superclass object, and a method table that maps method names to the a closure for that method. The closure contains the code for the method's body as well as the names of its formal parameters.

To explain how the dynamic dispatch mechanism for method calls works in Java and other OO languages, consider the call `ivl.size()`. To evaluate this expression, Java:

1. Evaluates `ivl`, producing a reference to an object, o (a pointer).
2. Finds the class of o (o.class), say this is the class whose class object is Iv.
3. Looks up the method code for the method named `size` (with no arguments) in the method table found via Iv.
4. Allocates space for the result of the call.
5. Creates a stack frame for the call, binding **this** to o (and in general also binding formals to actuals).
6. Runs the code in the new stack frame.
7. Executing a **return** E; statement evaluates the expression E, copies the value of E to the space allocated for it, and then pops the call's stack frame off the runtime stack.

Calling methods indirectly via the method table found at runtime from the receiver object is what makes this calling mechanism dynamic. Consider the call to `pick` in Fig. 3. The argument `iset` could be any subtype of `IntSet`, including `Interval`, `Interval2`, and even subtypes of `IntSet` that have not yet been programmed.

As another example, consider the call to `pick` shown in Fig. 13. In this figure, the argument has type `AbsInterval`, and thus the actual argument could

```
public void badTestPick(AbsInterval iv) {
    //@ assume iv.lb == 5 && iv.ub == 7;
    int p;
    //@ assert iv.lb <= iv.ub;
    //@ assert iv.size() > 0;     // checking method precondition
    p = iv.pick();
    //@ assume iv.contains(p);    // assumed method postcondition
    //@ assert p == 5;  // WRONG!
}
```

Fig. 13. A method that demonstrates the problems that dynamic dispatch causes for reasoning about method calls.

have a dynamic type that is `Interval`, `Interval2`, or any other subtype of `AbsInterval`. The integer returned by the call must be in the interval, but although `Interval`'s method will return 5, there is no guarantee that if `iv` denotes an object of dynamic type `Interval2` (or some other subtype) that the result will be 5, so the last assertion may fail. Thus the verification technique must take dynamic dispatch into account.

The essence of the problem is that specification and verification are done statically, before runtime, but the dynamic types of objects are only known (in general) at runtime. Furthermore, OO programs are "open" in the sense that new types may be added after the program is specified and verified, so even an exhaustive case analysis of the program's existing types will not be sound. Finally, not only is the code of the method that is run by a call determined dynamically, but the different subtypes may have different specifications for what the method should do. (However, for modular verification to be possible, we will always assume that methods correctly implement their specifications.)

To explain this problem in verification, imagine a verification technique that relies on a table of specifications for each method, indexed by dynamic types, and that verifies code involving method calls exhaustively, with a verification for each possible dynamic type of each call's receiver, using the dynamic type's specification. When new types are added to a program, all proofs must be examined and new cases must be added where needed to account for the new types. An advantage of this verification technique is that it would be very precise, as it could consider the exact effects of each method call. However, such a technique would not be scalable, since adding a new type to a program would require finding and reproving an unbounded number of assertions. The number of cases that would need to be considered would explode with the number of combinations of different dynamic types that are possible in a program fragment that is to be verified. In essence, such a technique would not be modular.

We would like a reasoning technique that is both static (so that specification and verification are done before runtime) and modular (so that adding new types to a program does not cause re-specification or re-verification). In addition, a suitable reasoning technique should be not much more difficult than reasoning about non-OO programs.

2.4   Supertype Abstraction

A reasoning technique for OO programs that is both static and modular is supertype abstraction [16,17,20,21]. Supertype abstraction relies on static type information to give upper bounds on the types of expressions; in a language without a built-in static type system, a separate static analysis could provide this information. Verification of a method call uses the specification of the method being called found in the receiver's static type. For validity, an overriding method in a subtype must obey all specifications for that method in all its supertypes, since these supertype specifications could be used in reasoning; that is, all subtypes must be behavioral subtypes [1–3,17,20–23]. In addition, if other properties of supertypes, such as invariants, can be used in reasoning, then subtype objects must also obey those properties.

An example of reasoning using supertype abstraction is shown in Fig. 2, which uses the specifications found in the supertype IntSet to verify the call to pick.

Behavioral subtyping, which is necessary for the validity of supertype abstraction [17], must be checked when new types are added to a program. These new types must each be behavioral subtypes of all of their supertypes (in particular of those that are already present in the program).

Even though supertypes generally have more abstract (less precise) specifications than subtypes, one can recover the precision of reasoning by using dynamic type information, while still using supertype abstraction. The way to do this is to use type tests (**instanceof** in Java) and downcasting to align the static types of receiver objects with dynamic type information. Figure 14 shows an example in which there is a supertype Staff of types Doctor and Nurse, and type tests and downcasting are used to specialize the static types of receivers. Then supertype abstraction can be used to verify the calls to methods on these subtypes. Thus by using supertype abstraction, one does not lose any ability to verify OO programs, compared to an exhaustive case analysis, since by using type tests and downcasts, one can add explicit case analysis on dynamic types.

```
/*@ requires p instanceof Doctor
  @          || p instanceof Nurse; @*/
public boolean isHead(final Staff p) {
    if (p instanceof Doctor) {
        Doctor doc = (Doctor) p;
        return doc.getTitle().startsWith("Head");
    } else {
        Nurse nrs = (Nurse) p;
        return nrs.isChief();
    }
}
```

Fig. 14. Using downcasting to do case analysis.

3   Semantics

In order to investigate the connection between supertype abstraction and behavioral subtyping, our *TOPLAS* paper [17] used a small "core" programming language that is similar to Java. To avoid repeating that formal development here, we will simply outline the main ideas and results.

3.1   A-Normal Form

A small problem with verification in a language such as Java is that expressions may, in general, have side effects. These side effects make it unsound to use substitution (of such expressions) in verification rules. To avoid these problems the core language used in the *TOPLAS* paper has a syntax that is in "A-normal form" [26]. In A-normal form, variables are used for certain expressions, such as the tests in while loops and if-statements, so that effects in such sub-expressions do not complicate the semantics. Although Java and JML do not require A-normal form syntax, we assumed it in presenting Hoare Logic rules for Java previously (in Fig. 9). Some verification tools (such as OpenJML) transform a complex expression in Java into A-normal form by rewriting the program; for example, if the condition x > y were used as the test in an if-statement, it would first declare a boolean variable, such as xGty, and assign xGty the value of that expression, as was done in Fig. 10. This transformation would be applied recursively to eliminate complex subexpressions within expressions. For example the code

```
if (a[i] > y) ...
```

would be transformed into A-normal form in a way similar to the following.[4]

```
int x; boolean xGty;
x = a[i];
xGty = (x > y);
if (xGty) ...
```

Such a program transformation would be carried out mechanically and would need to respect the semantics of Java expressions. The idea would be to allow Java expressions that involve at most one operation in an assignment statement, so that the semantics of that operator can be isolated from any side effects (or exceptions) caused by other operators.

Since method calls are expressions in Java, using A-normal form requires each actual argument be evaluated and its value stored in a variable, if it is not already a variable. Thus a call such as

```
iv.add(i+j);
```

would be transformed to something like the following (depending on the types of i and j, which the following assumes to be **int**).

---

[4] Note that the transformation must ensure that any variables declared are fresh.

```
int ipj;
ipj = i+j;
iv.add(ipj);
```

Henceforth let us assume that all programs have been converted to A-normal form.

3.2   Semantic Domains and Meaning Functions

In order to prove the soundness of a verification technique (i.e., that all conclusions reached are valid), one needs a semantics of the programming language and the specification language. To that end, the following development will discuss (but not precisely define all the details of) a denotational semantics for the programming and specification languages Java and JML. This subsection is adapted from our *TOPLAS* paper [17].

Java is a statically typed language, and our specification and verification approach requires that the static types of expressions are upper bounds of the types of values they may denote. We write typing judgments using a context (type environment), Γ, which is a finite mapping from names to types. Such finite maps are often treated as sets of pairs; for example, suppose $\Gamma_0 = [x : K, y : \mathbf{int}]$. Then the value of Γ_0 applied to x, $\Gamma_0(x)$, is K and $\Gamma_0(y)$ is $\mathbf{int}$. We extend such finite mappings using a comma, thus $[\Gamma_0, z : \mathbf{boolean}]$ is the finite map $[x : K, y : \mathbf{int}, z : \mathbf{boolean}]$. This extension notation (with the comma) is only used when the variable is not in the domain of the finite function; if it may be in the domain, then we use an override notation, such as $[\Gamma_0 \mid x : L]$, which is the finite map $[x : L, y : \mathbf{int}]$.

Types in Java can be either primitive (value) types, such as $\mathbf{int}$ and $\mathbf{boolean}$ or reference types, which are class or interface names (instantiated with type parameters if necessary). The notation *RefType* denotes the set of all reference types.

Our denotational semantics for a language like Java [17,18] assumes that the class and interface declarations of a program are available in a class table, CT, that maps reference types to their declarations. From now on the class table, CT, of the program being considered is assumed to be fixed.[5]

Types are partially ordered by the subtype relation $\leq$, which is derived from the reflexive-transitive closure of the declarations in classes and interfaces in the same way as in Java. Primitive types such as $\mathbf{int}$ are only subtypes of themselves. Subtyping for method types follows the usual contravariant ordering [6], although the formal parameter names must be identical. That is,

$$\overline{x : T} \rightarrow T_1 \quad \leq \quad \overline{y : U} \rightarrow U_1$$

if and only if $\overline{U} \leq \overline{T}$, $T_1 \leq U_1$, and $\overline{x}$ is identical to $\overline{y}$ [17].

---

[5] If classes can be created or loaded at runtime, then CT would contain all the classes that might be available to the program at runtime.

```
public abstract class AbsCounter {
  protected /*@ spec_public @*/ int count = 0;
  //@ requires count < Integer.MAX_VALUE;
  //@ assignable count;
  //@ ensures count > \old(count);
  public abstract void inc();
  //@ ensures \result == count;
  public /*@ pure @*/ int val() { return count; }
}

public class Counter extends AbsCounter {
  public void inc() { count++; }
}

public class Gauge extends AbsCounter {
  public void inc() {
    int cp2 = count+2;
    boolean ovfl = cp2 < count;
    if (!ovfl) {
      count = count+2;
    } else {
      count = Integer.MAX_VALUE;
    }
  }
}
```

Fig. 15. The classes AbsCounter two subtypes.

Example 2. Consider the interface and classes declared in Fig. 15 on the next page. This figure would produce a class table, call it CT_1, that maps AbsCounter to its declaration, Counter to its declaration, and Gauge to its declaration.

In this example Counter $\leq$ AbsCounter and Gauge $\leq$ AbsCounter, and each of these types is also a subtype of itself. ∎

As in Java, both expressions and commands (i.e., statements) can have effects. To model exceptions, our earlier work used a distinguished variable, **exc** in the post-state of a command; when no exception is thrown, **exc** is null, otherwise it contains the exception object thrown [17].

We formalize semantics uses the domains shown in Fig. 16 below.

We assume that there is a set, *Ref*, of *references*; these are the abstract addresses of objects.

To model the "class" field in an object's runtime representation that was shown in Fig. 12 we use a *ref context*, which is a finite partial function, r, that maps references to class names (and not interface names). The idea is that if $o \in dom(r)$ then o is allocated and moreover o points to an object of dynamic

Metavariable(s) $\in$ Domain		Description
o	$\in Ref$	references (addresses)
r	$\in RefCtx$	typing of allocated refs
o, v	$\in Val(T, r)$	value of type T in ref context r
Γ	$\in Context$	contexts (type environments)
s, t	$\in Store(\Gamma, r)$	stores for Γ
h	$\in Heap(r)$	heaps
σ, τ	$\in State(\Gamma)$	states for Γ
φ, ψ	$\in \Gamma_1 \rightsquigarrow \Gamma_2$	state transformers
η	$\in MethEnv$	method environment
$\dot{\eta}$	$\in XMethEnv$	extended method environment

Fig. 16. A guide to the domains used in the semantics, adapted from our earlier work [17].

type $r(o)$. We define the set of reference contexts:

$$RefCtx = Ref \rightharpoonup ClassName$$

where $\rightharpoonup$ denotes finite partial functions. For r and r' in $RefCtx$, $r \subseteq r'$ means that $dom(r) \subseteq dom(r')$ and, for objects allocated in r, the dynamic types are the same in r' [17].

For data type T its domain of values in a reference context r is defined by cases on T, where K is a class name and I is an interface name [17]:

$$
\begin{aligned}
Val(\textbf{int}, r) &= \{\ldots, -2, -1, 0, 1, 2, \ldots\} \\
Val(\textbf{boolean}, r) &= \{true, false\} \\
Val(K, r) &= \{null\} \cup \{o \mid o \in dom(r) \wedge r(o) \leq K\}, \qquad \text{if } K \in ClassName \\
Val(I, r) &= \{null\} \cup \{o \mid \exists K \cdot K \leq I \wedge o \in Val(K, r)\}, \text{if } I \in InterfaceName
\end{aligned}
$$

A *store*, s, for a context Γ is a dependent function from variables in scope to type-correct and allocated values. Thus for each $x \in dom(\Gamma)$, $s(x)$ is an element of $Val(\Gamma(x), r)$. In a store, **this** cannot be *null*.

$$
\begin{aligned}
&s \in Store(\Gamma, r) \\
&\iff s \in ((x : dom(\Gamma)) \to Val(\Gamma(x), r)) \wedge (\textbf{this} \in dom(\Gamma) \implies s(\textbf{this}) \neq null)
\end{aligned}
\tag{2}
$$

A *heap* h maps each allocated reference o to an object record, where the auxiliary function $fields$ returns a context for all the fields of the given class (taking inheritance into account) [17].

$$
\begin{aligned}
Obrecord(K, r) &\stackrel{\text{def}}{=} Store(fields(K), r) \\
Heap(r) &\stackrel{\text{def}}{=} (o : dom(r)) \to Obrecord(r(o), r)
\end{aligned}
$$

Given a type environment, Γ, a *state* for Γ is a tuple consisting of a ref context, r, together with an appropriate heap and store for r:

$$State(\Gamma) \stackrel{\text{def}}{=} (r : RefCtx) \times Heap(r) \times Store(\Gamma, r)$$

Example 3. An example of a state for the class table CT_1 (in Example 2) is as follows. Let the type environment Γ_2 be [c : AbsCounter, g : AbsCounter]. Let the store s_2 be [c : o_1, g : o_2]. Let a reference context, r_2 be [o_1 : Counter, o_2 : Gauge]. Let a heap for r_2 be defined by $h_2(o_1) = $ [count : 0] and $h_2(o_2) = $ [count : 2]. Then (r_2, h_2, s_2) is an element of $State(\Gamma_2)$. ∎

A *state transformer*, which is an element of $\Gamma \leadsto \Gamma'$ is a function φ that maps each state σ in $State(\Gamma)$ to either $\bot$ or a state $\varphi(\sigma)$ in $State(\Gamma')$, with a possibly extended heap, subject to some additional conditions.

$$\Gamma \leadsto \Gamma' \stackrel{\text{def}}{=}$$
$$(\sigma : State(\Gamma)) \to (\{\bot\} \cup \{\sigma' \mid \sigma' \in State(\Gamma'), extState(\sigma, \sigma'), imuThis(\sigma, \sigma')\})$$

The predicate $extState(\sigma, \sigma')$ says that the ref context of σ is extended by the ref context of σ'. The predicate $imuThis(\sigma, \sigma')$ says that **this** is not changed (if present in both states).

Example 4. Let Δ_3 be [**this** : Counter] and Δ_3' be [**res** : **void**, **exc** : Throwable]. A state transformer that is an element of $\Delta_3 \leadsto \Delta_3'$ is φ_3 defined by

$$\varphi_3(r, h, s) = (r, h', s')$$

where for some $o \in Ref$ and integer n, if $s(\textbf{this}) = o$ and $(h(o))(\text{count}) = n$, then the resulting heap is defined by $h' = [h \mid o : [h(o) \mid \text{count} : n+1]]$, and the resulting store is defined by $s' = [\textbf{res} : it, \textbf{exc} : null]$. (This state transformer would be appropriate for a call to Counter's method inc; see Fig. 15. This transformer uses **res** to hold the method's normal result. It also uses *it* as a value of type **void**, which avoids a special case for **void** state transformers.) ∎

State transformers are used for the meanings of expressions, commands, and methods as follows (where *mtype* returns the declared type of a method from the class table):

$$SemExpr(\Gamma, T) \stackrel{\text{def}}{=} \Gamma \leadsto [\textbf{res} : T, \textbf{exc} : \text{Throwable}]$$
$$SemCommand(\Gamma) \stackrel{\text{def}}{=} \Gamma \leadsto [\Gamma, \textbf{exc} : \text{Throwable}]$$
$$SemMeth(T, m) \stackrel{\text{def}}{=} \Gamma \leadsto [\textbf{res} : U, \textbf{exc} : \text{Throwable}]$$
$$\textbf{where } mtype(T, m) = \overline{z : U} {\to} U$$

Note that the meanings for expressions and method bodies are similar and neither contains **this** (or the formals in the case of methods). This means that expressions and method calls cannot change the store. Thus the conversion to A-normal form must make any expressions that have effects on the store that occur in a command or expression become commands that store the expression's value in a fresh variable, with this fresh variable replacing the expression with the effect. For example to convert a command such as the following

```
b = count ++ > 0;
```

into A-normal form, one would add extra commands to evaluate the expression count++ first, such as the following.

```
int ocount = count;
count = count+1;
b = ocount > 0;
```

In Java, arguments are passed by value,[6] so a method itself cannot change the formal parameters (or **this**).

Example 5. Let Γ_{xy} be [x : **int**, y : **int**]. A state transformer in $SemExpr(\Gamma_{xy}, \textbf{boolean})$ is the following. $\varphi_{xy}(r, h, s) \stackrel{\text{def}}{=} (r, h, s')$, where $s' = [\textbf{res} : s(x) > s(y), \textbf{exc} : null]$. The state transformer φ_{xy} would be the denotation of the expression x>y in the context Γ_{xy}.   ∎

Example 6. Exceptions in expressions and commands are handled by examining the special variable **exc** in the post-state. For example, the semantics of the Java assignment statement $x=E$; would be as follows.

$$\llbracket \Gamma \vdash x{=}E; \rrbracket(\eta)(r, h, s) \stackrel{\text{def}}{=}$$
$$\textbf{lets } (r_1, h_1, s_1) = \llbracket \Gamma \vdash E : T \rrbracket(\eta)(r, h, s)$$
$$\textbf{in if } s_1(\textbf{exc}) = null$$
$$\textbf{then } (r_1, h_1, [[s \mid x : s_1(\textbf{res})], \textbf{exc} : null])$$
$$\textbf{else } (r_1, h_1, [s, \textbf{exc} : s_1(\textbf{exc})])$$

If the expression goes into an infinite loop, then the meaning of the command is an infinite loop ($\bot$) also, since **lets** is a strict let expression in the notation. If the expression completes normally, then the state is updated with the variable being assigned bound to the result of the expression. Otherwise, if the expression threw an exception, then the command throws the same exception (and the store does not undergo any changes). (The meaning functions $\llbracket \cdot \rrbracket$ are curried functions that take a typing judgment and a method environment and then a state and produce a state of the appropriate type. Typing judgments for commands have no result type, but typing judgments for expressions do include a result type.)   ∎

Example 7. The state transformer φ_3 in Example 4 is an element of $SemMeth(\texttt{Counter}, \texttt{inc})$, where $\texttt{Counter}$ is defined in Fig. 15. The transformer φ_3 would be the denotation of $\texttt{Counter}$'s inc method.   ∎

A *normal method environment* is a table of denotations for all methods in all classes:

$$MethEnv \stackrel{\text{def}}{=} (K : ClassName) \times (m : Meths(K)) \to SemMeth(K, m).$$

---

[6] In Java, and Smalltalk-80 and C#, the values of expressions may be references, but the parameter passing mechanism is call by value, since one cannot write a method that modifies variables passed as actual parameters, such as swap. However, the semantics of method calls would need to be different for a language like C++ where parameters can be declared to be passed by reference (using &).

A normal method environment η is defined on pairs (K, m) where K is a class with method m; and $\eta(K, m)$ is a state transformer suitable to be the meaning of a method of type $mtype(K, m)$. In case m is inherited in K from class L, $\eta(K, m)$ will be the restriction of $\eta(L, m)$ to receiver objects of type K.

In our formulation of modular reasoning based on static types, we need to associate method meanings to interfaces as well as to classes, even though the receiver of an invocation is always an object of some class. So we define the set of *extended method environments* by

$$XMethEnv \stackrel{\text{def}}{=} (T : RefType) \times (m : Meths(T)) \to SemMeth(T, m).$$

The metavariable $\dot{\eta}$ is used to range over extended method environments; think of the dot as a reminder that interfaces are included.

3.3   Dynamic vs Static Semantics

Mathematically modeling supertype abstraction is essentially about modeling a reasoning process that uses static type information for method calls and comparing that to the actual (dynamic) semantics of the programming language. In our prior work [17] we avoided committing to a particular verification technique by using an imaginary semantics for the language that runs method calls using a state transformer for a called method that is based on a specification table, given statically, and the static types of receivers. Thus, following this prior work, we will work with two different semantics for Java:

– $\mathcal{D}[\![\cdot]\!]$, the *dynamic dispatch semantics*, which is the operationally accurate and models dynamic dispatch for method calls, and
– $\mathcal{S}[\![\cdot]\!]$, the *static dispatch semantics*, which models static reasoning by using a static dispatch semantics based on method specifications as the semantics for method calls.

These semantics differ primarily in the way they treat method calls.
The dynamic dispatch semantics of method call expressions is as follows [17]:

$$
\begin{aligned}
&\mathcal{D}[\![\Gamma \vdash x.m(\overline{y}) : U]\!](\eta)(r, h, s) \stackrel{\text{def}}{=} \\
&\quad \textbf{if } s(x) = null \\
&\quad \textbf{then } except(r, h, U, \texttt{NullPointerException}) \\
&\quad \textbf{else let } K = r(s(x)) \textbf{ in let } \overline{z} = formals(K, m) \textbf{ in} \\
&\quad\quad \textbf{let } s_1 = [\textbf{this} : s(x), \overline{z : s(y)}] \textbf{ in } (\eta(K, m))(r, h, s_1).
\end{aligned}
\tag{3}
$$

This semantic function's definition makes use of a helping function *except*, that returns a state that has the reference context and heap passed to it along with **res** bound to *null* and **exc** bound to a new object of type `NullPointerException` [17]. The auxiliary function *formals* returns the list of formal parameter names for a method. Note that in this semantics, K is the dynamic type of the receiver x and $\eta(K, m)$ is the meaning of the method m in the method environment, η. That method meaning is applied to a state, (r, h, s_1), which has bindings for **this** and the formal parameters $(\overline{z})$.

The static dispatch semantics of a method call uses the receiver's static type (T below) and a method meaning taken from an extended method environment, $\dot{\eta}$, which is ultimately determined by specifications [17]:

$$
\mathcal{S}[\![\Gamma \vdash x.m(\overline{y}) : U]\!](\dot{\eta})(r, h, s) \stackrel{\text{def}}{=}
$$
$$
\textbf{if } s(x) = \textit{null}
$$
$$
\textbf{then } \textit{except}(r, h, U, \texttt{NullPointerException}) \tag{4}
$$
$$
\textbf{else let } T = \Gamma(x) \textbf{ in let } \overline{z} = \textit{formals}(T, m) \textbf{ in}
$$
$$
\textbf{let } s_1 = [\textbf{this} : s(x), \overline{z : s(y)}] \textbf{ in } (\dot{\eta}(T, m))(r, h, s_1).
$$

Note that in the static dispatch semantics, not only is the method meaning taken from an extended method environment, but the type used to look up the method is based on the context (type environment) Γ, so the meaning can be determined statically.

There are both dynamic and static semantics for other expressions and statements, $\mathcal{D}[\![\cdot]\!]$ and $\mathcal{S}[\![\cdot]\!]$, which are constructed with identical definitions, except for their treatment of method call expressions.

The method environment for a program is constructed, using the dynamic disptach semantics $\mathcal{D}$, from the program's declarations (i.e., from the program's class table). Since methods may be mutually recursive, a chain of approximations is used to reach a fixed point [17,27]. We write $\mathcal{D}[\![CT]\!]$ for the method environment that is the least upper bound of this fixed point.

4 Specification Semantics

In order to formalize behavioral subtyping and supertype abstraction, we need to formalize specifications and refinement of specifications.

Recall that we think of the meaning of predicates as sets of states. For example, the meaning of the predicate x>y is $\{(r, h, s) \mid s(\text{x}) > s(\text{y})\}$. As another example, the meaning of the predicate **this**.num>0 would be $\{(r, h, s) \mid o = s(\textbf{this}), (h(o))(\text{num}) > 0\}$.

To consider the relationship between specifications in supertypes and subtypes, we need a notion of subtyping for contexts and state transformers.

Subtyping for type contexts, $\Gamma \leq \Delta$, holds when the domains of Γ and Δ are equal and for each x in their domain, $\Gamma(x) \leq \Delta(x)$. Since a subtype relation between types, $S \leq T$, implies that for each ref context r, $Val(S, r) \subseteq Val(T, r)$, states for Γ are a subset of the states for Δ when $\Gamma \leq \Delta$:

$$
\Gamma \leq \Delta \implies \textit{State}(\Gamma) \subseteq \textit{State}(\Delta). \tag{5}
$$

Subtyping for state transformer types follows the usual contravariant rule [6]:

$$
(\Gamma \rightsquigarrow \Gamma') \leq (\Delta \rightsquigarrow \Delta') \stackrel{\text{def}}{=} (\Delta \leq \Gamma) \wedge (\Gamma' \leq \Delta') \tag{6}
$$

4.1   Formalizing JML Specifications

In JML, postconditions specify a relationship between two states, by using the notation **\old()** to refer to the pre-state. We formalize such specifications as a pair of a predicate and a relation.

Definition 3 (Specification in two-state form). *Let Γ and Γ' be contexts, Then (P, R) is a* specification in two-state form *of type $\Gamma \rightsquigarrow \Gamma'$ if and only if P is a predicate on $State(\Gamma)$ and R is a relation between $State(\Gamma)$ and $State(\Gamma')$.*

However, Hoare logic typically uses one-state specifications, where each assertion only refers to a single state, as in our semantics for predicates above. JML does have a way to turn two-state postconditions into one-state postconditions, by using universal quantification over a specification.

Example 8. For example, the specification of AbsCounter's method inc in Fig. 15,

```
/*@ requires count < Integer.MAX_VALUE;
 @ assignable count;
 @ ensures count > \old(count);   @*/
```

can be written with JML's forall clause in an equivalent way as follows.

```
/*@ forall int oldCount;
 @ requires oldCount == count;
 @        && count < Integer.MAX_VALUE;
 @ assignable count;
 @ ensures count > oldCount;   @*/
```

The idea is that this specification applies for all values of oldCount that happen to equal the pre-state value of count.

One must also remember that references to field names such as count mean **this**.count in Java. Furthermore, since **this** is not available in the denotational semantics of the post-state, one also needs to use a **forall** to save the value of **this** and thereby allow the postcondition to access its fields. (This works because **this** cannot be changed by commands.) Thus the above should be rewritten as follows.

```
/*@ forall int oldCount; forall AbsCounter oldThis;
 @ requires oldThis == this && oldCount == this.count
 @        && this.count < Integer.MAX_VALUE;
 @ assignable oldThis.count;
 @ ensures oldThis.count > oldCount;   @*/
```

To approach Hoare logic even more closely, the formalization in the *TOPLAS* paper [17] assumed that the meaning of JML's assignable clauses could be written into the method's postcondition; these added postconditions would state that all locations that are not assignable are unchanged. For example, if the only other location in the program is the field `size`, then the above specification would be translated as follows into an equivalent specification.

```
/*@ forall int oldCount , oldSize; forall AbsCounter oldThis;
  @ requires oldThis == this && oldCount == this.count
  @         && oldSize == this.size
  @         && this.count < Integer.MAX_VALUE;
  @ ensures oldThis.count > oldCount
  @         && oldThis.size == oldSize;   @*/
```

(As can be seen from this example, this translation to eliminate assignable clauses is not modular, as it depends on the locations in the rest of the program.) ∎

Such specifications as last the one above, which have universally quantified variables, a precondition, and a postcondition, are termed "general specifications" in our *TOPLAS* paper [17].

Definition 4 (General Specification). *A general specification of type* $\Gamma \rightsquigarrow \Gamma'$ *is a triple of form* $(J, pre, post)$ *such that:*

1. *J is a non-empty set,*
2. *pre is a J-indexed family of predicates over Γ-states, i.e., a function from J to the powerset of $State(\Gamma)$, and*
3. *post is a J-indexed family of predicates over Γ'-states, i.e., a function from J to the powerset of $State(\Gamma')$.*

Example 9. Let Γ_3 be [**this** : AbsCounter] and Γ'_3 be [**res** : **void**, **exc** : Throwable]. Let J_{cst} be the set of triples of two integers and an AbsCounter reference. Let pre_{cst} and $post_{cst}$ be the functions defined by:

$$pre_{cst}(oc, os, ot) \stackrel{\text{def}}{=} \{(r, h, s) \mid s(\textbf{this}) = ot, (h(ot))(\texttt{count}) = oc,$$
$$(h(ot))(\texttt{size}) = os, oc < MaxInt\}$$
$$post_{cst}(oc, os, ot) \stackrel{\text{def}}{=} \{(r, h, s') \mid (h(ot))(\texttt{count}) > oc, (h(ot))(\texttt{size}) = os\}.$$

(We assume that `Integer.MAX_VALUE` denotes $MaxInt$.) Then $(J_{cst}, pre_{cst}, post_{cst})$ is a general specification of type $\Gamma_3 \rightsquigarrow \Gamma'_3$ that would be an appropriate meaning for the specification of AbsCounter's method inc (from Fig. 15) with the rewrites shown in Example 8. ∎

As a general technique, one can use the entire pre-state as the index set J, which allows one to access any features of the pre-state in postconditions [17]. This idea allows us to define an operator for converting specifications in two-state form into general specifications.

Definition 5 (Translation from two-state to general specifications). *Let* (P, R) *be a specification in two-state form of type* $\Gamma \rightsquigarrow \Gamma'$. *Then the translation of* (P, R) *into a general specification of type* $\Gamma \rightsquigarrow \Gamma'$ *is as follows.*

$$\langle\langle P, R\rangle\rangle \overset{\text{def}}{=} (J, pre, post)$$
$$\textbf{where } J = State(\Gamma)$$
$$\textbf{and } for \text{ all } \sigma \in State(\Gamma),$$
$$pre(\sigma) = \{\tau \mid \tau = \sigma \wedge \sigma \in P\}$$
$$post(\sigma) = \{\sigma' \mid (\sigma, \sigma') \in R\}$$

4.2   Satisfaction and Refinement

With the above semantics of Java and JML in hand, we can resume the study of their relationship.

4.2.1   Satisfaction

The key relation is satisfaction of a method specification by its implementation; in the formal model this boils down to satisfaction of the meaning of a specification by the meaning of a method implementation, which is a state transformer. For simple (pre/post) specifications (P, Q) of type $\Gamma \rightsquigarrow \Gamma'$, a state transformer $\varphi : \Delta \rightsquigarrow \Delta'$, whose type is a subtype of the specification's, $\Delta \rightsquigarrow \Delta' \leq \Gamma \rightsquigarrow \Gamma'$, we say that φ *satisfies* (P, Q), written $\varphi \models (P, Q)$, if and only if for all $\sigma \in State(\Gamma)$, $\sigma \in P \Rightarrow \varphi(\sigma) \in Q$. The definition for general specifications is analogous [17].

Definition 6 (Satisfaction). *Let $(J, pre, post)$ be a general specification of type $\Gamma \rightsquigarrow \Gamma'$. Let $\varphi : \Delta \rightsquigarrow \Delta'$ be a state transformer, where $\Delta \rightsquigarrow \Delta' \leq \Gamma \rightsquigarrow \Gamma'$. Then φ satisfies $(J, pre, post)$, written $\varphi \models (J, pre, post)$, if and only if for all $j \in J$, and for all $\sigma \in State(\Gamma)$,*

$$\sigma \in pre(j) \Rightarrow \varphi(\sigma) \in post(j).$$

This definition of satisfaction is a total correctness one, since the resulting state of a state transformer, $\varphi(\sigma)$, must be defined.

Example 10. Consider the general specification $(J_{cst}, pre_{cst}, post_{cst})$ from Example 9, which has the type:

$$[\textbf{this} : \texttt{AbsCounter}] \rightsquigarrow [\textbf{res} : \textbf{void}, \textbf{exc} : \texttt{Throwable}].$$

This is a formalization of the specification in `AbsCounter` for the method `inc` (from Fig. 15). Consider also the state transformer φ_3 from Example 4. This state transformer has type:

$$[\textbf{this} : \texttt{Counter}] \rightsquigarrow [\textbf{res} : \textbf{void}, \textbf{exc} : \texttt{Throwable}].$$

However, the type of φ_3 is not a subtype of the type of the specification, since `Counter` is a subtype of `AbsCounter`, but for subtyping of transformer types the argument contexts should be in a supertype relationship (as subtyping is contravariant on arguments) and the opposite is true. Thus φ_3 does not satisfy $(J_{cst}, pre_{cst}, post_{cst})$. ∎

4.2.2 Restrictions of Specifications

The above example shows that the type of the receiver argument (**this**) requires a careful treatment in an OO language like Java. The problem is that the dynamic dispatch mechanism will guarantee that the receiver for a method m in class K has a dynamic type that is a subtype of K, but the receiver's type is part of the context that is used to define the state spaces in the semantics, which leads to the subtyping problem in the above example.

In what follows, we use the auxiliary function *selftype*, which is defined as:

$$selftype(r, h, s) \overset{\text{def}}{=} r(s(\textbf{this})).$$

Using *selftype* we can define two restrictions on predicates.

Definition 7 (Exact Restriction). *Let T be a reference type and let Γ be a context which is defined on* this. *If pre is a predicate on State(Γ), then the exact restriction of pre to T, written $pre{\lfloor}T$, is the predicate on State($[\Gamma \mid$* this $: T]$) *defined by*

$$\sigma \in (pre{\lfloor}T) \overset{\text{def}}{=} selftype(\sigma) = T \wedge \sigma \in pre.$$

If $(J, pre, post)$ is a general specification of type, $\Delta \rightsquigarrow \Delta'$, where this *is in the domain of Δ, then the exact restriction of $(J, pre, post)$ to T, written $(J, pre, post){\lfloor}T$, is the general specification $(J, pre', post)$ of type $[\Delta \mid$* this $: T] \rightsquigarrow \Delta'$, where $pre'(j) \overset{\text{def}}{=} pre(j){\lfloor}T$.*

For simple specifications, $(P, Q){\lfloor}T$ is $(P{\lfloor}T, Q)$.

As methods may be inherited in subtypes in Java, they may be applied to receivers that do not have the exact type of the class in which they are defined. Thus it is useful to have a similar notion that permits the type of this to be a subtype of a given type.

Definition 8 (Downward Restriction). *Let T be a reference type and let Γ be a context that is defined on* this. *If pre is a predicate on State(Γ), then the downward restriction of pre to T, written $pre{\lfloor}^*T$, is the predicate on State($[\Gamma \mid$* this $: T]$) *defined by*

$$\sigma \in (pre{\lfloor}^*T) \overset{\text{def}}{=} selftype(\sigma) \leq T \wedge \sigma \in pre.$$

If $(J, pre, post)$ is a general specification of type $\Gamma \rightsquigarrow \Gamma'$ where this $\in dom(\Gamma)$, *then the downward restriction of $(J, pre, post)$ to T, written $(J, pre, post){\lfloor}^*T$, is the general specification $(J, pre', post)$ of type $[\Gamma \mid$* this $: T] \rightsquigarrow \Gamma'$, where $pre'(j) \overset{\text{def}}{=} pre(j){\lfloor}^*T$.*

Example 11. Consider the precondition specification $(J_{cst}, pre_{cst}, post_{cst})$ from Example 9, which has the type:

[**this** : AbsCounter] $\rightsquigarrow$ [**res** : **void**, **exc** : Throwable].

The exact restriction $(J_{cst}, pre_{cst}, post_{cst}) \lfloor \texttt{Counter}$, is $(J_{cst}, pre'_{cst}, post_{cst})$, where

$$pre'_{cst}(oc, os, ot) \overset{\text{def}}{=} \{(r, h, s) \mid s(\textbf{this}) = ot, (h(ot))(\texttt{count}) = oc,$$
$$(h(ot))(\texttt{size}) = os, oc < MaxInt$$
$$selftype(r, h, s) = \texttt{Counter}\}.$$

Note that $(J_{cst}, pre_{cst}, post_{cst}) \lfloor \texttt{Counter}$, has the type

$$[\textbf{this} : \texttt{Counter}] \rightsquigarrow [\textbf{res} : \textbf{void}, \textbf{exc} : \texttt{Throwable}].$$

Since the type of this exact restriction is the same as the type of φ_3 from Example 4, the reader can check that $\varphi_3 \models (J_{cst}, pre_{cst}, post_{cst}) \lfloor \texttt{Counter}$.

The downward restriction $(J_{cst}, pre_{cst}, post_{cst}) \lfloor^* \texttt{Counter}$ is $(J_{cst}, pre''_{cst}, post_{cst})$, where

$$pre''_{cst}(oc, os, ot) \overset{\text{def}}{=} \{(r, h, s) \mid s(\textbf{this}) = ot, (h(ot))(\texttt{count}) = oc,$$
$$(h(ot))(\texttt{size}) = os, oc < MaxInt$$
$$selftype(r, h, s) \leq \texttt{Counter}\}.$$

The reader can check that the type of this downward restriction is the same as the type of the state transformer φ_3 from Example 4, so that $\varphi_3 \models (J_{cst}, pre_{cst}, post_{cst}) \lfloor^* \texttt{Counter}$.   ∎

4.2.3   Refinement of Specifications

In general, a specification S_2 refines a specification S_1 if S_2 restricts the set of correct implementations such that every correct implementation of S_2 is a correct implementation of S_1. The importance of this is that if a verifier uses S_1, then any conclusions it draws are valid for implementations that satisfy S_2. This is exactly the property that supertype abstraction should have to permit modular reasoning about OO programs, hence refinement is key to the results reported in our *TOPLAS* paper [17].

Definition 9. *Let $spec_1$ be a specification of type $\Gamma \rightsquigarrow \Gamma'$ and let $spec_2$ be a specification of type $\Delta \rightsquigarrow \Delta'$ where $\Delta \rightsquigarrow \Delta' \leq \Gamma \rightsquigarrow \Gamma'$. Then $spec_2$ refines $spec_1$, written $spec_2 \sqsupseteq spec_1$, if and only if for all $\varphi : \Delta \rightsquigarrow \Delta'$,*

$$(\varphi \models spec_2) \Rightarrow (\varphi \models spec_1).$$

In terms of specifications, refinement can be characterized as follows [17].

Theorem 1. *Let $(I, pre, post)$ be a specification of type $\Gamma \rightsquigarrow \Gamma'$ and let $(J, pre', post')$ be a specification of type $\Delta \rightsquigarrow \Delta'$ where $\Delta \rightsquigarrow \Delta' \leq \Gamma \rightsquigarrow \Gamma'$. Then the following are equivalent:*

1. $(J, pre', post') \sqsupseteq (I, pre, post)$,

2. $\forall i \in I \cdot \forall \sigma \in State(\Gamma) \cdot$
   $\sigma \in pre(i)$
   $\Rightarrow ((\exists j \in J \cdot \sigma \in pre'(j))$
   $\wedge (\forall \tau \in State(\Delta') \cdot$
   $(\forall j \in J \cdot \sigma \in pre'(j) \Rightarrow \tau \in post'(j))$
   $\Rightarrow \tau \in post(i)))$

∎

Example 12. Imagine that in the abstract class `AbsInterval` the method `pick` was specified as follows:

```
//@ forall AbsInterval othis;
//@ requires this.lb < this.ub;
//@ ensures othis.lb <= \result && \result <= othis.ub;
public /*@ pure @*/ abstract int pick();
```

This JML specification corresponds to the general specification $(J_{pai}, pre_{pai}, post_{pai})$ of the type $[\textbf{this} : \texttt{AbsInterval}] \rightsquigarrow [\textbf{res} : \textbf{int}, \textbf{exc} : \texttt{Throwable}]$, where

$$J_{pai} \stackrel{\text{def}}{=} State([\textbf{this} : \texttt{AbsInterval}])$$

$$pre_{pai}(\sigma) \stackrel{\text{def}}{=} \{(r, h, s) \mid \sigma = (r, h, s), ot = s(\textbf{this}), (h(ot))(\text{lb}) < (h(ot))(\text{ub})\}$$

$$post_{pai}(r, h, s) \stackrel{\text{def}}{=} \{(r', h', s') \mid ot = s(\textbf{this}), r \subseteq r', h \subseteq h',$$
$$(h(ot))(\text{lb}) \leq s'(\textbf{res}), s'(\textbf{res}) \leq (h(ot))(\text{ub})\}$$

Consider the following JML specification for `pick` in the subtype `Interval`.

```
//@ also
//@    forall Interval othis;
//@    requires this.lb < this.ub;
//@    ensures othis.lb == \result;
public /*@ pure @*/ int pick() { /* ... */ }
```

This JML specification corresponds to the general specification $(J_{pi}, pre_{pi}, post_{pi})$, which has type $[\textbf{this} : \texttt{Interval}] \rightsquigarrow [\textbf{res} : \textbf{int}, \textbf{exc} : \texttt{Throwable}]$, where

$$J_{pi} \stackrel{\text{def}}{=} State([\textbf{this} : \texttt{Interval}])$$

$$pre_{pi}(\sigma) \stackrel{\text{def}}{=} \{(r, h, s) \mid \sigma = (r, h, s), ot = (h(ot))(s(\textbf{this})),$$
$$(h(ot))(\text{lb}) < (h(ot))(\text{ub})\}$$

$$post_{pi}(r, h, s) \stackrel{\text{def}}{=} \{(r', h', s') \mid r \subseteq r', h \subseteq h',$$
$$(h(ot))(\text{lb}) = s'(\textbf{res}), s'(\textbf{res}) < (h(ot))(\text{ub})\}$$

Then $(J_{pi}, pre_{pi}, post_{pi}) \sqsupseteq ((J_{pai}, pre_{pai}, post_{pai}) \lfloor \texttt{Interval})$, since

$$\varphi \models (J_{pi}, pre_{pi}, post_{pi}) \Rightarrow \varphi \models (J_{pai}, pre_{pai}, post_{pai}) \lfloor \texttt{Interval}.$$

To see this, let φ be such that $\varphi \models (J_{pi}, pre_{pi}, post_{pi})$ and consider an arbitrary pre-state $(r, h, s) \in State([\mathbf{this} : \mathtt{AbsInterval}])$ such that

$$(r, h, s) \in (pre_{pai} \lfloor \mathtt{Interval})(r, h, s).$$

The above means that $(r, h, s) \in pre_{pai}(r, h, s) \wedge selftype(r, h, s) = \mathtt{Interval}$. It follows that $(r, h, s) \in State([\mathbf{this} : \mathtt{Interval}])$ and $(r, h, s) \in pre_{pi}(r, h, s)$. Let reference ot be such that $(s(\mathbf{this})) = ot$. By assumption $\varphi(r, h, s) \in post_{pi}(r, h, s)$. Let (r', h', s') be $\varphi(r, h, s)$. Then by definition of $post_{pi}(r, h, s)$: $r \subseteq r', h \subseteq h', (h(ot))(\mathtt{lb}) = s'(\mathbf{res})$, and $s'(\mathbf{res}) < (h(ot))(\mathtt{ub})$. It follows that $(h(ot))(\mathtt{lb}) \leq s'(\mathbf{res})$ and $s'(\mathbf{res}) \leq (h(ot))(\mathtt{ub})$, so $\varphi(r, h, s) = (r', h', s') \in post_{pai}(r, h, s)$. ∎

As in the above example, due to subtyping and inheritance, it is useful to consider combinations of refinement with exact or downward restrictions of specifications (from supertypes). So we make the following definitions [17].

Definition 10 (Refinement at a subtype). *Let $spec_1$ be a specification of type $\Gamma \rightsquigarrow \Gamma'$, where $\mathbf{this} \in dom(\Gamma)$. Let $spec_2$ be a specification of type $[\Delta \mid \mathbf{this} : T] \rightsquigarrow \Delta'$, which is such that $([\Delta \mid \mathbf{this} : T] \rightsquigarrow \Delta') \leq (\Gamma \rightsquigarrow \Gamma')$.*

Then $spec_2$ refines $spec_1$ at exact subtype T, written $spec_2 \sqsupseteq^T spec_1$, iff $spec_2 \sqsupseteq (spec_1 \lfloor T)$.

Further, $spec_2$ refines $spec_1$ at downward subtype T, written $spec_2 \sqsupseteq^{*T} spec_1$, if and only if $spec_2 \sqsupseteq (spec_1 \lfloor^* T)$.

Example 13. Consider the specifications $(J_{pai}, pre_{pai}, post_{pai})$ and $(J_{pi}, pre_{pi}, post_{pi})$ from Example 12. Since that example showed that

$$(J_{pi}, pre_{pi}, post_{pi}) \sqsupseteq ((J_{pai}, pre_{pai}, post_{pai}) \lfloor \mathtt{Interval})$$

it follows that $(J_{pi}, pre_{pi}, post_{pi}) \sqsupseteq^{\mathtt{Interval}} (J_{pai}, pre_{pai}, post_{pai})$. The reader can check that it is also the case that $(J_{pi}, pre_{pi}, post_{pi}) \sqsupseteq^{*\mathtt{Interval}} (J_{pai}, pre_{pai}, post_{pai})$. ∎

It happens that the downward restriction of a specification refines the exact restriction of that specification (at the same type), and so downward refinement implies exact refinement [17]. Thus downward refinement is a stronger notion than exact refinement.

Corollary 1. *Let $spec_1$ be a specification of type $\Gamma \rightsquigarrow \Gamma'$, where $\mathbf{this} \in dom(\Gamma)$. Let $spec_2$ be a specification of type $[\Delta \mid \mathbf{this} : T] \rightsquigarrow \Delta'$, which is such that $([\Delta \mid \mathbf{this} : T] \rightsquigarrow \Delta') \leq (\Gamma \rightsquigarrow \Gamma')$. Then $spec_2 \sqsupseteq^{*T} spec_1$ implies $spec_2 \sqsupseteq^T spec_1$.* ∎

5 Supertype Abstraction

Armed with the understanding of the semantics of specifications and programs discussed above, we can return to the topic of supertype abstraction and its soundness and completeness.

Recall that we want verification to be modular, so that one can verify OO programs in a way that will remain valid when new subtypes are added to the program. In addition, for the verification technique to be practical, it should be able to verify one method at a time, using the specifications of all other methods (to allow for mutually-recursive methods).

5.1   Specification Tables

The method specifications available in a program are modeled [17] in a *specification table*, ST, which is a function from pairs of reference types and method names to general specifications. That is, for all reference types T and method names m such that $mtype(T, m) = \overline{x : U} \to V$:

$$ST(T, m) : [\text{this} : T, \overline{x : U}] \rightsquigarrow [\text{res} : V, \text{exc} : \text{Throwable}]. \tag{7}$$

An element of ST, $ST(T, m)$ is a general specification, and thus models the meaning of specification of m in type T, taking into account all of the specification language's semantics.

Each method in a program should satisfy its specification; this can be summarized by saying that the method environment satisfies the specification table.

Definition 11 (Satisfaction of ST by a method environment). *Let ST be a specification table.*

An extended method environment $\dot\eta$ satisfies ST, written $\dot\eta \models ST$, if and only if for all reference types T and method names $m \in Meths(T)$, $\dot\eta(T, m) \models ST(T, m)$.

A normal method environment η satisfies ST, written $\eta \models ST$, if and only if for all class types K and methods $m \in Meths(K)$, $\eta(K, m) \models ST(K, m)$.

5.2   Modular Verification

Verification is modular with respect to methods if it relies on the specifications of called methods, from the specification table for a program, not on the code of those methods (from the class table). The main advantage of modular verification is that it is scalable, since verification can proceed one method at a time and does not depend on how many other methods are called in a method (or how deep the call graph is in a program). Another advantage is that modular verification does not need to be changed when the code changes. For example, code in a method may be changed in any way (e.g., to make it more efficient), and as long as it correctly implements the method's specification (and that specification is unchanged), then verification of method calls that uses that method does not need to change. Another important example is that one should be able to add new subtypes to a program without re-verifying it. The main disadvantage of modular verification is that when the specifications used (to make it modular) are too weak, then one will not be able to draw all the conclusions that might be valid operationally.

In Java all code is part of a method. If every method has a (JML) specification, then satisfaction of the specification table means that the program is correct. That is, a program with class table CT and specification table ST is correct if and only if $\mathcal{D}[\![CT]\!] \models ST$, i.e., when the method environment constructed by the dynamic semantics satisfies the specification table, so that every method correctly implements its specification. This models the way a verification logic would prove the implementation of each method separately, using the specifications of all methods as assumptions.

To formalize that reasoning is not dependent on method implementations, but only relies on the specifications of methods, one can quantify over all correct method implementations, as in the following.

Definition 12. *Let ST be a specification table, let Γ be a context, and let C be a command that type checks in the context Γ, i.e., $\Gamma \vdash C$. Then C modularly satisfies spec with respect to ST, written $ST, (\Gamma \vdash C) \models^{\mathcal{D}} spec$, if and only if for all $\eta \in MethEnv$,*

$$(\eta \models ST) \Rightarrow (\mathcal{D}[\![\Gamma \vdash C]\!](\eta) \models spec).$$

We will use a similar notation for any phrase-in-context (i.e., typing judgment), $\mathcal{P}$, so that $ST, \mathcal{P} \models^{\mathcal{D}} spec$ if and only if in every correct method environment for ST, $\mathcal{D}[\![\mathcal{P}]\!](\eta) \models spec$. The idea is that modular satisfaction can only depend on the specifications in ST, since all correct method environments must satisfy the specification.

Example 14. Let ST be such that $ST(\texttt{AbsCounter}, \texttt{inc})$ is the general specification from Example 9: $(J_{cst}, pre_{cst}, post_{cst})$. Let Γ_3 and Γ_3' be as in Example 9. Let the command C_{inc} be as follows.

$$\texttt{this . count = this . count +1 ;}$$

Then $\Gamma_3 \vdash C$ is a valid typing judgment. Let η be a method environment that satisfies ST and in particular $\eta(\texttt{AbsCounter}, \texttt{inc})$ is the state transformer φ_3. Since C_{inc} does not involve any method calls, the following is independent of the type environment η.

$$\mathcal{D}[\![\Gamma_3 \vdash C]\!](\eta)(r, h, s) = (r, h', s')$$
$$\textbf{where } s' = [\textbf{res} : it, \textbf{exc} : null]$$
$$\textbf{and } ot = h(s(\textbf{this}))$$
$$\textbf{and } h' = [h \mid ot : [h(ot) \mid \texttt{count} : ((h(ot))(\texttt{count})) + 1]]$$

Then $ST, (\Gamma_3 \vdash C) \models (J_{cst}, pre_{cst}, post_{cst})$ follows (ignoring overflow and the field $\texttt{size}$, which is mentioned in the specification). ∎

More interesting examples involve method calls. For example, the verification shown in Fig. 4 is modular, as it only uses the specifications from $\texttt{IntSet}$ to verify several commands in sequence. We formalize such modular reasoning using the specifications associated with static types as follows [17].

Definition 13. *Let ST be a specification table. Let $\mathcal{P}$ be a phrase-in-context. Let spec be a specification. Then $\mathcal{P}$ modularly satisfies spec with respect to ST under static dispatch, written $ST, \mathcal{P} \models^{\mathcal{S}} spec$, if and only if for all extended method environments $\dot{\eta} \in XMethEnv$,*

$$(\dot{\eta} \models ST) \Rightarrow (\mathcal{S}[\![\mathcal{P}]\!](\dot{\eta}) \models spec).$$

5.3   Supertype Abstraction

Supertype abstraction allows one to prove modular correctness using the static dispatch semantics. What we call strong supertype abstraction is formalized as modular satisfaction under static dispatch implying modular satisfaction [17].

Definition 14 (strong supertype abstraction). *Let ST be a specification table. Then ST allows strong supertype abstraction if and only if for all phrases-in-context $\mathcal{P}$ and specifications spec,*

$$(ST, \mathcal{P} \models^{\mathcal{S}} spec) \Rightarrow (ST, \mathcal{P} \models^{\mathcal{D}} spec).$$

Specification tables that allow strong supertype abstraction thus have the property that one can reason in a modular way using just specifications based on static type information, and yet can draw conclusions that are dynamically valid, in spite of subtyping and dynamic dispatch.

Of course, we would like to reason in a way that is more economical than considering all possible extended method environments. The approach for doing this is to use specifications in reasoning, as in JML.

5.4   Supertype Abstraction and Behavioral Subtyping

Leaving aside many technical details, we can point to the main theoretical result of our *TOPLAS* paper [17].

One approach to more economical reasoning is to treat calls of the form $x.m(\overline{y})$, where x has static type T as indicated in the introduction as predicate transformers. If $ST(T, m)$ is the simple specification $(pre, post)$, then the call can be treated as a specification statement that asserts *pre* and then assumes *post*, which in JML can be written as follows.

```
requires pre;
ensures post;
```

Following the *TOPLAS* paper [17], we can give semantics to such specification statements as weakest precondition (wp) predicate transformers, which map postconditions to the weakest preconditions that guarantee the postcondition will be reached. Recall that one can think of predicates as set of states, so a predicate transformer can also be thought of as mapping sets of states to sets of states. We write $\{[(pre, post)]\}$ for the weakest precondition predicate transformer above that maps the predicate *post* to the predicate *pre*. One can also think of this as mapping the set of all states that satisfy *post* to the set of all states that satisfy *pre*.

The weakest precondition transformer for a general specification [17] $(J, pre, post)$ of type $\Gamma \rightsquigarrow \Gamma'$, written $\{[(J, pre, post)]\}$, is defined such that for any state σ and predicate Q:

$$\sigma \in \{[(J, pre, post)]\}(Q) \stackrel{\mathrm{def}}{=} (\exists j \in J \cdot \sigma \in pre(j))$$
$$\wedge (\forall \tau \cdot (\forall i \in J \cdot \sigma \in pre(i) \Rightarrow \tau \in post(i)) \Rightarrow \tau \in Q)$$

The *TOPLAS* paper used such *wp* predicate transformers to define an environment of predicate transformers derived from the specifications of each method. That is, the method environment, $\{[ST]\}$, is such that for all types T and method names m, the transformer for the method m in type T is the weakest precondition predicate transformer that corresponds to the specification of that method:

$$\{[ST]\}(T, m) \stackrel{\mathrm{def}}{=} \{[ST(T, m)]\}.$$

This extended method environment is called the *least refined specification table* [17].

The least refined specification table and predicate transformers provide another characterization of modular verification [17]. This notion of modular verification uses a static dispatch predicate transformer semantics ($\mathcal{S}\{[\cdot]\}$) and the least refined specification table that satisfies ST ($\{[ST]\}$), to avoid quantifying over all extended method environments.

Definition 15 (Modular Verification). *Let ST be a specification table. Let Γ be a type context that type checks a command C, i.e., $\Gamma \vdash C$. Let spec be a specification of type $\Gamma \rightsquigarrow [\Gamma, exc: \mathtt{Throwable}]$. Then C is modularly verified for spec with respect to ST if and only if*

$$\mathcal{S}\{[\Gamma \vdash C]\}(\{[ST]\}) \sqsupseteq \{[spec]\}.$$

Supertype abstraction means that one can establish modular correctness using supertype specifications and static type information. Our *TOPLAS* paper [17] formalized this in two ways. Weak supertype abstraction uses the idea of modular verification above.

Definition 16 (Weak supertype abstraction). *Let ST be a specification table. Then ST allows weak supertype abstraction if and only if for every phrase-in-context $\mathcal{P}$ and every specification spec:*

$$(\mathcal{S}\{[\mathcal{P}]\}(\{[ST]\})) \Rightarrow (ST, \mathcal{P} \models^{\mathcal{D}} spec).$$

We explained the notion of strong supertype abstraction above (Definition 14). Strong supertype abstraction says that any conclusions drawn using the static dispatch semantics are valid using the dynamic dispatch semantics. Thus strong supertype abstraction generalizes from any particular reasoning technique.

Behavioral subtyping is a property of a specification table, as it relates the specifications of subtypes to their supertypes. There are two notions of behavioral subtyping, corresponding to exact refinement and downward refinement of specifications.

Behavioral subtyping means that each overriding method in a class K refines the specification of that method at exact type K (i.e., assuming that the type of **this** is equal to K).

Definition 17 (Behavioral Subtyping). *Let ST be a specification table. Then ST has behavioral subtyping if and only if for all reference types U, method names $m \in Meths(U)$ and classes K:*

$$(K \leq U) \Rightarrow (ST(K,m) \sqsupseteq^K ST(U,m)).$$

Robust Behavioral subtyping means that each overriding method in a class K downward refines the specification of that method at type K (i.e., assuming that K is an upper bound on the type of **this**).

Definition 18 (Robust Behavioral Subtyping). *Let ST be a specification table. Then ST has robust behavioral subtyping if and only if for all reference types U, method names $m \in Meths(U)$ and classes K:*

$$(K \leq U) \Rightarrow (ST(K,m) \sqsupseteq^{*K} ST(U,m)).$$

Note that in neither case is there any necessary relationship between specifications in interfaces. Although JML insists that overriding methods in interfaces (downward) refine the specifications in the interfaces that they override, this is not needed for such specifications that appear in interfaces. What is needed is that overriding methods in classes refine all specifications in their supertypes (including interfaces).

Practical examples seem to have robust behavioral subtyping, which corresponds to what JML enforces. Even Parkinson and Bierman's Cell and DCell examples [25], which make liberal use of a **selftype** primitive in specifications, exhibit robust behavioral subtyping [17, Example 8.5].

Since downward refinement is stronger than exact refinement, robust behavioral subtyping implies behavioral subtyping [17].

The main result in our *TOPLAS* paper is the following theorem [17, Theorem 8.15].

Theorem 2. *Let ST be a specification table that is satisfiable. Then the following are equivalent:*

1. *ST has behavioral subtyping,*
2. *ST allows strong supertype abstraction, and*
3. *ST allows weak supertype abstraction.*

6   Specification Inheritance

Because supertype abstraction is desirable for modular reasoning about OO programs, and because the validity of supertype abstraction is equivalent to specifications having behavioral subtyping, it is desirable to have a way to either: (a) check that specifications have behavioral subtyping, or (b) construct specifications with behavioral subtyping. Some authors (e.g., Findler and Felleisen [8]) take the view that it is the responsibility of the specifier to ensure behavioral subtyping, and thus that tools should check that what has been specified satisfies some definition of behavioral subtyping. An advantage of this approach is that specifiers will know exactly what specifications are being used for each type. A disadvantage is that writing such specifications may be more work than with the other approach.

JML uses specification inheritance to force all subtypes to be behavioral subtypes [7,16], which implicitly constructs specifications with behavioral subtyping. An advantage of this approach is that behavioral subtyping is automatic. A disadvantage is that specifiers need to be aware of how specifications are automatically constructed.

In this section we will explain the formal model of specification inheritance developed in our prior work [17] and how it forces behavioral subtyping.

6.1   Joining Specifications

The idea of specification inheritance is that the obligations for a method should be inherited from supertypes in a way that is similar to the way code is inherited. This makes the construction of new subtypes easier, approaching the ease of constructing new subclasses in code.

The approach that is adopted in JML is due to Alan Wills, whose mechanism for Smalltalk [32] combines method specifications from supertypes. The basic idea is simple: all the specifications from all supertypes are combined so that an implementation that satisfies the combined specification also satisfies each inherited specification (considered separately). In JML a method specification may have several "specification cases," each of which can be formally modeled with a general specification. Methods must correctly implement each of these specification cases [33]. Conversely, a client, when calling a method, may choose any of a method's specification cases to use when verifying a call to the method (by checking the precondition of that case and assuming its postcondition).

Example 15. Consider the method pick, specified in both the interface IntSet and the subtype Interval. The specifications of this method from IntSet (see Fig. 1) and from Interval (see Fig. 6) are combined by JML into the specification shown in Fig. 17. This combined specification has two specification cases, separated by **also**. The first specification case is the specification inherited from IntSet. The second specification case is the one added for the type Interval.

This textual combination form is the source of the **also** that must precede added specifications in overriding methods in JML [19].   ∎

```
//@    requires size() > 0;
//@    assignable state;
//@    ensures contains(\result);
//@ also
//@    requires lb <= ub;
//@    assignable state;
//@    ensures lb == \old(lb) && ub == \old(ub);
//@    ensures \result == (int)lb;
public int pick() { /* ... */ }
```

Fig. 17. The combined specification (for the class `Interval`) of the method `pick`.

To connect the idea of specification inheritance to the formal model developed so far, we need a way to combine several method specifications into one specification. This will also serve to explain the meaning of how method specifications are combined. As with behavioral subtyping, however, one must be careful about typing. However, unlike the typing of specification refinement related to behavioral subtyping, for specification inheritance the problem is not the type of **this**, which can be handled by a (downward) restriction, but the type of the result.

Example 16. Imagine a method in a supertype T has a general specification $(J, pre', post')$ of type $\Gamma \rightsquigarrow \Gamma'$. A subtype K can also write a specification for the same method, $(I, pre, post)$ of type $\Delta \rightsquigarrow \Delta'$. The type system ensures that $(\Delta \rightsquigarrow \Delta') \leq ([\Gamma \mid \textbf{this} : K] \rightsquigarrow \Gamma')$, (i.e., $[\Gamma \mid \textbf{this} : K] \leq \Delta$ and $\Delta' \leq \Gamma'$).

Suppose $I \cap J = \emptyset$ and we combined these disjoint partial specifications to form the general specification $(I \cup J, pre \cup pre' |^*K, post \cup post')$ for the subtype's method. This nearly formalizes the idea of combining specification cases [7,32], since a call can satisfy the precondition by choosing either $i \in I$ or $j \in J$ such that $pre(i)$ or $pre'(j)|^*K$ holds, and then, given the choice for i or j, the corresponding postcondition can be assumed. Conversely, an implementation must satisfy all these partial specifications, due to the definition of satisfaction of a general specification by a predicate transformer (Definition 6), which requires the transformer to satisfy the specification for each index.

However, this specification should have a type appropriate for the subtype, i.e., $\Delta \rightsquigarrow \Delta'$. For the arguments, $[\Gamma \mid \textbf{this} : K] \leq \Delta$, so for any $j \in J$, $pre'(j)|^*K \in State(\Delta)$, which works. However, for the result $\Delta' \not\leq \Gamma'$, since for some $j \in J$, $post'(j)$ may not be contained in $State(\Delta')$, so the postcondition cannot be inherited in this way. ■

The problem shown in the above example is the type of the method's result. In a method specification, the domain of the result context always contains just **res** and **exc**. The type of **exc** is always `Throwable`, so that does not cause any difficulties. The problem is that in a supertype's method, the type of **res** may be a supertype of the type of the result type in the subtype's method, so $post'$ needs to be strengthened to make the result have the type needed ($\Delta'(\textbf{res})$).

(Note that if one writes code in the subtype for an overriding method, the type checker will ensure that the result has the declared type, but that type might be a subtype of the declared type of the result in the method being overridden.)

To solve this problem, our earlier work [17] used an operator $⋒$, defined as follows.

Definition 19 (Restricting Postconditions). *Let X be a set of states of type $State(\Gamma')$ and let $post'$ be a J-indexed family of predicates of type $State(\Gamma')$. Then $(post' ⋒ X)$ is the J-indexed family of predicates defined by:*

$$(post' ⋒ X)(j) \overset{\text{def}}{=} (post'(j) \cap X).$$

This operator can be used to define the join of two general specifications with disjoint index sets.

Definition 20 (Inheriting Join of Specifications). *Suppose I and J are disjoint non-empty sets. Let $(I, pre, post) : \Delta \rightsquigarrow \Delta'$ where $\Delta(\texttt{this}) = T$, and $(J, pre', post') : \Gamma \rightsquigarrow \Gamma'$ be general specifications such that $\Delta \rightsquigarrow \Delta' \le [\Gamma \mid \texttt{this} : T] \rightsquigarrow \Gamma'$. Then the* inheriting join *of these specifications, a general specification of type $\Delta \rightsquigarrow \Delta'$ is defined by:*

$$(I, pre, post) \sqcup (J, pre', post') \overset{\text{def}}{=} (I \cup J, pre \cup (pre' \upharpoonright^* T), post \cup (post' ⋒ State(\Delta'))).$$

To illustrate this using the `pick` method's specifications as in Example 15, a formal model of those specifications is needed. Since the `pick` method's specification involves pure method calls, we define the following notation for evaluating Boolean expressions to help shorten the presentation of these models.

$$beval[\![\Gamma \vdash E]\!](r, h, s) \overset{\text{def}}{=} \text{ lets } (r', h', s') = \mathcal{D}[\![\Gamma \vdash E : \textbf{boolean}]\!](r, h, s)$$
$$\text{ in if } s'(\textbf{exc}) = null \text{ then } s'(\textbf{res}) \text{ else } \bot$$

The result of $beval[\![\Gamma \vdash E]\!]$ in a given state will thus be either *true* or *false* (or $\bot$).

To deal with index sets that may have a non-empty intersection, we define [17]:

$$I + J \overset{\text{def}}{=} \{(i, 0) \mid i \in I\} \cup \{(j, 1) \mid j \in J\}.$$

with injections $inl : I \to (I + J)$ and $inr : J \to (I + J)$ defined by $inl(i) = (i, 0)$ and $inr(j) = (j, 1)$.

Example 17. Consider the two specification cases for the `pick` method in Fig. 17.

Ignoring the assignable clauses, the first specification case (from `IntSet`) can be thought of as the general specification of type $\Gamma_{is} \rightsquigarrow \Gamma_{ir}$, $(State(\Gamma_{is}), pre_{is}, post_{is})$, where the context Γ_{is} is $[\texttt{this} : \texttt{IntSet}]$, $\Gamma_{ir} = [\textbf{res} : \textbf{int}, \textbf{exc} : \texttt{Throwable}]$, and

$$pre_{is}(r, h, s) \overset{\text{def}}{=} \{(r, h, s) \mid beval[\![\Gamma_{is} \vdash \texttt{this}.\texttt{size}() > 0]\!](r, h, s)\}$$
$$post_{is}(r, h, s) \overset{\text{def}}{=} \{(r', h', s') \mid s'(\textbf{res}) = n, s'' = [s, \textbf{res} : n], \Gamma_{isr} = [\Gamma_{is}, \textbf{res} : \textbf{int}],$$
$$beval[\![\Gamma_{isr} \vdash \texttt{this}.\texttt{contains}(\textbf{res}) > 0]\!](r, h, s'')\}$$

The second specification case (from `Interval`) can modeled as the general specification of type $\Gamma_{iv} \rightsquigarrow \Gamma_{ir}$, $(State(\Gamma_{iv}), pre_{iv}, post_{iv})$, where the context Γ_{iv} is [**this** : `Interval`], Γ_{ir} is as above, and (assuming $long2int$ converts a value from a **long** to an **int**):

$$pre_{iv}(r, h, s) \stackrel{\text{def}}{=} \{(r, h, s) \mid s(\textbf{this}) = ot, (h(ot))(\texttt{lb}) \leq (h(ot))(\texttt{ub})\}$$
$$post_{iv}(r, h, s) \stackrel{\text{def}}{=} \{(r', h', s') \mid s(\textbf{this}) = ot, (h'(ot))(\texttt{lb}) = (h(ot))(\texttt{lb}),$$
$$(h'(ot))(\texttt{ub}) = (h(ot))(\texttt{ub}),$$
$$s'(\textbf{res}) = long2int((h'(ot))(\texttt{lb}))\}$$

So the inheriting join of the above two general specifications is

$$(State(\Gamma_{iv}) + State(\Gamma_{is}),$$
$$(pre_{iv} \circ inl^{-1}) \cup (pre_{is} |^* \texttt{Interval} \circ inr^{-1}),$$
$$(post_{iv} \circ inl^{-1}) \cup (post_{is} \circ inr^{-1})).$$

This general specification has type $\Gamma_{iv} \rightsquigarrow \Gamma_{ir}$. The ⋒ operator is not needed to form the postcondition in this case, as the same result context, Γ_{ir}, is used for both specifications.

Thus the precondition of the join is equivalent to the following.

$$pre((r, h, s), 0) = \{(r, h, s) \mid s(\textbf{this}) = ot, (h(ot))(\texttt{lb}) \leq (h(ot))(\texttt{ub})\}$$
$$pre((r, h, s), 1) = \{(r, h, s) \mid selftype(r, h, s) \leq \texttt{Interval},$$
$$beval[\![\Gamma_{is} \vdash \textbf{this.size()>0}]\!](r, h, s)\}$$

Similarly the postcondition of the join is equivalent to the following.

$$post((r, h, s), 0) = \{(r', h', s') \mid s(\textbf{this}) = ot, (h'(ot))(\texttt{lb}) = (h(ot))(\texttt{lb}),$$
$$(h'(ot))(\texttt{ub}) = (h(ot))(\texttt{ub}),$$
$$s'(\textbf{res}) = long2int((h'(ot))(\texttt{lb}))\}$$
$$post((r, h, s), 1) = \{(r', h', s') \mid s'(\textbf{res}) = n, s'' = [s, \textbf{res} : n], \Gamma_{isr} = [\Gamma_{is}, \textbf{res} : \textbf{int}],$$
$$beval[\![\Gamma_{isr} \vdash \textbf{this.contains(res)>0}]\!](r, h, s'')\}$$

■

As in the above example, it is possible to combine the index sets of general specifications as if they were disjoint, by using the operator $+$ as shown above [17]. Thus the inheriting join can always be used to combine general specifications.

The inheriting join is a "join" in the sense of lattice theory, as it is the least upper bound in the refinement ordering.

Lemma 1. *Suppose I and J are disjoint sets $(I, pre, post)$ is a general specification of type $\Delta \rightsquigarrow \Delta'$, $\Delta(\textbf{this}) = T$, and $(J, pre', post')$ is a general specification of type $\Gamma \rightsquigarrow \Gamma'$ such that $\Delta \rightsquigarrow \Delta' \leq [\Gamma \mid \textbf{this} : T] \rightsquigarrow \Gamma'$. Then the inheriting join $(I, pre, post) \sqcup (J, pre', post')$ is the least upper bound of $(I, pre, post)$ and*

$(J, pre', post' \cap State(\Delta'))$ *with respect to the refinement ordering for specifications of type* $\Delta \rightsquigarrow \Delta'$. *That is, for all* $spec : \Delta \rightsquigarrow \Delta'$,

$$spec \sqsupseteq (I, pre, post) \sqcup (J, pre', post')$$

if and only if the following both hold:

$$spec \sqsupseteq (I, pre, post),$$
$$spec \sqsupseteq (J, pre', post' \cap State(\Delta')).$$

As the above lemma states, the join of two specifications refines both of them. However, satisfying two specifications simultaneously may be impossible.

Example 18. Consider the following JML specification, which has two specification cases.

```
//@    ensures \result == lb;
//@ also
//@    ensures \result == ub;
public abstract /*@ pure @*/ int pick();
```

These specification cases can be modeled formally as follows. Let the type context $\Gamma_{iv} = [\mathbf{this} : \texttt{Interval}]$. The first specification case is then modeled as $(State(\Gamma_{iv}), true, post_{lb})$, where

$$post_{lb}(r, h, s) = \{(r', h', s') \mid s(\mathbf{this}) = ot, (h'(ot))(\texttt{lb}) = s'(\mathbf{res}),$$
$$(h'(ot))(\texttt{lb}) = (h(ot))(\texttt{lb}), (h'(ot))(\texttt{ub}) = (h(ot))(\texttt{ub})\}$$

The second specification case is similarly modeled as $(State(\Gamma_{iv}), true, post_{ub})$, where

$$post_{ub}(r, h, s) = \{(r', h', s') \mid s(\mathbf{this}) = ot, (h'(ot))(\texttt{ub}) = s'(\mathbf{res}),$$
$$(h'(ot))(\texttt{lb}) = (h(ot))(\texttt{lb}), (h'(ot))(\texttt{ub}) = (h(ot))(\texttt{ub})\}$$

Since the index sets are the same $(State(\Gamma_{iv}))$, the join is the specification

$$(State(\Gamma_{iv}) + State(\Gamma_{iv}), true \circ inl^{-1} \cup true \circ inr^{-1}, post_{lb} \circ inl^{-1} \cup post_{ub} \circ inr^{-1}).$$

This is equivalent to the general specification $(State(\Gamma_{iv}) \times \{0, 1\}, true, post_c)$, where the family of postconditions $post_c$ is equivalent to the following.

$$post_c((r, h, s), 0) = \{(r', h', s') \mid s(\mathbf{this}) = ot, (h'(ot))(\texttt{lb}) = s'(\mathbf{res}),$$
$$(h'(ot))(\texttt{lb}) = (h(ot))(\texttt{lb}), (h'(ot))(\texttt{ub}) = (h(ot))(\texttt{ub})\}$$
$$post_c((r, h, s), 1) = \{(r', h', s') \mid s(\mathbf{this}) = ot, (h'(ot))(\texttt{ub}) = s'(\mathbf{res}),$$
$$(h'(ot))(\texttt{lb}) = (h(ot))(\texttt{lb}), (h'(ot))(\texttt{ub}) = (h(ot))(\texttt{ub})\}$$

However, $post_c$ is unsatisfiable. Why? Because an implementation will need to produce a state with a fixed value for **res**; if it makes **res** be the value of $\texttt{lb}$, then it will not satisfy $post_c$ when the state passed is paired with 1, but in the formal model it must satisfy $post_c$ for all indexes, as the precondition is always satisfied. (One might think of the 0 or 1 passed in a pair with a state as an input that the program cannot observe.) Thus, if the values of lb and ub can be different, then it will not be possible to write a correct implementation of this specification, since the result cannot simultaneously have two different values.

In more detail, recall that an implementation is modeled as a state transformer, φ, which is a function. To satisfy a general specification, such as $(State(\Gamma_{iv}) \times \{0,1\}, true, post_c)$, φ must be such that for each $((r,h,s),j) \in State(\Gamma_{iv}) \times 0,1$, if $\sigma \models true$ then $\varphi(\sigma) \models post_c((r,h,s),j)$. However, if $\varphi(\sigma) \models post_c((r,h,s),0)$, so that **res** is lb's value, then $\varphi(\sigma) \not\models post_c((r,h,s),1)$, assuming that ub's value is different.   ∎

Expressed in JML, the join of two specification cases

```
//@ requires pre_1;
//@ ensures post_1;
```

and

```
//@ requires pre_2;
//@ ensures post_2;
```

is the JML specification

```
//@ requires pre_1 || pre_2;
/*@ ensures (\old(pre_1) ==> post_1)
  @        && (\old(pre_2) ==> post_2);   @*/
```

This combined specification [7,16,19,33], requires the implementation to satisfy both of the separate specification cases (which corresponds to the formal requirement that the specification be satisfied at all indexes). Note that if both pre_1 and pre_2 are true, then both post_1 and post_2 must hold.

Thus in JML, and in the formal model, the join of two specifications may be unsatisfiable. Another way of looking at this is that joining specifications can only add more constraints to a specification, and that may result in a specification that cannot be correctly implemented [7,16,17].

6.2   Constructing the Specification Table

Overall, the goal of specification inheritance, in our formal model, is to construct a specification table that has behavioral subtyping. Thus we can state the goals of a technique for constructing a specification table as follows [17]:

1. It should refine the written specifications,
2. It should have behavioral subtyping.
3. It should be the least refined specification table with these properties.
4. It should provide the most complete modular verification in the sense whenever conclusions are modularly correct, then these conclusions can be verified using the technique.

Our *TOPLAS* paper [17] discussed several technical approaches to constructing a specification table and compared each against the above goals.

Refinement for specification tables is defined pointwise, that is,

$$ST' \sqsupseteq ST \stackrel{\text{def}}{=} (\forall T, m \cdot ST'(T,m) \sqsupseteq ST(T,m)). \tag{8}$$

From this definition, it follows that if $ST' \sqsupseteq ST$, then for all phrases-in-context $\mathcal{P}$,

$$ST', \mathcal{P} \models^{\mathcal{S}} spec \Rightarrow ST, \mathcal{P} \models^{\mathcal{S}} spec.$$

One way to formalize the construction of a specification tables with behavioral subtyping is to define a function that takes a specification table argument and returns a specification table based on the argument, which has behavioral subtyping.

Definition 21 (Robust Class Inheritance). *Let ST be a specification table. Then the specification table $rki(ST)$ is defined for class names K and interface names I by:*

$$(rki(ST))(K,m) \stackrel{\text{def}}{=} \sqcup\{ST(T,m)|^*K \mid m \in Meths(T), K \leq T\}$$
$$(rki(ST))(I,m) \stackrel{\text{def}}{=} ST(I,m)$$

The following is closest to what JML does.

Definition 22 (Robust RefType Inheritance). *Let ST be a specification table. Then the specification table $rrti(ST)$ is defined for reference types U by:*

$$(rrti(ST))(U,m) \stackrel{\text{def}}{=} \sqcup\{ST(T,m)|^*U \mid m \in Meths(T), U \leq T\}$$

A variant of the above uses exact restriction instead of a downward restriction.

Definition 23 (Exact RefType Inheritance). *Let ST be a specification table. Then the specification table $erti(ST)$ is defined for reference types U by:*

$$(erti(ST))(U,m) \stackrel{\text{def}}{=} \sqcup\{ST(T,m){\lfloor}U \mid m \in Meths(T), U \leq T\}$$

In our prior work, we showed that both of the robust flavors of inheritance produce specification tables that refine the original table: $rki(ST) \sqsupseteq ST$ and $rrti(ST) \sqsupseteq ST$. However, it is not the case that $erti(ST)$ refines ST, because in general exact restrictions do not produce refinements.

Both robust flavors of inheritance produce specification tables with robust behavioral subtyping, although **etri** only produces a specification table with behavioral subtyping (not robust behavioral subtyping). It turns out [17] that if **rki**(ST) is satisfiable, then it is the least refinement of ST that is satisfiable and has robust behavioral subtyping. So **rki** satisfies our first three goals. However, **rrti** also satisfies these first three goals and also provides the most complete modular verification [17].

7 Conclusions

Supertype abstraction allows for modular reasoning about OO programs that is both powerful and simple. In combination with rewriting code to use downcasts, it can be used to reach any conclusions that an exhaustive case analysis could.

Our definition of behavioral subtyping [17] is both necessary and sufficient for sound supertype abstraction.

Robust behavioral subtyping, which itself implies behavioral subtyping, can be obtained by specification inheritance.

7.1 Future Work

Our prior work [17] did not give a modular treatment of framing and how to modularly specify and verify frame conditions in OO programs. Thus an important area of future work is to provide such a modular treatment of framing with supertype abstraction and behavioral subtyping. This work would benefit practical tools. Bao has been working on solving this problem [5].

An interesting line of future work would be to conduct human studies with programmers to see what the true advantages and disadvantages of using supertype abstraction are for reasoning about OO programs.

Acknowledgments. Thanks to David Cok for comments on an earlier draft and for fixing some errors with the IntSet example. Thanks also to David for his work on the OpenJML tool (see http://www.openjml.org/) and his help with using it.
Notations. As an aid to the reader, we present a table of defined notations in Fig. 18 on the next page.

Notation	description	Location
(P, Q)	simple specification	Section 2.2
$\{P\}\ C\ \{Q\}$	Hoare Triple	Section 2.2
σ	state	Section 2.2
$\sigma \models \{P\}\ C\ \{Q\}$	$\{P\}\ C\ \{Q\}$ is valid in σ	Section 2.2
$\models \{P\}\ C\ \{Q\}$	$\{P\}\ C\ \{Q\}$ is valid	Section 2.2
$Impls(P, Q)$	set of commands that implement (P, Q)	Section 2.2
$(P', Q') \sqsupseteq (P, Q)$	Def. Def. 2	
CT	class table	Section 3.2
$\leq$	subtype of relation	Section 3.2
res	distinguished variable for normal results	Section 3.2
exc	distinguished variable for exceptions	Section 3.2
r	reference context	Section 3.2
Γ, Δ	context (type environment)	Section 3.2
s, t	store	Section 3.2
h	heap	Section 3.2
σ	state	Section 3.2
φ, ψ	state transformers	Section 3.2
$\Gamma \rightsquigarrow \Gamma'$	state transformer type	Section 3.2
η	method environment	Section 3.2
$\dot{\eta}$	extended method environment	Section 3.2
$\mathcal{D}[\![\cdot]\!]$	dynamic dispatch semantics	Section 3.3
$\mathcal{S}[\![\cdot]\!]$	static dispatch semantics	Section 3.3
$(J, pre, post)$	general specification	Def. 4
$\varphi \models spec$	φ satisfies $spec$	Section 4.2 and Def. 6
$pre \lfloor T$	exact restriction of pre	Def. 7
$(J, pre, post) \lfloor T$	exact restriction of $(J, pre, post)$	Def. 7
$spec \lfloor^* T$	downward restriction of $spec$	Def. 8
$spec_2 \sqsupseteq^T spec_1$	$spec_2$ refines $spec_1$ at exact subtype T	Def. 10
$spec_2 \sqsupseteq^{*T} spec_1$	$spec_2$ refines $spec_1$ at downward subtype T	Def. 10
ST	specification table	Section 5.1
$\mathcal{P}$	phrase in context (typing judgment)	Section 5.2
$\dot{\eta} \models ST$	$\dot{\eta}$ satisfies ST	Def. 11
$ST, (\Gamma \vdash C) \models^{\mathcal{D}} spec$	C modularly satisfies $spec$ with respect to ST	Def. 12
$\{\![(J, pre, post)]\!\}$	weakest precondition (wp) transformer	Section 5.4
$\{\![ST]\!\}$	least refined specification table	Section 5.4
$\mathcal{S}\{\![\cdot]\!\}$	static dispatch wp predicate transformer	Section 5.4
$(post \cap X)$	postcondition restriction	Def. 19
$spec_1 \sqcup spec_2$	inheriting join of $spec_1$ and $spec_2$	Def. 20
rki(ST)	robust class inheritance	Def. 21
rrti(ST)	robust ref tyep inheritance	Def. 22
erti(ST)	exact ref type inheritance	Def. 23

Fig. 18. Table of notations used in this paper.

References

1. America, P.: Inheritance and subtyping in a parallel object-oriented language. In: Bézivin, J., Hullot, J.-M., Cointe, P., Lieberman, H. (eds.) ECOOP 1987. LNCS, vol. 276, pp. 234–242. Springer, Heidelberg (1987). https://doi.org/10.1007/3-540-47891-4_22

2. America, P.: A behavioural approach to subtyping in object-oriented programming languages. Technical report 443, Philips Research Laboratories, Nederlandse Philips Bedrijven B. V., April 1989. Revised from the January 1989 version

3. America, P.: Designing an object-oriented programming language with behavioural subtyping. In: de Bakker, J.W., de Roever, W.P., Rozenberg, G. (eds.) REX 1990. LNCS, vol. 489, pp. 60–90. Springer, Heidelberg (1991). https://doi.org/10.1007/BFb0019440

4. Apt, K.R., Olderog, E.: Verification of Sequential and Concurrent Programs. Graduate Texts in Computer Science Series, 2nd edn. Springer, New York (1997). https://doi.org/10.1007/978-1-4757-2714-2

5. Bao, Y.: Reasoning about frame properties in object-oriented programs. Technical report CS-TR-17-05, Computer Science, University of Central Florida, Orlando, Florida, December 2017. https://goo.gl/WZGMiB, the author's dissertation

6. Cardelli, L.: A semantics of multiple inheritance. Inf. Comput. **76**(2/3), 138–164 (1988)

7. Dhara, K.K., Leavens, G.T.: Forcing behavioral subtyping through specification inheritance. In: Proceedings of the 18th International Conference on Software Engineering, Berlin, Germany, pp. 258–267. IEEE Computer Society Press, Los Alamitos, March 1996. https://doi.org/10.1109/ICSE.1996.493421, a corrected version is ISU CS TR #95 20c, http://tinyurl.com/s2krg

8. Findler, R.B., Felleisen, M.: Contract soundness for object-oriented languages. In: OOPSLA 2001 Conference Proceedings of Object-Oriented Programming, Systems, Languages, and Applications, 14–18 October 2001, Tampa Bay, Florida, USA, pp. 1–15. ACM, New York, October 2001

9. Floyd, R.W.: Assigning meanings to programs. Proc. Symp. Appl. Math. **19**, 19–31 (1967)

10. Guttag, J., Horning, J.J.: The algebraic specification of abstract data types. Acta Informatica **10**(1), 27–52 (1978). https://doi.org/10.1007/BF00260922

11. Hennessy, M.: The Semantics of Programming Languages: An Elementary Introduction Using Structural Operational Semantics. Wiley, New York (1990)

12. Hoare, C.A.R.: An axiomatic basis for computer programming. Commun. ACM **12**(10), 576–580, 583 (1969). http://doi.acm.org/10.1145/363235.363259

13. Huisman, M., Jacobs, B.: Java program verification via a hoare logic with abrupt termination. In: Maibaum, T. (ed.) FASE 2000. LNCS, vol. 1783, pp. 284–303. Springer, Heidelberg (2000). https://doi.org/10.1007/3-540-46428-X_20

14. Landin, P.J.: The mechanical evaluation of expressions. Comput. J. **6**, 308–320 (1964). See also Landin's paper "A Lambda-Calculus Approach" in Advances in Programming and Non-Numerical Computation, L. Fox (ed.), Pergamon Press, Oxford, 1966

15. Landin, P.J.: The next 700 programming languages. Commun. ACM **9**(3), 157–166 (1966)

16. Leavens, G.T.: JML's rich, inherited specifications for behavioral subtypes. In: Liu, Z., He, J. (eds.) ICFEM 2006. LNCS, vol. 4260, pp. 2–34. Springer, Heidelberg (2006). https://doi.org/10.1007/11901433_2

17. Leavens, G.T., Naumann, D.A.: Behavioral subtyping, specification inheritance, and modular reasoning. TOPLAS **37**(4), 13:1–13:88 (2015). https://doi.acm.org/10.1145/2766446
18. Leavens, G.T., Naumann, D.A., Rosenberg, S.: Preliminary definition of Core JML. CS Report 2006–07, Stevens Institute of Technology, September 2006. http://www.cs.stevens.edu/~naumann/publications/SIT-TR-2006-07.pdf
19. Leavens, G.T., et al.: JML Reference Manual, September 2009. http://www.jmlspecs.org
20. Leavens, G.T., Weihl, W.E.: Reasoning about object-oriented programs that use subtypes (extended abstract). In: Meyrowitz, N. (ed.) OOPSLA ECOOP 1990 Proceedings. ACM SIGPLAN Notices, vol. 25, no. 10, pp. 212–223. ACM, October 1990. https://doi.org/10.1145/97945.97970
21. Leavens, G.T., Weihl, W.E.: Specification and verification of object-oriented programs using supertype abstraction. Acta Informatica **32**(8), 705–778 (1995). https://doi.org/10.1007/BF01178658
22. Liskov, B.H., Wing, J.M.: A behavioral notion of subtyping. ACM Trans. Program. Lang. Syst. **16**(6), 1811–1841 (1994). https://doi.org/10.1145/197320.197383
23. Meyer, B.: Object-Oriented Software Construction. Prentice Hall, New York (1988)
24. Meyer, B.: Object-Oriented Software Construction, 2nd edn. Prentice Hall, New York (1997)
25. Parkinson, M., Bierman, G.: Separation logic, abstraction and inheritance. In: Wadler, P. (ed.) ACM Symposium on Principles of Programming Languages, pp. 75–86. ACM, New York, January 2008
26. Sabry, A., Felleisen, M.: Reasoning about programs in continuation passing style. Lisp Symb. Comput. **6**(3/4), 289–360 (1993)
27. Schmidt, D.A.: Denotational Semantics: A Methodology for Language Development. Allyn and Bacon Inc., Boston (1986)
28. Scott, D.S., Strachey, C.: Toward a mathematical semantics for computer languages. In: Proceedings Symposium on Computers and Automata. Microwave Institute Symposia Series, vol. 21, pp. 19–46. Polytechnic Institute of Brooklyn, New York (1971)
29. Stoy, J.: Denotational Semantics: The Scott-Strachey Approach to Programming Language Theory. The MIT Press, Cambridge (1977)
30. Strachey, C.: Towards a formal semantics. In: IFIP TC2 Working Conference on Formal Language Description Languages for Computer Programming, pp. 198–220. North-Holland, Amsterdam (1966)
31. Strachey, C.: Fundamental concepts in programming languages. In: Notes International Summer School in Computer Programming (1967)
32. Wills, A.: Capsules and types in Fresco. In: America, P. (ed.) ECOOP 1991. LNCS, vol. 512, pp. 59–76. Springer, Heidelberg (1991). https://doi.org/10.1007/BFb0057015
33. Wing, J.M.: A two-tiered approach to specifying programs. Technical report TR-299, Massachusetts Institute of Technology, Laboratory for Computer Science (1983)

Formalizing Hoare Logic in PVS

Natarajan Shankar[(✉)] [iD]

Computer Science Laboratory, SRI International, Menlo Park, CA 94025, USA
shankar@csl.sri.com

Abstract. We formalize a Hoare logic for the partial correctness of *while* programs in PVS and prove its soundness and relative completeness. We use the PVS higher-order logic to define the syntax and semantics of a small imperative programming language, and describe a proof system for Hoare triples involving programs in this language. We prove the soundness of the proof system by demonstrating that only valid triples are provable. We also demonstrate the relative completeness of the proof system by defining the *weakest liberal precondition* operator and using it to prove that all valid Hoare triples are provable *modulo* the assertion logic. Finally, we verify a verification condition generator for Hoare logic Variants of Hoare logic have been formalized before in PVS and using other interactive proof assistants. We use Hoare logic as a tutorial exercise to illustrate the effective use of PVS in capturing the syntax and semantics of embedded logics. The embedding of Hoare logic is simple enough to be easily reproduced by the reader, but it also illustrates some of the nuances of formalization and proof using PVS, in particular, and higher-order logic, in general.

1 Introduction

The assertional style of reasoning about program correctness was already used by Turing in 1947 (see Morris and Jones [15]) and by von Neuman and Goldstine [18] in 1948. In the early 1960 s, McCarthy [13] introduced a formalism for reasoning about recursive programs and showed that it could also capture assertional reasoning. In 1967, Floyd [8] laid out a systematic way of reasoning about properties of flowchart programs decorated with annotations. Hoare [11] in 1969 introduced an assertional proof system, Hoare logic, centered around the idea of a Hoare triple. The soundness and relative completeness of Hoare logic was established by Cook [6] in 1976. Since then, assertional reasoning formalisms have been developed for a number of programming notations covering nondeterminism, concurrency, and distributed computing. Apt [2] gives a readable summary of the early research on Hoare logic. The development of Hoare logic using higher-order logic as shown here follows Gordon's presentation [9]. The textbook *Concrete Semantics* by Klein and Nipkow [19] also provides a

---

Dedicated to the memory of Mike Gordon, FRS (1948–2017), dear friend, inspiring mentor, and a pioneering researcher in interactive theorem proving, and hardware and software verification.

© Springer Nature Switzerland AG 2018
J. P. Bowen et al. (Eds.): SETSS 2017, LNCS 11174, pp. 89–114, 2018.
https://doi.org/10.1007/978-3-030-02928-9_3

cogent introduction to the metatheory of Hoare logic along quite similar lines. The author's chapter [23] in the *Handbook of Model Checking* [5] covers the basics of Hoare logic, and that presentation forms the foundation of the formalization described in this paper.

The present paper is a tutorial on the formalization of the syntax and semantics of a program logic using SRI's Prototype Verification System (PVS) [20,21]. The formalization of Hoare logic is a useful example for the purposes of this tutorial for several reasons. One, Hoare logic is interesting in its own right as a systematic approach to program proving. Two, the example is simple enough that these proofs can be replicated by the reader using PVS in a few hours. Three, the example highlights some of the nuances and peculiarities of formalization using PVS's higher-order logic. Four, lessons learned from this exercise can be easily generalized to other more complex proofs that cover advanced properties of more complex languages.

We first look at an example of the use of Hoare logic. Consider the program in Fig. 1 for computing the *maximum segment sum* of an array of integers [4], where a segment sum is $\Sigma_{j=l}^{h}a[j]$, the sum of contiguous elements $a[l], \ldots, a[h]$ for $0 \leq l, h < N$, for an array a of size N. Note that an empty segment has segment sum of 0 since $\Sigma_{j=l}^{h}a[j] = 0$ when $h < l$, this is the lowest answer that can be returned. For example, if the array elements are $a[0] = -3, a[1] = 4, a[2] = -2, a[3] = 6, a[4] = -5$, then the maximum segment sum is 8, which is the sum of $a[1], a[2]$, and $a[3]$. As it scans the array prefix $a[0 \ldots i-1]$, the program maintains two maxima: maxsum, which is the maximal segment sum from the scanned prefix of the array, and maxcurrentsum, which is the maximal segment sum for a segment ending at the current index being scanned. The program maintains two invariants. One, that maxsum = $\max_{0 \leq l, h < i \leq N}\Sigma_{j=l}^{h}a[j]$, the maximum segment sum for any subsegment of the array within 0 and $i - 1$. We abbreviate this invariant as $P(\text{maxsum}, i)$. Two, that maxcurrentsum = $\max_{0 \leq l \leq i \leq N}\Sigma_{j=l}^{i-1}a[j]$, which we abbreviate as $Q(\text{maxcurrentsum}, i)$. This asserts that the value of maxcurrentsum is the maximum of a segment sum for segment ending in $i - 1$.

2   First-Order Hoare Logic

We now describe the Hoare calculus and show how it can be used to construct a correctness proof for the maxsegsum program. We first introduce the concept of a first-order language. Let f range over function symbols (e.g., $+$ is a two-place function symbol) and p range over predicate symbols (e.g., $<$ is a two-place predicate symbol). A 0-ary predicate p yields a propositional atom $p()$ that can take on truth values $\top$ when the proposition is logically true, or $\bot$, otherwise. A first-order signature Σ is a partial map from the set of function and predicate symbols to their arity, so that if $\Sigma(p) = n$, for $n \geq 0$, then p represents an n-ary predicate symbol, e.g., $\Sigma(<) = 2$ if $<$ is in the signature as a two-place predicate. Similarly, if $\Sigma(f) = n$, then f represents an n-ary function symbol, e.g., $\Sigma(+) = 2$ if $+$ is in Σ as a two-place function symbol. A Σ-term is either a variable x or it is of the form $f(a_1, \ldots, a_n)$ where $\Sigma(f) = n$ and $a_1, \ldots, a_n$

$$\{\texttt{true}\}$$
$$(\texttt{maxsum}, \texttt{maxcurrentsum}, \texttt{i}) := (0,0,0);$$
$$\{P(\texttt{maxsum}, \texttt{i}) \wedge Q(\texttt{maxcurrentsum}, \texttt{i})\}$$
$$\texttt{while}(\texttt{i} < N))$$
$$\qquad S(\texttt{maxsum}, \texttt{maxcurrentsum}, \texttt{i})$$
$$\{P(\texttt{maxsum}, N)\}$$

where

$$S(\texttt{maxsum}, \texttt{maxcurrentsum}, \texttt{i})$$
$$= \begin{pmatrix} \texttt{maxsum} \\ \texttt{maxcurrentsum} \\ \texttt{i} \end{pmatrix} := \begin{pmatrix} \max(\texttt{maxsum}, \texttt{maxcurrentsum} + a[\texttt{i}]) \\ \max(0, \texttt{maxcurrentsum} + a[\texttt{i}]) \\ \texttt{i} + 1 \end{pmatrix}$$
$$P(\texttt{maxsum}, i)$$
$$= (\texttt{maxsum} = \max_{0 \le l, h < i \le N} \Sigma_{j=l}^{h} a[j])$$
$$Q(\texttt{maxcurrentsum}, i)$$
$$= (\texttt{maxcurrentsum} = \max_{0 \le l \le i \le N} \Sigma_{j=l}^{i-1} a[j])$$

Fig. 1. Program for computing the maximum segment sum of an array of integers

are n Σ-terms. For example $+(x, +(y, x))$ is a Σ-term. A Σ-atom is either an equality of the form $a = b$ for two Σ-terms a, b, or is of the form $p(a_1, \ldots, a_n)$ where $\Sigma(p) = n$ and $a_1, \ldots, a_n$ are n Σ-terms. For example $< (+(x, 1), x)$ is a Σ-atom.[1] A Σ-formula A is either a Σ-atom, a *negation* $\neg B$, a *conjunction* $A_1 \wedge A_2$, or an *existential quantification* $\exists x.B$, where A_1, A_2, and B are Σ-formulas. Disjunction $A_1 \vee A_2$ can be defined as $\neg(\neg A_1 \wedge \neg A_2)$, implication $A_1 \implies A_2$ as $\neg A_1 \vee A_2$, and universal quantification $\forall x.B$ as $\neg \exists x.\neg B$.

Semantics. The semantics for a first-order Σ-term is given by a Σ-structure M with a non-empty set $|M|$ (the *domain*) and an interpretation of the n-ary function and predicate symbols of Σ as n-ary functions and predicates over $|M|$. If $\Sigma(f) = n$, then $M(f)$ is a map from $|M|^n$ to $|M|$, and if $\Sigma(p) = n$, then $M(p)$ is a map from $|M|^n$ to $\{\top, \bot\}$. An M-*assignment* ρ maps each variable to elements of $|M|$. The assignment $\rho\{x \mapsto \mathbf{a}\}$ maps x to $\mathbf{a}$, and maps any y, $y \not\equiv x$, to $\rho(y)$. The semantics of a Σ-term a, written as $M[\![a]\!]\rho$, is defined so that $M[\![x]\!]\rho = \rho(x)$ and $M[\![f(a_1, \ldots, a_n)]\!]\rho = M(f)(M[\![a_1]\!]\rho, \ldots, M[\![a_n]\!]\rho)$. The semantics of a formula $M[\![A]\!]\rho$ is either $\top$ or $\bot$, where

---

[1] Informally, we abuse notation to employ infix versions of the familiar function and predicate symbols so that the Σ-atom $< (+(x, 1), x)$ will be written as $x + 1 < x$.

$$M[\![a = b]\!]\rho = (M[\![a]\!]\rho = M[\![b]\!]\rho)$$
$$M[\![p(a_1,\ldots,a_n)]\!]\rho = M(p)(M[\![a_1]\!]\rho,\ldots,M[\![a_n]\!]\rho)$$
$$M[\![\neg A]\!]\rho = \neg M[\![A]\!]\rho$$
$$M[\![A_1 \wedge A_2]\!]\rho = M[\![A_1]\!]\rho \wedge M[\![A_2]\!]\rho$$
$$M[\![\exists x.A]\!]\rho = M[\![A]\!]\rho\{x \mapsto d\} \text{ for some } d \in |M|$$

The satisfaction relation $M, \rho \models A$ holds iff $M[\![A]\!]\rho = \top$. The set of free variables $vars(a)$ of a term a is defined as $vars(x) = \{x\}$ and $vars(f(a_1,\ldots,a_n)) = \bigcup_i vars(a_i)$. The set of free variables of a formula $vars(A)$ is defined as

$$vars(p(a_1,\ldots,a_n)) = \bigcup_i vars(a_i)$$
$$vars(\neg A) = vars(A)$$
$$vars(A \wedge B) = vars(A) \cup vars(B)$$
$$vars(\exists x.A) = vars(A) - \{x\}$$

If X is a set of variables, a Σ-term a is said to be a $\Sigma[X]$-term if $vars(a) \subseteq X$. Similarly, a Σ-formula A is a $\Sigma[X]$-formula if $vars(A) \subseteq X$. A Σ-sentence A is a $\Sigma[\emptyset]$-formula, i.e., one with no free variables so that $vars(A) = \emptyset$. If a is a $\Sigma[X]$-term, $\overline{x}$ is a sequence $x_1,\ldots,x_n$ of length n of pairwise distinct variables covering a subset X' of X, and $\overline{e}$ is a sequence $e_1,\ldots,e_n$ of $\Sigma[Y]$-terms, the $a[\overline{e}/\overline{x}]$ is a $\Sigma[(X - X') \cup Y]$-term that is obtained by substituting e_i for x_i in a, for $1 \leq i \leq n$. The free variables in a formula are implicitly universally quantified so that a Σ-formula A is valid if $M[\![A]\!]\rho = \top$ for all Σ-structures M and M-assignments ρ.

First-Order Programs. A *program term* e is a $\Sigma[Y]$-term, i.e., $vars(e)$ contains only program variables. A $\Sigma[Y]$-statement is one of

1. A *skip* statement *skip*.
2. A *simultaneous assignment* statement $\overline{y} := \overline{e}$ where $\overline{y}$ is a sequence of n distinct program variables from Y, e is a sequence of n $\Sigma[Y]$-terms.
3. A *conditional* statement $C \,?\, S_1 \,:\, S_2$, where C is a $\Sigma[Y]$-formula, and S_1 and S_2 are $\Sigma[Y]$-statements.[2]
4. A *loop* statement *while C do S*, where C is a $\Sigma[Y]$-formula and S is a $\Sigma[Y]$-statement. Here too, C can be an arbitrary first-order $\Sigma[Y]$-formula.
5. A *sequential composition* $S_1; S_2$, where S_1 and S_2 are $\Sigma[Y]$-statements.

A Hoare triple in a given signature Σ has the form $\{P\}S\{Q\}$, where P and Q are *assertions*, i.e., $\Sigma[X \cup Y]$ formulas for some finite disjoint sets X and

---

[2] Note that C can be an arbitrary first-order $\Sigma[Y]$-formula so that programs might not necessarily be computable. The metatheorems on Hoare logic presented here are valid even in this generalized setting.

Y of logical and program variables, respectively, where S is a $\Sigma[Y]$ statement. We call such a triple a $\Sigma[X, Y]$-triple. The logical variables X occur only in assertions, whereas the program variables can occur in both the statement S and the assertions P and Q. The logical variables have the same assignment in the precondition and the post-condition, whereas the interpretation of program variables can be different in the two assertions to reflect the change from the input state to the output state of the program.

The inference rules of the Hoare calculus, assuming all triples are $\Sigma[X, Y]$-triples, are as shown in Fig. 2. The Skip rule preserves any precondition assertion. The Assignment rule asserts that for an assignment statement $\overline{y} := \overline{e}$, the post-condition P over the program variables $\overline{y}$ follows from the same precondition P with $\overline{e}$ substituted for $\overline{y}$. The Conditional rule has two premises, one for each of the branches of the conditional statement, that the post-condition must hold of then (else) branch when the precondition has been strengthened with the condition (negation of the condition). The Loop rule has the premise that the assertion P is a loop invariant. The Composition rule introduces an intermediate assertion R that is a post-condition to the first statement S_1 and a precondition to the statement S_2. The Consequence rule derives the conclusion triple by strengthening the precondition and weakening the post-condition of the premise triple.

Skip	$\{P\}skip\{P\}$
Assignment	$\{P[\overline{e}/\overline{y}]\}\overline{y} := \overline{e}\{P\}$
Conditional	$\dfrac{\{C \wedge P\}S_1\{Q\} \quad \{\neg C \wedge P\}S_2\{Q\}}{\{P\}C\ ?\ S_1\ :\ S_2\{Q\}}$
Loop	$\dfrac{\{P \wedge C\}S\{P\}}{\{P\}while\ C\ do\ S\{P \wedge \neg C\}}$
Composition	$\dfrac{\{P\}S_1\{R\} \quad \{R\}S_2\{Q\}}{\{P\}S_1; S_2\{Q\}}$
Consequence	$\dfrac{P \Rightarrow P' \quad \{P'\}S\{Q'\} \quad Q' \Rightarrow Q}{\{P\}S\{Q\}}$

Fig. 2. A Hoare calculus for While programs

Returning to our `maxsegsum` example, we can construct the proof as shown in Fig. 3.

3 Higher-Order Logic

The PVS specification language is based on higher-order logic. In first-order logic, there is a single domain and the variables range over all of the domain elements. First-order logic can be extended to *many-sorted logic* where variables can be tagged with sorts such as, say, books, authors, cities, etc. Sorts, can thus be seen

Step No.	Triple	Explanation
1	$\{(P(0,0) \land Q(0,0))\}$ $(\mathtt{maxsum}, \mathtt{maxcurrentsum}, \mathtt{i}) := (0,0,0)$ $\{P(\mathtt{maxsum}, \mathtt{i}) \land Q(\mathtt{maxcurrentsum}, \mathtt{i})\}$	Assignment
2	$\{\mathtt{true}\}$ $(\mathtt{maxsum}, \mathtt{maxcurrentsum}, \mathtt{i}) := (0,0,0)$ $\{P(\mathtt{maxsum}, \mathtt{i}) \land Q(\mathtt{maxcurrentsum}, \mathtt{i})\}$	Consequence[1]
3	$\left\{ \begin{array}{l} \mathtt{i} < N \\ \land\, P(\max(\mathtt{maxsum}, \mathtt{maxcurrentsum} + a[\mathtt{i}]), \mathtt{i}+1) \\ \land\, Q(\max(0, \mathtt{maxcurrentsum} + a[\mathtt{i}]), \mathtt{i}+1) \end{array} \right\}$ $S(\mathtt{maxsum}, \mathtt{maxcurrentsum}, \mathtt{i})$ $\{P(\mathtt{maxsum}, \mathtt{i}) \land Q(\mathtt{maxcurrentsum}, \mathtt{i})\}$	Assignment
4	$\left\{ \begin{array}{l} \mathtt{i} < N \\ \land\, P(\mathtt{maxsum}, \mathtt{i}) \\ \land\, Q(\mathtt{maxcurrentsum}, \mathtt{i}) \end{array} \right\}$ $S(\mathtt{maxsum}, \mathtt{maxcurrentsum}, \mathtt{i})$ $\{P(\mathtt{maxsum}, \mathtt{i}) \land Q(\mathtt{maxcurrentsum}, \mathtt{i})\}$	Consequence[3]
5	$\{P(\mathtt{maxsum}, \mathtt{i})\}$ $\mathtt{while}(\mathtt{i} < N)$ $\quad S(\mathtt{maxsum}, \mathtt{maxcurrentsum}, \mathtt{i})$ $\{\mathtt{i} \geq N \land P(\mathtt{i})\}$	While[4]
6	$\{P(\mathtt{maxsum}, \mathtt{i})\}$ $\mathtt{while}(\mathtt{i} < N))$ $\quad S(\mathtt{maxsum}, \mathtt{maxcurrentsum}, \mathtt{i})$ $\{P(\mathtt{maxsum}, N)\}$	Consequence[5]
5	$\{\mathtt{true}\}$ $(\mathtt{maxsum}, \mathtt{maxcurrentsum}, \mathtt{i}) := (0,0,0);$ $\mathtt{while}(\mathtt{i} < N)$ $\quad S(\mathtt{maxsum}, \mathtt{maxcurrentsum}, \mathtt{i})$ $\{P(\mathtt{maxsum}, N)\}$	Composition[2, 5]

Fig. 3. Hoare Logic proof of $\mathtt{maxsegsum}$ program

as restricting the range of a variable to a well-defined subset of the domain. In higher-order logic, there is a hierarchy of types. The base types can be first-order sorts like numbers, vertices, and edges. One such type can be the type of Booleans $\mathtt{bool}$ containing the constants $\mathtt{TRUE}$ and $\mathtt{FALSE}$, where $\mathtt{TRUE} \neq \mathtt{FALSE}$.[3] A new type T can be constructed by forming an n-tuple $[T_1, \ldots, T_n]$ of n types, or a function space $[T_1 \rightarrow T_2]$ of a domain type T_1 and a range type T_2. With such higher types, the type of predicates is just a function space where the range type is the type $\mathtt{bool}$ of the Booleans. Negation, conjunction, disjunction, and implication are operations on the type $\mathtt{bool}$. For a type T, the everywhere-true

---

[3] Unlike $\top$ and $\bot$ which are in the semantic universe of first-order logic, $\mathtt{TRUE}$ and $\mathtt{FALSE}$ are constants in the PVS higher-order logic.

predicate maps each element of T to TRUE, which is written as $\lambda(x : T).$TRUE. For a predicate p, we can define $\forall p$ as $p = \lambda(x : T).$TRUE.

The stratification of types so that the order $order(T)$ of a base type T is 1, the order of a function type $order([T_1, \ldots, T_n])$ is the maximum of $order(T_i)$ for $1 \leq i \leq n$, and the order of a function type $[T_1 \rightarrow T_2]$ is the maximum of $1 + order(T_1)$ and $order(T_2)$. The order of bool is 1. The order of $[$bool$\rightarrow[$bool$\rightarrow$bool$]]$ is 2 since this is the type of a function that takes an argument of order 1 and returns a function that also takes an argument of order 1. The order of $[[$bool$\rightarrow$bool$]\rightarrow$bool$]$ is 3 since this is the type of a function that takes an argument of order 2. The order of $[$bool$, [$bool$\rightarrow$bool$]]$ is 2. Higher-order logic can express

1. Induction over the natural numbers: For any p, a predicate on natural numbers, if $p(0)$ and $\forall x.p(x) \implies p(S(x))$, then $\forall x.p(x)$, where the natural numbers are constructed from 0 using the successor operator S.
2. The well-ordering property over the natural numbers: Any nonempty predicate p on the natural numbers, when viewed as a set, contains a least element x such that $p(x)$.
3. The completeness property of the reals: Any nonempty set of reals that has an upper bound has a least upper bound.

For the purpose of formalizing Hoare logic, higher-order logic has the advantage of being able to capture the predicates and predicate transformers used in reasoning about program correctness.

4   Hoare Logic in PVS

A PVS specification is a collection of theories. Theories can have formal parameters that are types or individuals. We define Hoare logic in a theory that takes as a parameter, a (nonempty) type value representing the type of values that a program variable can take. Writing TYPE+ instead of TYPE indicates that the type is required to be nonempty since PVS allows types to be empty. A theory such as HoareLogic can be imported into another theory with actual parameters for the formal parameters, e.g., the type int of integers for value. An example of this appears in Sect. 6. The body of the HoareLogic theory is presented below.

```
HoareLogic[value: TYPE+] : THEORY
  BEGIN
    :
    :
    END HoareLogic
```

We embed Hoare logic in the higher-order logic of PVS using a mixture of a shallow (semantic) embedding which defines some of the Hoare logic operators by corresponding PVS operations, and a deep (syntactic) embedding where other operators are syntactically represented by data structures defined in PVS. In PVS, the base types are the Boolean bool and the real numbers real (and its subtypes like the rationals rat and the integers int). A tuple type $[T_1, \ldots, T_n]$

is constructed from component types T_i, for $1 \leq i \leq n$. For example, [bool, int] is a tuple type and if x is a variable of this type, then it can take on a tuple value (TRUE, -3), and x'1 represents the first component TRUE, and x'2, the second component -3. A record type has the form $[\#l_1 : T_1, \ldots, l_n : T_n\#]$, where each l_i is a distinct field name and each T_i, for $1 \leq i \leq n$ is a type. For example, if r is a variable of record type [#age : nat, weight : real#], then r'age and r'weight return the age and weight components, respectively. A function type has the form $[T_1 \rightarrow T_2]$ with domain T_1, and range T_2. If the domain type is a tuple of the form $[S_1, \ldots, S_n]$, then the function type can be written as $[S_1, \ldots, S_n \rightarrow T_2]$, instead of $[[S_1, \ldots, S_n] \rightarrow T_2]$. A function f of type [int, real$\rightarrow$real], can be applied as f(-3, sqrt(2)), if sqrt is itself a function of type [real$\rightarrow$real]. Some dyadic function symbols like +, *, /, -, <, and <=, have an infix syntax in PVS. An expression of function type, e.g., [real$\rightarrow$real], can be constructed as a *lambda expression*, e.g., (LAMBDA (x: real): x + x). For any type T and an expression A of type bool, the type $\{x : T \mid A\}$ represents the *predicate subtype* of T. An expression e of type T has the type $\{x : T \mid A\}$ if A[e/x] (the expression obtained by substituting e for x in A) holds. For example, a subrange of the integers from -5 to 5 can be defined as $\{x : \text{int} \mid -5 <= x <= 5\}$. The expression 6/2 when typechecked with the expected type $\{x : \text{int} \mid -5 <= x <= 5\}$ generates two proof obligations: one requiring that 6/2 is an integer, and the second that -5 <= 6/2 <= 5 holds. In addition to the above type constructions, there is a DATATYPE mechanism for defining inductive datatypes like lists, trees, and programs that is described below.

4.1   Representing Programs in PVS

In PVS, the body of a theory is a sequence of declarations/definitions of types, constants, and formulas (axioms, lemmas, and theorems). In our embedding, the state of a program is represented as a finite sequence of values given by finseq[value]. The type finseq is defined in the PVS prelude, the default background library, as a record type with length field and a seq field that is of type [below(length)$\rightarrow$value], which is essentially an array of length length.

```
finite_sequence: TYPE = [# length: nat, seq: [below[length] -> T] #]
finseq: TYPE = finite_sequence
```

The finite_sequence type is an example of a *dependent type* since the type of the seq field depends on the length field.[4] An expression of type finseq[value] can be constructed, for example, as (# length := 3, seq := (LAMBDA (i : below(3)): V(i)) #), where V maps the index variable i to an element of the type value. If s is a finite sequence, then s'length represents the contents of the length field of s, and s'seq is the sequence itself, and s'seq(i)

---

[4] Type dependencies of this sort can occur within record types, as in the finite_sequence example, as well as in tuple types, function types, and inductive datatypes.

is the i'th element of the sequence. The idea is that the variables of a program have indices 0, 1, etc., that are used to retrieve the value bound to a program variable in the state. The value of the variable with index i is the i'th element of the sequence representing the state. The indices $0, \ldots, s'\text{length} - 1$ for a state s represent the program variables Y from the informal presentation of Hoare logic in Sect. 2. The finite sequence representation is not actually exploited in this presentation so that the state type could have been declared without a specific definition. We could also use other definitions for the state type such as a map from strings representing variable names to the value type, or a record type with fields representing the variables. Such definitions do not adequately support the stacking discipline needed to handle block structure and functions.

The embedding of Hoare logic in PVS does not use variables, terms, nor assignments of terms to variables. The sequence representation becomes relevant when the programming language is extended with function calls. The type test is defined as a predicate on state, that is a function from state to bool. The type of an assignment is a map from state to state preserving the length of the state sequence. The range type of an assignment {t : state | t'length = s'length} is a *predicate subtype* of state according to the predicate constraint t'length = s'length. The type assignment is a dependent function type since the range type depends on the domain element s. When given an expression representing an assignment, the PVS typechecker generates a proof obligation to ensure that the assignment operation does not change the length of the state sequence.

```
state: TYPE = finseq[value]
test: TYPE = pred[state]
assignment: TYPE = [s : state -> {t : state | t'length = s'length}]
```

The syntax of **While** programs is specified by an inductive datatype program that introduces constructors for skip statements, assign statements, conditional statements, while loops, and sequencing. The body of a datatype definition is a sequence of constructor specifications. For example, the assign constructor takes a single argument of type assignment. The label update is the corresponding accessor operation. The label assign? names the corresponding recognizer predicate. An assignment statement contains an update operation that, as we saw before, maps an input state to an output state. The condition in a conditional statement is a test, a predicate on state. Typechecking the datatype declaration generates a number of declarations. These declarations introduce the type program with constructor operations skip, assign, ift, while, and seq. For example, the assign constructor is introduced with the type [assignment→program] so that assign(A) has type program if A has type assignment. Each constructor has a corresponding recognizer, either skip?, assign?, ift?, while?, or seq?, all of type [program→bool]. Each constructor has zero or more accessors. For example, the skip constructor has no accessors, but the assign constructor has the accessor update such that update(assign(A)) = A. Axioms are generated corresponding to the properties of constructors, recognizers, and accessors, including induction principles for the datatype and definitions for some basic operation. These generated declarations can be optionally viewed (using the Emacs command M-x prettyprint-expanded) but not edited.

```
program : DATATYPE
  BEGIN
    skip: skip?
    assign(update : assignment): assign?
    ift(ifcond: test, thenprog: program, elseprog: program): ift?
    while(wcond: test, body : program): while?
    seq(left, right: program): seq?
  END program
```

4.2   Program Semantics

We now present a trace semantics for programs in higher-order logic. The next sequence of declarations introduce variable names for programs, tests, and assignments. These declarations are merely a convenience to indicate that a variable occurrence with the name C has the default type test in the definitions that follow. These defaults can be over-ridden through local declarations. The variables in the PVS formalization do not necessarily line up with the metavariables used in the informal exposition in Sect. 2.

```
S, S1, S2: VAR program
C : VAR test
A : VAR assignment
s, r, t: VAR state
```

The type trace is defined as a finite sequence of states of length at least 2 to indicate that each trace contains a distinct start and end state. We define the semantics of a program as a set of traces rather than as a relation between the start and end states. The latter relational semantics would require the semantics of a while statement to be given as an inductive relation, whereas with traces, the semantics defined by the meaning operation below is by recursion on the length of the trace. A Hoare triple $\{P\}S\{Q\}$ is valid (as defined below) only under the assumption that the program S terminates on any state satisfying the precondition P.

The definition of the trace type is also a predicate subtype. It is important to be able to specify types at this level of specificity. The operations first and last extract the first and last element of a given trace, respectively. The definition of first generates a proof obligation requiring that the access X'seq(0) is safe, i.e., X'length is at least 1.

```
first_TCC1: OBLIGATION FORALL (X: trace): 0 < X'length;
```

This follows from the type constraint in the definition of **trace** that required X'length to be at least 2. Similarly, for the definition of last, X'length - 1 must be at least 1, and smaller than X'length.

```
last_TCC1: OBLIGATION
  FORALL (X: trace): X'length - 1 >= 0 AND X'length - 1 < X'length;
```

Both proof obligations are also easily discharged. The **splice** operation appends two traces together but only if the, *join point*, i.e., the last state of the first trace, is identical to the first state of the second trace. The **splice** operation could have been defined to avoid the duplication of the join point, but there is no significant value to achieving this kind of efficiency. The o operation for concatenating two finite sequences is defined in the PVS prelude library which is a standard part of PVS. Later, in the proof of completeness, the o operation is also used for function composition, and this kind of overloading is not unusual in PVS formalizations.

```
trace : TYPE = {x : finseq[state] | x'length > 1}
X, Y, Z: VAR trace
first(X): state = X'seq(0)
last(X): state = X'seq(X'length - 1)
splice(X, (Y | first(Y) = last(X))): trace = X o Y
```

We need a notion of program size that can be used in termination arguments. The recursive definition of **programSize** below assigns a size of 1 to skip and assignment statements, and computes the size of conditional, loop, and sequencing statements from the size of the constituent programs. It uses a CASES construction to perform a pattern-matching case-split on the constructor forms in the **program** datatype. The termination argument for the definition of **programSize** itself is given by the well-founded subterm relationship << on the program datatype.

```
programSize(S): RECURSIVE nat =
CASES S OF
  skip: 1,
  assign(A): 1,
  ift(C, S1, S2): 1 + programSize(S1) + programSize(S2),
  while(C, S1): 1 + programSize(S1),
  seq(S1, S2): programSize(S1) + programSize(S2)
ENDCASES
  MEASURE S BY <<
```

The semantics of programs is given in terms of sets of traces. A trace X is in the set corresponding to the meaning of program S iff **meaning(S)(X)** holds. The recursive definition of **meaning** generates proof obligations corresponding to subtyping as well as termination. Note that the termination measure in this case is a lexicographic pair of ranking functions consisting of the length of the trace X and the program size of S.

```
meaning(S)(X): RECURSIVE bool =
CASES S OF
 skip: (X'length = 2 AND last(X) = first(X)),
 assign(A): (X'length = 2 AND last(X) = A(first(X))),
 ift(C, S1, S2): (IF C(first(X))
                      THEN meaning(S1)(X)
                      ELSE meaning(S2)(X) ENDIF),
 while(C, S1): (IF C(first(X))
                    THEN (EXISTS Y, Z: first(Z) = last(Y)
                          AND X = splice(Y, Z)
                          AND meaning(S1)(Y)
                          AND meaning(S)(Z))
                    ELSE (X'length = 2 AND last(X) = first(X))
                    ENDIF),
 seq(S1, S2): (EXISTS Y, Z: first(Z) = last(Y)
                          AND X = splice(Y, Z)
                          AND meaning(S1)(Y)
                          AND meaning(S2)(Z))
ENDCASES
MEASURE lex2(X'length, programSize(S))
```

4.3   Representing Hoare Logic in PVS

We introduce the concept of a Hoare triple, the semantics of triples, and the
proof rules of Hoare logic. The type **assertion** is defined as a predicate on the
state type, namely, the type [state→bool].

```
assertion: TYPE = [state -> bool]
```

A few variables are first declared to range over assertions. The variables
a, b, and c range over the **parameter** type, and are not to be confused with
the metavariables a, b, and c ranging over terms. The **triple_holds** relation
is defined on **pre**, S, and **post** to return a predicate on traces. The predicate
triple_holds(pre, S, post) holds of a trace X when X is a trace of the program S, i.e., when meaning(S)(X), then **post** holds of the last state of X if **pre**
holds of the first state of X. The Hoare triple consisting of **pre**, S, and **post**
is a valid triple, as defined by **valid_triple**, if for any program trace X of S,
pre(first(X)) implies **post(last(X))**.

```
P, Q, R, pre, post: VAR assertion

triple_holds(pre, S, post)(X): bool =
  pre(first(X)) AND meaning(S)(X) => post(last(X))

triple_valid(pre, S, post): bool =
  (FORALL X: triple_holds(pre, S, post)(X))
```

The next sequence of lemmas introduce semantic versions of the Hoare logic
inference rules and demonstrate that each inference rule preserves validity: if the
premises of the inference rule are valid triples, then so is the conclusion. The first
of these asserts the soundness of the skip rule. This lemma is proved with a single

grind proof command using the PVS proof assistant which expands definitions, applies various built-in simplifications, skolemizes any universal-strength quantifiers, and heuristically instantiates any existential-strength quantifiers through pattern-matching.

```
skip_rule: LEMMA
  triple_valid(P, skip, P)
```

The soundness of the assignment rule asserts that the triple with precondition P o A (P composed with A), the assignment statement assign(A), and a post-condition assertion P, is valid. This lemma is also proved by the grind proof command.

```
assignment_rule: LEMMA
  triple_valid(P o A, assign(A), P)
```

We define two operations before presenting the conditional rule of Hoare logic. The first operation forms the conjunction (⊓) of two assertions P and Q, and second operation forms the negation of an assertion. These definitions employ unicode symbols for ⊓, ∧, and ¬.

```
⊓(P, Q)(s): bool = P(s) ∧ Q(s);

neg(C)(s): bool  = ¬C(s)
```

The soundness of the conditional rule asserts that the triple consisting of the precondition P, the program ift(C, S1, S2), and the post-condition post is valid if the triple corresponding to the S1 branch is valid with precondition (pre ⊓ C), and the triple corresponding to the S2 branch is valid with precondition (pre ⊓ neg(C)). This rule is also discharged by the grind proof command.

```
conditional_rule: LEMMA
    triple_valid(pre ⊓ C, S1, post)
    AND triple_valid(pre ⊓ neg(C), S2, post)
    => triple_valid(pre, ift(C, S1, S2), post)
```

The soundness of the while rule is a similarly straightforward rendering of the informal rule presented in Fig. 2. The proof of this rule is nontrivial. We have to expand the definition of triple_valid in the consequent to expose the universal quantifier over trace X. Then we apply measure induction on the length of X. The inductive hypothesis when composed with the antecedent formula, which represents one execution of the loop body, can be used to prove the induction goal. This proof takes twelve interactive steps and is described in Sect. 5.1.

```
while_rule:  LEMMA
    triple_valid(P ⊓ C, S, P)
    => triple_valid(P, while(C, S), P ⊓ neg(C))
```

The soundness of the composition rule is easily stated and also proved using the `grind` proof command.

```
composition_rule: LEMMA
  triple_valid(P, S1, Q) AND triple_valid(Q, S2, R)
  => triple_valid(P, seq(S1, S2), R)
```

The soundness of the consequence rule, the final rule in Fig. 2, is also trivial. The relation `conseq` checks that the assertion Q is a consequence of P. The `conseq_rule` lemma is also proved using the `grind` proof command.

```
conseq(P, Q): bool =
(FORALL s: P(s) => Q(s))

P1, Q1: VAR assertion

conseq_rule: LEMMA
  conseq(P, P1) AND conseq(Q1, Q)
  AND triple_valid(P1, S, Q1)
  => triple_valid(P, S, Q)
```

4.4 Hoare Logic Proofs

Next, we define a representation for proofs constructed through the application of the Hoare logic rules. The type `triple` is defined as a record type with fields `prog`, `pre`, and `post`.

```
triple: TYPE = [# prog: program, pre, post: assertion #]
H, G: VAR triple
```

The datatype `preProof` introduces constructors for the proof rules, but these proof representations build from these constructors have to be checked before they can be viewed as correct proofs. Each constructor has an accessor slot labelled `conclusion` representing the triple that is the conclusion of the proof rule. Some constructors like `ift_step`, `while_step`, `seq_step`, and `conseq_step` have recursive sub-proof slots.

```
preProof: DATATYPE
BEGIN
  skip_step(conclusion: triple): skip_step?
  assign_step(conclusion: triple): assign_step?
  ift_step(conclusion: triple, thenProof, elseProof: preProof)
    : ift_step?
  while_step(conclusion: triple,  bodyProof: preProof): while_step?
  seq_step(conclusion: triple, left, right: preProof): seq_step?
  conseq_step(conclusion: triple, subProof: preProof): conseq_step?
END preProof
```

We first declare some variables that range over pre-proofs.

```
M, M1, M2: VAR preProof
```

```
Proof?(M): RECURSIVE bool =
  CASES M OF
    skip_step(H): skip?(H'prog) AND H'pre = H'post,
    assign_step(H): assign?(H'prog)
                    AND H'pre = H'post o update(H'prog),
    ift_step(H, M1, M2): ift?(H'prog)
                    AND conclusion(M1)'pre
                         = (H'pre ⊓ ifcond(H'prog))
                    AND conclusion(M2)'pre
                         = (H'pre ⊓ neg(ifcond(H'prog)))
                    AND conclusion(M1)'post = H'post
                    AND conclusion(M2)'post = H'post
                    AND conclusion(M1)'prog = thenprog(H'prog)
                    AND conclusion(M2)'prog = elseprog(H'prog)
                    AND Proof?(M1)
                    AND Proof?(M2),
    while_step(H, M1): while?(H'prog)
                    AND conclusion(M1)'pre
                         = (H'pre ⊓ wcond(H'prog))
                    AND conclusion(M1)'post = H'pre
                    AND conclusion(M1)'prog = body(H'prog)
                    AND H'post = (H'pre ⊓ neg(wcond(H'prog)))
                    AND Proof?(M1),
    seq_step(H, M1, M2): seq?(H'prog)
                    AND conclusion(M1)'pre = H'pre
                    AND conclusion(M2)'pre = conclusion(M1)'post
                    AND conclusion(M2)'post = H'post
                    AND conclusion(M1)'prog = left(H'prog)
                    AND conclusion(M2)'prog = right(H'prog)
                    AND Proof?(M1)
                    AND Proof?(M2),
    conseq_step(H, M1): conseq(H'pre, conclusion(M1)'pre)
                    AND conseq(conclusion(M1)'post, H'post)
                    AND conclusion(M1)'prog = H'prog
                    AND Proof?(M1)
  ENDCASES
  MEASURE M BY <<
```

Fig. 4. The Hoare proof checker

The predicate `Proof?` defined in Fig. 4 is a recursive proof checker for Hoare logic proofs. It checks that each step in the proof is a proper application of the corresponding proof rule from Fig. 2. Since PVS is a logic with a fairly basic syntax and semantics, the pattern-matching in the `CASES` destructures only the surface constructors of the proof M. Each case of the definition addresses one of the proof constructors to check that all recursive sub-proofs are correct and that the `conclusion` slot contains a well-formed triple reflecting the application of the proof rule. In the `while_step` case, for example, the `H'pre` slot contains the loop invariant.

Soundness. The predicate `valid` simply checks if the triple H is valid according to the `triple_valid` predicate. The soundness lemma asserts that the conclusion of a proof M that has been checked by `Proof?` is always valid. The interactive proof consists of fourteen steps and is described in more detail in Sect. 5.2. First, we employ induction on the structure of M, which yields 6 branches, one for each proof rule. Each of these branches is proved by rewriting or forward-chaining on the corresponding soundness lemma above.

```
valid(H): bool = triple_valid(H'pre, H'prog, H'post)

soundness: LEMMA
  Proof?(M) => valid(conclusion(M))
```

Completeness. The completeness of Hoare logic is proved by constructing proofs
for valid Hoare triples by induction on the program syntax. The completeness
proof is quite simple. First, we define the *weakest liberal precondition* operator
wlp which maps a program S and assertion Q to an assertion wlp(S)(Q) which
holds of any state s such that whenever s is the first state of a trace for S, then
assertion Q holds of the last state of the trace. The lemma wlp_valid is just
a sanity check that the wlp operator does in fact return a valid precondition.
It has no other role in the proof of completeness. This lemma is proved with a
ten-step proof that employs induction on the structure of the program S.

```
wlp(S)(Q)(s) : bool =
   (FORALL X: meaning(S)(X) AND s = first(X) =>  Q(last(X)))

wlp_valid: LEMMA
   triple_valid(wlp(S)(Q), S, Q)
```

The operation **Proves** checks that M is a Hoare logic proof with the conclusion
triple H.

```
Proves(M, H): bool =
   Proof?(M) AND conclusion(M) = H
```

The lemma wlp_proof is the key to the completeness proof and the PVS proof
steps are presented in Sect. 5.3. It asserts that the Hoare triple with precondition
wlp(S)(Q), program S, and post-condition Q is provable. The PVS proof is by
induction on the structure of S.

```
wlp_proof: LEMMA
   EXISTS M: Proves(M, mkTriple(wlp(S)(Q), S, Q))
```

The proof goes as follows.

- If S is a skip statement, the triple {wlp(skip)(Q)}skip{Q} is just
  {Q}skip{Q}. The latter triple is proved by the skip rule of Fig. 2.
- If S is an assignment statement with assignment A, the triple

$$\{\texttt{wlp(assign(A))(Q)}\}\texttt{assign(A)}\{\texttt{Q}\}$$

can be rewritten using the function composition operation ∘ as

$$\{\texttt{Q} \circ \texttt{A}\}\texttt{assign(A)}\{\texttt{Q}\},$$

which is easily proved using the assignment rule of Fig. 2.
- If S is a conditional statement of the form ift(C, S1, S2), the induction
  hypothesis yields the triples

1. $\{\texttt{wlp(S1)(Q)}\}\texttt{S1}\{\texttt{Q}\}$, for which we know that

$$\texttt{conseq}((\texttt{wlp(S)(Q)} \sqcap C), \texttt{wlp(S1)(Q)})$$

by the definition of $\texttt{wlp}$. By the consequence rule, we can derive the triple

$$\{(\texttt{wlp(S)(Q)} \sqcap C)\}\texttt{S1}\{Q\}.$$

2. $\{\texttt{wlp(S2)(Q)}\}\texttt{S2}\{\texttt{Q}\}$, for which we know that

$$\texttt{conseq}((\texttt{wlp(S)(Q)} \sqcap \texttt{neg}(C)), \texttt{wlp(S2)(Q)})$$

by the definition of $\texttt{wlp}$. By the consequence rule, we can derive the triple

$$\{(\texttt{wlp(S)(Q)} \sqcap \texttt{neg}(C))\}\texttt{S2}\{\texttt{Q}\}.$$

We can then apply the conditional rule to derive the triple $\{\texttt{wlp(S)(Q)}\}\texttt{S}\{\texttt{Q}\}$.
- If S is of the form $\texttt{while(C, S1)}$, then we can construct a proof of the triple $\{\texttt{wlp(S)(Q)}\}\texttt{S}\{\texttt{Q}\}$ with the following steps:
  1. By the induction hypothesis, we have $\{\texttt{wlp(S1)(wlp(S)(Q))}\}\texttt{S1}\{\texttt{wlp(S)(Q)}\}$.
  2. Then by the consequence rule, we have

$$\{(\texttt{wlp(S)(Q)} \sqcap C)\}\texttt{S1}\{\texttt{wlp(S)(Q)}\},$$

  since $\texttt{conseq}((\texttt{wlp(S)(Q)} \sqcap C), \texttt{wlp(S1)(wlp(S)(Q))})$.
  3. The while rule yields

$$\{\texttt{wlp(S)(Q)}\}\texttt{while(C, S)}\{(\texttt{wlp(S)(Q)} \sqcap \texttt{neg}(C))\}.$$

  4. Finally, the consequence rule yields

$$\{\texttt{wlp(S)(Q)}\}\texttt{while(C, S)}\{\texttt{Q}\}.$$

- If S is of the form $\texttt{seq(S1, S2)}$, the proof of the triple follows from the induction hypotheses on S1 and S2 by observing that $\texttt{wlp(seq(S1, S2))(Q)} = \texttt{wlp(S1)(wlp(S2)(Q))}$.

5   PVS Proofs About Hoare Logic

We take a brief look at the use of the PVS proof assistant to construct the proofs described in Sect. 4. Typechecking the theory HoareLogic generates twenty type correctness conditions (TCCs) as proof obligations. These correspond to subtype constraints and termination conditions. All of these are discharged by the default proof strategy for proving these TCCs.

5.1   Proof of the while_rule lemma

The first nontrivial proof in the development is that of the while_rule lemma demonstrating the soundness of the while proof rule. Though we present the proof steps with an informal explanation, the best way to understand the proof is to actually step through it with PVS. Proofs in PVS are constructed through a read-eval-print loop that displays a proof goal followed by a prompt Rule? asking the user for a proof rule to apply. Each proof goal is presented in a sequent form as

$$\{-1\}A_1$$
$$\vdots$$
$$\{-m\}A_m$$
$$\vdash$$
$$\{1\}C_1$$
$$\vdots$$
$$\{n\}C_n$$

Here the formulas $A_1, \ldots, A_m$ are the *antecedent* formulas, and $C_1, \ldots, C_n$ are *consequent* formulas. The interpretation of a sequent is that the implication $\bigwedge_{i=1}^m A_k \implies \bigvee_{j=1}^n C_j$ must be shown to be valid. The proof commands include those for

- Propositional simplification:
  - flatten which simplifies top-level negations, consequent disjunctions and implications, and antecedent conjunctions,
  - split which simplifies top-level antecedent disjunctions and implications, and consequent conjunctions to derive subgoals for each of the conjuncts, and
  - prop which is a strategy that applies flatten and split to completion.
- Quantifier reasoning:
  - skolem, skolem!, and skeep for replacing top-level antecedent existential quantifiers and consequent universal quantifiers with fresh constants (skolemization),
  - inst, inst? for instantiating top-level antecedent universal quantifiers and consequent existential quantifiers with witnessing terms
- Equational reasoning:
  - replace which applies any antecedent equations as rewrites to replace equals for equals,
  - assert which simplifies the antecedent formulas and the negations of the consequent formulas and asserts these to a decision procedure in order to see if the negation of the sequent is unsatisfiable,
  - apply-extensionality which uses extensionality to demonstrate that two functions (records, tuples, datatype expressions) are equal by showing that they are componentwise equal, and
  - replace-eta which applies the eta axiom to replace a variable of a constructor subtype in a datatype with constructor expression.

- Combined strategies:
  - **ground** which combines propositional simplification with **assert**,
  - **grind** which extends **ground** with skolemization and heuristic quantifier instantiation,
  - **induct** and **measure-induct+** which apply induction to the sequent to generate base and induction subgoals, and
  - **induct-and-simplify** and **measure-induct-and-simplify** which apply induction to the sequent to then simplify the resulting subgoals.

The typical strategy is to see if the lemma can be proved using the **grind** command. This is a somewhat brute-force command which can fail due to incorrect quantifier instantiation, overly aggressive definition expansion, divergent rewriting, or because a more sophisticated proof strategy is needed. The **grind** command takes a number of flags and options that can be used to control its behavior. There are also more powerful variants of **grind** like **lazy-grind**, as well as less powerful variants like **bash** and **reduce**.

With the **while_rule** lemma, the proof needs a bit of manual intervention since it requires induction. First, we need to expose the variable on which we can perform induction. The **skeep** step skolemizes the universally quantified variables in the lemma P, C, and S. It then expands the definition of **triple_valid** to create a proof goal that now includes a universal quantified trace variable X. The **measure-induct+** step performs measure induction over the well-founded measure function X'length. The proof then follows by expanding the definition of **triple_holds** and **meaning** on the induction goal. We then do another round of skolemization using **skeep**, simplify the formula using propositional simplification and decision procedures with the **ground** command, then instantiate the induction hypothesis variables, and conclude the proof with **grind** step. The definition of **meaning** is excluded since it is not needed for completing the proof, and it can trigger an expansion loop. One useful feature of this query/response approach to interactive proof is that one typically constructs the proof more through improvisation than planning. The combination of automation and interactivity makes it easy to explore proof paths, backtrack when a path looks fruitless. Through such exploration, one can also find and fix incorrect definitions and conjectures.

```
(""
 (skeep)
 (expand "triple_valid")
 (measure-induct+ "X'length" "X")
 (expand "triple_holds")
 (expand "meaning" +)
 (skeep)
 (ground)
 (("1" (skeep) (inst - "Z") (inst - "Y") (grind :exclude "meaning"))
  ("2" (grind :exclude "meaning")))))
```

5.2   Proof of the soundness Theorem

The proof of the lemma **soundness** is shown below. It requires a top-level induction on the structure of the proof M. Each subgoal corresponds to one proof constructor. Each one is proved using a variant of grind using the appropriate soundness lemma. In some cases grind is unable to use the rule directly in which case the forward-chain rule is applied to instantiate the lemma based on formulas in the proof goal. The replace-eta step is needed to replace a variable of a constructor type such as (ift?) with the corresponding constructor expression.

```
(""
 (induct "M")
 (("1" (grind :rewrites "skip_rule"))
  ("2" (grind :rewrites "assignment_rule"))
  ("3"
   (grind :if-match nil :exclude "triple_valid")
   (forward-chain "conditional_rule")
   (replace-eta "ift_step1_var!1'prog" "(ift?)"))
  ("4"
   (grind :if-match nil :exclude "triple_valid")
   (forward-chain "while_rule")
   (replace-eta "while_step1_var!1'prog" "(while?)"))
  ("5"
   (grind :if-match nil :exclude "triple_valid")
   (forward-chain "composition_rule")
   (replace-eta "seq_step1_var!1'prog" "(seq?)"))
  ("6"
   (grind :exclude ("conseq" "triple_valid"))
   (forward-chain "conseq_rule"))))
```

5.3 Proof of the wlp_proof Lemma

The proof of the wlp_proof lemma is a little too long to present in detail. We restrict ourselves to the case of the skip statement. At the top level, the proof is by induction on the structure of the program S. This yields five cases. In each case, one first skolemizes the subgoal, instantiates the existential quantifier for the proof (possibly using the subproofs yielded by the induction hypothesis), followed by a few routine steps of simplification and instantiation.

```
(""
 (induct "S")
 (("1"
   (skeep)
   (inst + "skip_step(mkTriple(wlp(skip)(Q), skip, Q))")
   (grind)
   (apply-extensionality)
   (grind)
   (inst - "(: x!1, x!1 :)")
   (("1" (grind)) ("2" (grind))))
   .
   .
   .
)
```

6   Verification Condition Generation

Klein and Nipkow [19] present a treatment of verification condition generation to reduce the verification of a Hoare triple for an annotated program to the discharging of certain proof obligations (*verification conditions*) in the assertion logic. The formalization of verification condition generation is also a useful exercise that the reader is encouraged to replicate in PVS. The relevant definitions and theorems are captured in a PVS theory called **HoareVC**. This theory has the same parameter **value** as the theory **HoareLogic**. The **HoareVC** theory imports the corresponding instance of the **HoareLogic** theory. The variable declarations are local to a theory and so the **HoareVC** theory reintroduces these declarations. The contents of the theory are presented below.

```
HoareVC  [ value : TYPE+ ]: THEORY
  BEGIN
   IMPORTING HoareLogic[value]

   P, Q, C, I: VAR assertion
   s: VAR state
   S, S1, S2: VAR program
   A: VAR assignment
    :
    :
  END HoareVC
```

We first define the judgement P ⊏ Q that an assertion P is uniformly stronger than another assertion Q. We also define the dual operation to ⊓ where P ⊔ Q is the assertion that holds of those states on which either P or Q holds.

```
   ⊏(P, Q): bool = (∀ s: P(s) => Q(s));
   ⊔(P, Q)(s): bool =  P(s) ∨ Q(s);
```

To capture the idea of an annotated program, we define a datatype that is a small variant of the **program** datatype defined in Sect. 4.1. The only difference is that the **while** constructor has a slot **invariant** which contains the putative loop invariant.

```
annotatedProgram : DATATYPE
  BEGIN
    skip: skip?
    assign(update : assignment): assign?
    ift(ifcond: test, thenprog: annotatedProgram,
        elseprog: annotatedProgram): ift?
    while(wcond: test, body : annotatedProgram,
          invariant: assertion): while?
    seq(left, right: annotatedProgram): seq?
  END annotatedProgram
```

The **extract** operation defined below deletes the invariant annotation to generate the unannotated program corresponding to an annotated one.

```
extract(SS): RECURSIVE program =
  CASES SS OF
   skip: skip,
   assign(A): assign(A),
   ift(C, SS1, SS2): ift(C, extract(SS1), extract(SS2)),
   while(C, SS1, I): while(C, extract(SS1)),
   seq(SS1, SS2): seq(extract(SS1), extract(SS2))
  ENDCASES
  MEASURE SS BY <<
```

Verification condition generation is defined by two operations `pre` and `vc`. The expression `pre(SS)(Q)` takes an annotated program `SS` and a post-condition assertion `Q`, and yields the weakest liberal precondition for the program `SS` relative to its invariant annotations. The definition of `pre` is by recursion on the structure of `SS`, and for a `while` statement, the precondition is the invariant annotation itself.

```
SS, SS1, SS2: VAR annotatedProgram

pre(SS)(Q) : RECURSIVE assertion =
 CASES SS OF
  skip: Q,
  assign(A): Q o A,
  ift(C, SS1, SS2): (C ⊓ pre(SS1)(Q)) ⊔ (neg(C) ⊓ pre(SS2)(Q)),
  while(C, SS1, I): I,
  seq(SS1, SS2): pre(SS1)(pre(SS2)(Q))
  ENDCASES
  MEASURE SS BY <<
```

The `pre` operation does not verify if the invariant annotations in the annotated program is actually a valid invariant. The expression `vc(SS)(Q)` generates the proof obligations to ensure that the annotated program contains only valid invariants that entail the post-condition. The definition of `vc` is also by recursion on the structure of the annotated program using the `pre` operation to construct the preconditions needed to verify each invariant annotation. The output of `vc(SS)(Q)` is a Boolean formula representing the conjunction of proof obligations.

```
vc(SS)(Q): RECURSIVE bool =
 CASES SS OF
  skip: TRUE,
  assign(A): TRUE,
  ift(C, SS1, SS2): vc(SS1)(Q) AND vc(SS2)(Q),
  while(C, SS1, I): vc(SS1)(I)
                    AND (C ⊓ I ⊑ pre(SS1)(I))
                    AND (neg(C) ⊓ I ⊑ Q),
  seq(SS1, SS2): vc(SS2)(Q) AND vc(SS1)(pre(SS2)(Q))
  ENDCASES
  MEASURE SS BY <<
```

The main claim about verification condition generation is that when the proof obligations corresponding the invariant annotations are valid, then the triple {`pre(SS)(Q)`}`extract(SS)`{`Q`} is valid. Its proof is by induction on the structure of the annotated program `SS`.

```
vc_pre: LEMMA
   vc(SS)(Q) => triple_valid(pre(SS)(Q), extract(SS), Q)
```

7   Observations

The careful reader would have noticed several discrepancies between our presentation of a first-order Hoare logic in Sect. 2 and the embedding of Hoare logic in the PVS higher-order logic presented in Sect. 4. One difference is in the treatment of state. The notion of state is implicit in the presentation of Hoare logic. The logic itself only mentions logic and program variables, and program statements can only mention program variables. In the PVS embedding, there is an explicit notion of state used in programs as well as assertions. The test part of a conditional is a predicate on states. The assignment statement uses an explicit state transformer. It is possible to formalize Hoare logic in such a way that the state is implicit, and it can be shown that such a language is an instance of the Hoare logic embedding given here. That would have the advantage that we are not mixing the host logic of the embedding, namely PVS, with the target language of **While** programs.

The PVS embedding does not have a notion of logic variables. PVS variables appearing in assertions serve the role of logic variables. For example, in verifying a **While** program that sorts an array, we need to maintain the invariant that the intermediate array is a permutation of the input array. The value of the input array is recorded in a PVS variable used in the precondition and post-condition.

The Hoare logic for **While** programs can be extended in several ways. One extension is to introduce function calls with return values. Semantically, each function call extends the stack representing the state with bindings for the actual parameter values. The stack is popped when the function body has been executed. The return value is also written to the stack. Given a program as a sequence Δ of function definitions of the form $g(\overline{x}) := S$, where the program variables in S are drawn from the sequence $\overline{x}$ augmented with a variable $return$ to hold the return value. The proof rule for function invocations is shown below.

$$\frac{\{P\}S\{Q\}}{\{P[\overline{e}/\overline{x}]\}y := g(\overline{e})\{Q[y/return]\}}$$

Other extensions of the Hoare logic embedding include separation logic [22] to cover heap-manipulating programs, probabilistic programs [14], and data refinement [7]. PVS has already been used to embed a number of other logics including the Duration Calculus [24], the B Method [1,17], object-oriented programs [10], Timed I/O Automata [3], and the Alloy calculus [12,16]. However, there are many other logics that can benefit from a mix of deep and shallow embedding, including several modal and temporal logics.

8   Conclusions

We have presented an embedding of Hoare logic in the PVS higher-order logic as a modest-sized tutorial exercise in the application of interactive proof tools to the definition of program logics. Achieving expertise with a modern highly automated proof assistant like PVS requires a careful exploration of the power and limitations of the PVS language and the kind of automation employed by the proof commands. On the one hand, the automation in PVS is focused on the contextual simplification of formulas in order to enhance readability. In other words, when the simplifier simplifies a sub-expression, it takes into account the assertions that hold in the context in which this sub-expression occurs. For example, when simplifying an expression of the form IF A THEN B ELSE C ENDIF, the simplifier first simplifies A to A', and then simplifies B in a context where A' is asserted to be true, and simplifies C in a context where A' is asserted false.

By judiciously combining manual proof commands that suggest induction, case analysis, and selective definition expansion with the more brute-force commands, an expert user can be quite productive in both debugging incorrect specifications and proof attempts, as well as in maintaining and improving completed proofs. In a formalization, modelling and specification can be more challenging than proof construction. Specification languages like PVS offer a wide range of ways in which concepts can be formalized, and it is quite hard to predict the impact of these choices on the effort needed to produce proofs. For example, why did we use a finite sequence representation for state instead of a list datatype? The list representation is better when the stack representation is being used through a push and pop interface, whereas the finite sequence representation supports random-access lookup and update as needed for evaluating expressions and defining the semantics of assignment statements. Lists and finite sequences are inter-convertible through the use of *conversions* in PVS.

The use of predicate subtypes and dependent types makes it possible to capture the entire specification for an operation within its type. However, it is not always a good idea to place too many type constraints into the signature of an operation since these can produce many repeated proof obligations during a proof. Though the PVS specification language and the proof assistant are both easy to learn, it can take a several weeks of experimentation to master the nuances of the language and to learn to live with the idiosyncrasies of the theorem prover. Embedding other logics into the PVS higher-order logic makes it possible to exploit the automation for the host logic in the guest logic. For example, in our Hoare logic embedding, the verification conditions generated in a proof can be discharged directly with PVS itself. The main point to keep in mind is that the language and automation features of PVS make it fairly easy to develop formalizations of the kind described here. The formal development of the Hoare logic occupied only a handful of hours of work compared to the weeks of effort involved in crafting a readable informal presentation of the same concepts and results.

Acknowledgments. The author is grateful to Zhiming Liu for his excellent organization of the SETTS 2017 school, to Jonathan Bowen for his patient editing, and to the anonymous referees for their insightful comments and helpful suggestions for improving the paper. This work was funded by DARPA under agreement number FA8750-16-C-0043. The views and conclusions contained herein are those of the authors and should not be interpreted as necessarily representing the official policies or endorsements, either expressed or implied, of DARPA or the U.S. Government.

References

1. Abrial, J.-R.: The B-Book: Assigning Programs to Meanings. Cambridge University Press, Cambridge (1996)
2. Apt, K.R.: Ten years of Hoare's logic: a survey - part 1. ACM Trans. Program. Lang. Syst. **3**(4), 431–483 (1981)
3. Archer, M., Heitmeyer, C.: Mechanical verification of timed automata: a case study. In: IEEE Real-Time Technology and Applications Symposium (RTAS 1996), Brookline, MA, June 1996, pp. 192–203. IEEE Computer Society (1996)
4. Bentley, J.L.: Programming pearls: algorithm design techniques. Commun. ACM **27**(9), 865–871 (1984)
5. Clarke, E.M., Henzinger, T.A., Veith, H., Bloem, R. (eds.): Handbook of Model Checking. Springer, Heidelberg (2018). https://doi.org/10.1007/978-3-319-10575-8
6. Cook, S.A.: Soundness and completeness of an axiom system for program verification. SIAM J. Comput. **7**(1), 70–90 (1978)
7. de Roever, W.-P., Engelhardt, K.: Data Refinement: Model-Oriented Proof Methods and their Comparrison. Cambridge Tracts in Theoretical Computer Science, vol. 47. Cambridge University Presss (1998)
8. Floyd, R.W.: Assigning meanings to programs. In: Mathematical Aspects of Computer Science, Proceedings of Symposia in Applied Mathematics, vol. XIX, pp. 19–32. American Mathematical Society, Providence (1967)
9. Gordon, M.J.C.: Mechanizing programming logics in higher order logic. Technical Report CCSRC-006, SRI International, Cambridge Computer Science Research Centre, Suite 23, Millers Yard, Mill Lane, Cambridge CB2 1RQ, England, September 1988
10. Hensel, U., Huisman, M., Jacobs, B., Tews, H.: Reasoning about classes in object-oriented languages: logical models and tools. Technical Report CSI-R9718, Computing Sciences Institute, Katholieke Universiteit Nijmegen, Nijmegen, The Netherlands, October 1997
11. Hoare, C.A.R.: An axiomatic basis for computer programming. Comm. ACM **12**(10), 576–583 (1969)
12. Jackson, D.: Automating first-order relational logic. In: Proceedings of ACM SIGSOFT Conference on Foundations of Software Engineering, November 2000
13. McCarthy, J.: Towards a mathematical science of computation. In: Proceedings of IFIP Congress, pp. 21–28. North-Holland (1962)
14. McIver, A., Morgan, C.: Abstraction, Refinement and Proof for Probabilistic Systems. Technical Monographs in Computer Science. Springer, New York (2005). https://doi.org/10.1007/b138392
15. Morris, F.L., Jones, C.B.: An early program proof by Alan Turing. IEEE Ann. Hist. Comput. **6**, 139–143 (1984)
16. Moscato, M.M., Pombo, C.L., Frias, M.F.: Dynamite: a tool for the verification of Alloy models based on PVS. ACM Trans. Softw. Eng. Methodol **23**(2), 20:1–20:37 (2014)
17. Muñoz, C.: PBS: support for the B-method in PVS. Technical Report SRI-CSL-99-1, Computer Science Laboratory, SRI International, Menlo Park, CA, February 1999
18. von Neumann, J., Goldstine, H.H.: Planning and coding of problems for an electronic computing instrument. Institute for Advanced Study, Princeton, New Jersey (1948). Reprinted in [25]

19. Nipkow, T., Klein, G.: Concrete Semantics - With Isabelle/HOL. Springer, Heidelberg (2014). https://doi.org/10.1007/978-3-319-10542-0
20. Owre, S., Rushby, J.M., Shankar, N.: PVS: a prototype verification system. In: Kapur, D. (ed.) CADE 1992. LNCS, vol. 607, pp. 748–752. Springer, Heidelberg (1992). https://doi.org/10.1007/3-540-55602-8_217
21. Owre, S., Rushby, J., Shankar, N., von Henke, F.: Formal verification for fault-tolerant architectures: prolegomena to the design of PVS. IEEE Trans. Softw. Eng. **21**(2), 107–125 (1995). PVS home page: http://pvs.csl.sri.com
22. Reynolds, J.C.: Separation logic: a logic for shared mutable data structures. In: LICS, pp. 55–74. IEEE Computer Society (2002)
23. Shankar, N.: Combining Model Checking and Deduction. In: Clarke, E., Henzinger, T., Veith, H., Bloem, R. (eds.) Handbook of Model Checking, pp. 651–684. Springer, Cham (2018). https://doi.org/10.1007/978-3-319-10575-8_20
24. Skakkebæk, J.U., Shankar, N.: Towards a duration calculus proof assistant in PVS. In: Langmaack, H., de Roever, W.-P., Vytopil, J. (eds.) FTRTFT 1994. LNCS, vol. 863, pp. 660–679. Springer, Heidelberg (1994). https://doi.org/10.1007/3-540-58468-4_189
25. von Neumann, J.: Collected Works, vol. V. Pergamon Press, Oxford (1961)

Modeling Concurrency in Dafny

K. Rustan M. Leino[1,2(✉)] iD

[1] Microsoft Research, Redmond, WA, USA
leino@acm.org
[2] Imperial College London, London, UK

Abstract. This article gives a tutorial on how the Dafny language and
verifier can be used to model a concurrent system. The running example
is a simple ticket system for mutual exclusion. Both safety and, under
the assumption of a fair scheduler, liveness are verified.

1 Introduction

Knowing how to reason about the correctness of programs is an important skill
for every software engineer. In some situations, functional correctness is so important that it makes sense to reason formally. This is done by being precise about
the *pre- and postcondition specifications* of procedures, the *invariants* of data
structures, and the justifications for why the program upholds these specifications and invariants. Today's tools make it possible to carry out and check this
reasoning mechanically. In other situations, functional correctness is deemed less
critical. Still, the concepts of pre- and postconditions and invariants apply and
guide good program design, even if these are not checked rigorously in every
possible execution of the program.

In my lectures at SETSS 2017, I taught program-correctness concepts like
pre- and postconditions and invariants through many examples. I used the programming language Dafny [18,20], which includes specification constructs and
has an automated program verifier that checks that programs meet their specifications. The literature already contains some tutorials that use Dafny for this
purpose [6,11,14,17,19]. So, instead of repeating those tutorials, I am using these
lecture notes to explain a more advanced use of Dafny, namely the modeling of
a simple concurrent algorithm in Dafny. The reasoning that I show here is representative of how several popular formal systems reason about the behavior of
concurrent threads of execution. A benefit you get from doing the modeling in
Dafny is the automated verification.

If you are looking to learn to do this kind of modeling on your own, I suggest
you follow along by entering the Dafny declarations into a buffer in the Dafny
IDE for VS Code, Visual Studio, or Emacs. You can install Dafny and an IDE
plug-in from https://github.com/Microsoft/dafny/. Alternatively, you can enter
the declarations in your web browser at http://rise4fun.com/dafny, periodically
clicking on the Play button to let Dafny check your program for syntactic and
semantic correctness.

© Springer Nature Switzerland AG 2018
J. P. Bowen et al. (Eds.): SETSS 2017, LNCS 11174, pp. 115–142, 2018.
https://doi.org/10.1007/978-3-030-02928-9_4

2 Concurrency

A concurrent system consists of a number of processes that each executes some code. If we think of the execution of a process as a sequence of tiny steps, then we can model the entire system as an *interleaving* of these tiny-step sequences. To make sure our model captures every possible behavior of the concurrent system, it is important that each tiny step is so tiny that we can think its execution as taking place all by itself, impossibly interrupted or interfered with by the execution of other tiny steps. We call such a tiny step an *atomic event* (or *atomic step*, or *atomic action*). In a typical model, atomic events are limited to one read or write of a shared variable.

To model a concurrent system, we consider what possible atomic events may take place during the running of the system. This is the common idea in formalisms and tools like Chandy and Misra's UNITY [5], Back and Sere's action systems [4], Abrial's Event-B [1] (implemented in the Rodin tool [3]), and Lamport's TLA+ [15]. As designers of a model, we decide what each atomic event stands for. By choosing an appropriate level of abstraction for the events, we can use the same modeling techniques when writing a high-level specification as when writing a low-level implementations. To see how this kind of thinking can lead to nice specifications, see for example Leslie Lamport's TLA+ lectures [16] or Jean-Raymond Abrial's Event-B lectures [2].

Code executed by a process is authored as a program where control flow is implicit. To model such code, we introduce an explicit control state for each process. In the extreme, the control state can be a program counter, but many times we don't need to be as concrete as that.

Dafny is a programming language designed to support formal reasoning [18]. Even though the language is sequential, we can use it to model concurrent systems in the way I just alluded to. For instance, we can write each event as a little body of code, and we can give such a piece of code a name by declaring it as a procedure, which in Dafny is known as a *method*. An approach like this makes use of some programming constructs in Dafny, but mostly, it uses Dafny as a logical foundation for the modeling.

To illustrate this approach, I will describe a simple ticket system for mutual exclusion and model this in Dafny. I will use two different models. The first model defines atomic events by methods that change the program state. The second model defines atomic events by predicates over pairs of consecutive states. The main theorem to be proved about the ticket system is that, at any one time, at most one process is in its critical section. This is called a *safety property* and can be proved in either model. Another theorem of interest is that a process in the ticket system never gets stuck. This is called a *liveness property* and is most easily described in the second model. More complex applications of Dafny to specifying and implementing concurrent systems are found in the IronFleet project [10].

3   The Ticket System

The concurrent system we are going to reason about can be described as follows.

A fixed number of philosophers are gathered in a library. Mostly, they just sit around and think. Sometimes, a philosopher may become hungry and need to eat. Attached to the library is a kitchen. Unfortunately, the kitchen is undergoing some renovations, so it would be dangerous to have more than one person in the kitchen at any one time. To manage the contention for the shared kitchen resource, a ticket system has been installed.

The ticket system has a ticket dispenser that dispenses numbered tickets in increasing sequential order. There is no upper limit on these numbers. It is very quick to dispense a ticket, so we consider obtaining a ticket to be an atomic event.

The ticket system also includes a display that says "serving" and shows a number. The philosophers decide that only a philosopher whose ticket number agrees with the display is allowed into the kitchen. The button that advances the "serving" display to the next number is located in the kitchen. Upon leaving the kitchen, a philosopher presses the button to advance the number displayed.

4   Pseudo Code

Each philosopher operates as described by the following pseudo code:

```
forever repeat
{
  Thinking:
  // ...

  t, ticket := ticket, ticket + 1;   // Request
  Hungry:

  wait until serving = t;   // Enter
  Eating:
  // ...
  serving := serving + 1;   // Leave
}
```

A philosopher can be in one of three states: thinking, hungry, or eating. It starts in the thinking state. What exactly a philosopher is thinking about is not relevant to the algorithm, so the pseudo code abstracts over it.

To enter the hungry state, a philosopher grabs the next ticket, an operation I will refer to as Request. The ticket number obtained is recorded into a variable t that is local to the philosopher.

In the hungry state, a philosopher waits until the "serving" display shows t. The philosopher then enters the kitchen, which is represented as the eating state.

This `Enter` operation can take place only when the given condition holds. Alternatively, you can think of `Enter` as an operation that is attempted repeatedly, each attempt being one atomic event, until the given condition holds.

When a philosopher is done in the kitchen, it increments the "serving" display and returns back to the thinking state. I will refer to this operation as `Leave`. What exactly the philosopher prepares and eats in the kitchen is not relevant to the algorithm, so the pseudo code abstracts over it.

5   Formalizing the Ticket System

To formalize the ticket system in Dafny, we need to encode the ticket dispenser and the "serving" display. We also need a way to talk about each philosopher, which from now on I will call a *process*, along with the state of the process and any ticket it may be holding.

5.1   Processes as an Uninterpreted Type with Equality

To model the identity of processes, we introduce a type. In the most abstract way, we can do that by:

```
type Process
```

which introduces `Process` as the name of an uninterpreted type. Dafny allows us to be more concrete. For example, we can say that `Process` is just a synonym for the integers:

```
type Process = int
```

Or we can define `Process` to be an enumeration of a specific set of names, perhaps inspired by the names of our friends:

```
datatype Process = Agnes | Agatha | Germaine | Jack
```

In our case, we don't need more than an uninterpreted type. Almost. We do need to know that the type comes equipped with the ability to compare its values with equality. The notation for saying this is:

```
type Process(==)
```

(This `"(==)"` suffix is among the most cryptic of syntactic constructs in Dafny. It is unfortunate that, in this example, it's the first thing we need.)

5.2   Names of Process Control States

We need names for the program labels in our pseudo code. We define these in an enumeration type that we call `CState` (for *control state*):

```
datatype CState = Thinking | Hungry | Eating
```

5.3   Ticket System as a Class

Representing the ticket dispenser and "serving" display requires some state. For what I want to show in this article about the method formulation of events, it is simplest to declare this state as fields of a class. A class in Dafny is like a class in object-oriented languages, but there is nothing object-oriented in our example, so it is not particularly useful to think of our class like that. For our present purposes, all we need to know about a class is the following:

- A class can have state, which is introduced by var declarations inside the class. Borrowing from object-oriented terminology, these variables are sometimes called *fields*.
- A class can have methods, which are named bodies of code that operate on the state.
- A class has a *constructor* that initializes the state.
- A class can also declare *functions* and *lemmas*. I'll describe these when we need them.

In fact, for our purposes, there is not much difference between a class and what might be a module with some procedures and global variables. There are no global variables in Dafny, so that is why I use a class for our example.

The class itself is declared as follows:

```
class TicketSystem
{
}
```

All remaining declarations that I describe in this section and the next are to be placed inside the curly braces of this class declaration. Two of those declarations are for the ticket dispenser and "serving" display, each of which is represented by an integer:

```
var ticket: int
var serving: int
```

It will be convenient to have a name for the fixed set of processes, so we introduce a variable to store that set:

```
var P: set<Process>
```

In fact, since P will never change once it has been initialized, we can declare it to be an immutable field:

```
const P: set<Process>
```

Next, we introduce the state for each process. This state consists of a control-state value (that is, thinking, hungry, or eating) and an integer that denotes the value of the ticket held by the process. The ticket value is relevant only if the process is hungry or eating; when the process is thinking, we don't care what the value of this integer is.

But how do we introduce this state for each process? There's more than one way to do this in Dafny. We will use a way that perhaps would be most natural to someone familiar with TLA+, or for that matter, someone familiar with Alloy [13]. It is to use maps from processes to values. We introduce a map cs from each process in P to a control state and a map t from each process in P to an integer:

```
var cs: map<Process, CState>
var t: map<Process, int>
```

To look up the CState value for a process p, we consult the map cs using the expression cs[p].

We need these maps only for processes in P, but (unlike in TLA+) you cannot use a state variable P as the domain of these maps. (Actually, in TLA+, P would not be a variable, but a logical constant.) That's why we declare the domain type of these maps to be Process, which includes not just the processes in our instance of the ticket system, but every conceivable process. This is no problem, because a map in Dafny is a (possibly) partial map, anyway. Stated differently, the domain of a map in Dafny is some subset of the values denoted by the domain type of the map. In other words, if you think of a map as a set of key-value pairs, then this set may or may not contain a key-value pair for every value of the map-domain type.

5.4   System Invariant

When we access one of our maps for a particular process, say p, we need to know that p is in the domain of the map (that is, that p is among the *keys* of the map). In our ticket system, it will always be the case that the domain of the maps is P. (Actually, we will never have occasion to access these maps outside P, so the important property is that P is a *subset* of the domain of each map.) We call this an *invariant* of the system, and (we will show that) it holds initially and is maintained by every atomic operation.

If we are given arbitrary values for our variables, then this invariant condition may or may not hold. We introduce a function that tells us whether or not the condition holds. We'll give this function the name Valid:

```
predicate Valid()
  reads this
{
  cs.Keys == t.Keys == P
}
```

There are several points to explain about the definition of Valid.

- A function that returns a boolean is synonymously known as a *predicate*. The predicate declaration is just a nice way to write function Valid(): bool.
- In Dafny, functions are allowed to depend on the program state, but they must declare which parts of the program state they depend on. This concept

is called *framing* (see, for example, [9]). For this purpose, a function (and also a predicate, since a predicate is just a function that returns a boolean) has a reads clause. Here, a bit of object-oriented notation creeps in: the keyword this. By declaring the function with reads this, we are saying that it may depend on the values of the fields declared in the class. Framing is not central to our problem here, but you have to include the reads clause or Dafny would complain that the function body illegally reads cs and t.

- The value of the function—here, of type boolean—is given by its body, which is an expression enclosed in the curly braces that follow the function signature and specification.
- Equality in Dafny uses the syntax so familiar to all C and Java programmers: ==.
- In Dafny, a number of operators, including equality, are *chaining*. This means that you can string them together, just like you would in a mathematical textbook. In particular, cs.Keys == t.Keys == P is equivalent to the conjunction ("and") of cs.Keys == t.Keys and t.Keys == P. By the way, conjunction is written && and disjunction ("or") is written ||.
- The domain of a map is a set that is retrieved by the member .Keys.

(As I remarked above, we only need that P is a subset of the keys of each map. If we had chosen to formalize that, we would instead have written P <= cs.Keys && P <= t.Keys in the body of Valid. In Dafny, <= applied to sets denotes the subset relation.)

As we go along, we will find more things to add to the body of Valid. Remember, we think of Valid() as describing the invariant of our system, but as far as Dafny is concerned, Valid is just a function that sometimes returns false and sometimes returns true. What makes it appropriate to think of Valid() as an invariant has to do with the way we use it. We'll see this soon.

5.5 Initializing the Ticket System

We are now ready to write a little code to initialize the ticket system. This code is placed in a special method called a *constructor*. We parameterize the constructor by a set of processes.

```
constructor (processes: set<Process>)
  ensures Valid()
{
  P := processes;
  ticket, serving := 0, 0;
  cs := map p | p in processes :: Thinking;
  t := map p | p in processes :: 0;
}
```

The specification of the TicketSystem constructor has a *postcondition*, which is declared by an ensures clause. It expresses that, upon termination of the constructor, Valid() will hold. Dafny checks this, of course. In other words, this postcondition says that initialization establishes the invariant. For this reason, it is important to include a constructor—otherwise, we may accidentally write down an invariant that is equivalent to false, in which case all of the theorems we prove about the system will hold trivially.

The body of the constructor uses imperative programming statements that can change the state. In the second line, I am using a *parallel assignment*, because I think it looks nice. It would be equally good to write this as two separate assignments. Likewise, it would be equally good to write all five assignments as one parallel assignment.

The assignments to cs and t make use of map comprehensions. The first of these can be read as "the map from p, where p is a process in processes, to the value Thinking". Dafny infers the type of p to be Process.

In the map comprehension used to initialize the map t, we are being overly specific when we say that t maps each process to 0. Since every process is initially thinking, this value is irrelevant. However, to establish the invariant, we do need to assign to t a map whose domain is processes, which our assignment achieves.

All concurrency formalisms have some way to describe the possible initial states of the system. For example, in UNITY, an **initially** clause gives a predicate that describes the possible initial states. In TLA+ and Event-B, too, the initial condition is phrased as a predicate.

At this point, we have declared all types and variables involved in the modeling of our system. We have also declared an invariant and provided a constructor that initializes the system to satisfy the invariant. What remains to be done is to formalize the atomic steps of the system. And, of course, to state and verify a correctness theorem about the system.

5.6   Specifying the Atomic Events

There are three atomic events for us to formalize: Request, Enter, and Leave. Actually, we need to formalize each of these for each process. To do that, we parameterize each atomic event by a process. As I have mentioned before, we will model each atomic event by a method. To parameterize the description of an atomic event, we simply declare the method to take a parameter.

The parameter, which I will name p, is of type Process. We only want to model atomic events for processes in our system, so we write a *precondition*, which is declared by a requires clause. Moreover, we are only interested in modeling behavior from states that satisfy the invariant, so we also include Valid() as a precondition of our methods.

An atomic event for a process is typically enabled only in certain circumstances. These circumstances depend on the control state of the process. For example, the atomic event Request(p) is enabled only when p is thinking. Therefore, we add a constraint on cs[p], like cs[p] == Thinking, to the precondition.

It is important that each atomic event maintain the invariant. To express and check this property, we add Valid() as a postcondition of each method, just as for the constructor.

There is one more detail. Recall that a function must declare (in a `reads` clause) which parts of the program state it depends on. In a similar way, a method must declare (in a `modifies` clause) which parts of the program state it updates. By declaring our methods with `modifies this`, we are saying that they may update the fields in the class. This framing does not really play a role in our example, but we have to declare it or Dafny would complain that the method body illegally updates the fields.

In summary, each atomic operation in our example will be modeled by a method whose signature and specification look like this:

```
method AtomicStep(p: Process)
  requires Valid() && p in P && cs[p] == ...
  modifies this
  ensures Valid()
```

5.7 Implementing the Atomic Events

Having laid down the foundation, we can now easily define the three atomic events of our example. As you check these, you may want to compare them with the pseudo code above.

```
method Request(p: Process)
  requires Valid() && p in P && cs[p] == Thinking
  modifies this
  ensures Valid()
{
  t, ticket := t[p := ticket], ticket + 1;
  cs := cs[p := Hungry];
}
```

The notation `t[p := ticket]` is a map-update expression. It stands for a map that is like `t`, except that it maps `p` to `ticket`. (In TLA+, such an expression is written [t **EXCEPT** ![p] = ticket].) The body of `Request` thus records the current ticket as the ticket number held by `p`, increments the current ticket, and changes the control state of `p` to `Hungry`.

In the body of `Request`, I happen to be using one parallel assignment (updating both `t` and `ticket`) followed by one other assignment (updating `cs`), because I think this looks nice in the program text. However, there are many other sequences of assignments that achieve the same effect. By using a method to model an atomic event, the intermediate states inside the method body are not relevant, so the cosmetic choices we make inside the method body have no bearing on the model.

```
method Enter(p: Process)
  requires Valid() && p in P && cs[p] == Hungry
  modifies this
  ensures Valid()
```

```
{
  if t[p] == serving {
    cs := cs[p := Eating];
  }
}

method Leave(p: Process)
  requires Valid() && p in P && cs[p] == Eating
  modifies this
  ensures Valid()
{
  serving := serving + 1;
  cs := cs[p := Thinking];
}
```

These three methods model the three atomic events in our system.

5.8   On the Atomicity of Events

To justify calling a method in our model an *atomic* event, we need to make sure that the method body is something that really can be completed without interference of other processes in the system we are modeling. Typically, this means that the body is allowed at most one read or write of one shared variable. Updating a map at a process p counts as an update that is local to p. In other words, we think of cs[p] as a local variable, not as a shared variable. In our example, two of our methods read or write a shared variable more than once, so why do we think our modeling is done properly? Let's take a closer look at these two methods.

Method Request reads ticket twice and writes it once, with the effect of incrementing ticket and recording its previous value. One way to achieve this in an actual implementation of our system would be to use a mutual-exclusion lock. But if we had such a lock, then we could use that lock as the way for a philosopher to enter the kitchen (that is, for a process to enter its critical section). The whole point of the ticket system is to *implement* a mutual-exclusion lock. Luckily, there are less heavy-handed ways than a lock to implement these accesses of ticket. For example, these accesses can be implemented by a hardware-supported atomic-increment operation, which is found in many modern machines. Such an operation increments the value stored in a memory location and at the same time returns its value from before the increment. With such an operation in mind, we feel justified in thinking about method Request as an atomic event.

The other method that reads or writes a shared variable more than once is Leave, which increments serving. We could justify this increment by a hardware atomic-increment operation as well, but for Leave, there is a less imposing justification. The serving variable is incremented only by the philosopher in the kitchen (that is, by the process in the critical section), so (if our ticket system does indeed provide mutual exclusion, then) serving is stable in Leave. That justifies calling Leave an atomic event without appealing to any hardware support.

In fact, there's yet one more way to deal with the atomicity of Leave. By the time a Leave(p) event takes place, the ticket held by p is equal to serving. Thus, instead of reading the shared variable serving as in the code above, we can read the local t[p]. If you want to check that what I'm saying is true, you can insert the following statement at the beginning of the body of Leave:

```
assert t[p] == serving;
```

In the program we have developed so far, the verifier will flag this assertion as an error, but once we're done with our correctness theorem below, the verifier will be able to verify it. (This assertion introduces yet one more read of the shared variable serving. But it is okay, because an assertion is to be considered as specification-only, so we don't need to worry about which variables it mentions.)

This completes our encoding of the atomic events in our model. What remains to do is to state and prove a correctness theorem that shows that the ticket system does indeed provide mutual exclusion.

5.9   Notes About Other Formalisms

In Event-B, the state transition of an event is given as a set of assignment statements. These assignments are performed in parallel, so the order in which you list them does not matter. In Dafny, the order of statements matters. However, whenever you use a parallel assignment, all right-hand sides are evaluated before any state change takes place. So, if you want an Event-B style body in Dafny, use one parallel assignment statement.

In UNITY, a state transition is also given as a parallel assignment. The syntax of the assignment is more like that in Dafny.

In TLA+, events are specified as two-state predicates, where a primed variable is used to refer to the value of the variable in the post-state. For example, the increment of ticket in Request is written ticket' = ticket + 1 in TLA+. I will show such predicates in Sect. 8.3.

6   Correctness Theorem

The correctness of our ticket system comes down to showing that no two processes are ever in the eating state at the same time. To show that this condition holds in every state of the system, we prove a theorem that the invariant (which holds in every state) implies the condition. This can be stated in Dafny using a lemma declaration. A lemma in Dafny is really just a method, except that it will not be compiled into code. Like any method, a lemma has a pre- and postcondition. The precondition denotes the *antecedent* of the lemma and the postcondition is its *conclusion* (also known as its *proof goal*).

We state our correctness theorem as follows:

```
lemma MutualExclusion(p: Process, q: Process)
  requires Valid() && p in P && q in P
  requires cs[p] == Eating && cs[q] == Eating
  ensures p == q
{
}
```

The lemma is parameterized by two processes, p and q. It says that if the system is in a valid state (that is, the variables have values that satisfy the invariant) and if p and q are processes, each of which is in the eating state, then p and q are the same process.

The proof of a lemma is given as a method body. It follows the same rules as in Floyd/Hoare logic [7,8,12], namely that, starting from any state in which the precondition holds, every path through the body must be shown to reach the end of the body in a state where the postcondition holds. We supply a body of the lemma by a pair of curly braces, just like for the other method bodies we have seen. For the ticket-system example, it turns out that the proof can be done automatically, so I will not say more about writing proofs here.

When you supply the empty body { } of the lemma, the verifier complains that it cannot prove p == q. For this condition to follow from the lemma's antecedent, the invariant must be sufficiently strong. Our task is now to strengthen the invariant until the verifier can prove the lemma (or until we find an error in our model).

6.1   Strengthening the Invariant

The invariant is recorded in predicate Valid. So far, our invariant speaks only about P and the domains of cs and t. Writing an invariant requires a good bit of thinking and practice. Here, I will describe the additional pieces of the invariant that we need; a more comprehensive tutorial on how to write and debug invariants is out of the scope of this article.

A property we expect to hold of the ticket machinery is that the ticket dispenser may run ahead of the "serving" display, but never the other way around. We formalize this by strengthening the invariant with the condition serving <= ticket:

```
predicate Valid()
  reads this
{
  cs.Keys == t.Keys == P &&
  serving <= ticket
}
```

Having added this conjunct to Valid, Dafny immediately flags method Leave as possibly not establishing its postcondition. It frequently happens that, while strengthening an invariant, we find that showing the stronger invariant to be maintained by our operations requires further strengthenings of the invariant. So let's not be too discouraged by the fact that our strengthening increased the number of errors reported by the verifier.

The new error can help us get ideas about how to strengthen the invariant next. When `Leave(p)` increments `serving`, we expect that `ticket` is already strictly larger than `serving`—when p got its ticket, it would have incremented `ticket`, and ticket is never decreased by any process. This leads us to think about the property that every ticket number held by a process lies in the range from `serving` to `ticket`. Thus, we strengthen the invariant to the following condition:

```
predicate Valid()
  reads this
{
  cs.Keys == t.Keys == P &&
  serving <= ticket &&
  forall p :: p in P && cs[p] != Thinking ==> serving <= t[p] < ticket
}
```

In the new conjunct, `!=` is the operator for "not equals", `==>` is logical implication, and `<=` and `<` are the usual arithmetic comparison operators that we have chained together. The binding power of `==>` is lower than that of `&&`, as is suggested by the fact that `==>` is wider than `&&` (3 ASCII characters wide for implication versus 2 for conjunction). The relative binding powers of the other operators are like in C and Java. The type of the bound variable p, namely `Process`, is inferred by Dafny. (If you wonder what type is inferred, you can hover the mouse over the identifier in the Dafny IDE for Visual Studio and a tool tip will tell you this information. Of course, you can also specify the type manually, if you prefer or if the type inference were ever to fail.)

The new conjunct allows the verifier to prove the previous conjunct, but the verifier now complains that `Leave` may fail to maintain the new conjunct. The error message gives us more precise information:

```
TS.dfy(78,2): Error: A postcondition might not hold on this return path.
TS.dfy(77,12): Related location: This is the postcondition that might not hold.
TS.dfy(36,4): Related location
TS.dfy(36,56): Related location
```

It says, in the respective lines, that `Leave` may fail to establish the postcondition, that `Valid()` is the postcondition that is not established, that the `forall` is the conjunct inside `Valid()` that is not established, and that `serving <= t[p]` is the conjunct inside the quantification that is not established. Apparently, the verifier imagines a situation where some other process also has a t value that is equal to `serving`—if so, incrementing `serving` would violate the quantifier we just wrote. But we expect processes to have unique ticket numbers. Let's write that down by strengthening the invariant again:

```
predicate Valid()
  reads this
{
  cs.Keys == t.Keys == P &&
```

```
    serving <= ticket &&
    (forall p :: p in P && cs[p] != Thinking ==> serving <= t[p] < ticket) &&
    (forall p,q ::
        p in P && q in P && p != q && cs[p] != Thinking && cs[q] != Thinking
        ==> t[p] != t[q])
}
```

Note the parentheses we now need around the first quantifier. I also added parentheses around the second quantifier, to make the two quantifiers cosmetically more alike.

The introduction of the new conjunct did not eliminate the complaint about the previous error. Apparently, uniqueness of ticket numbers among the processes is not enough. We also need to know that the process that is leaving the critical section is indeed one that holds a ticket number that agrees with serving. We update Valid() once more:

```
predicate Valid()
    reads this
{
    cs.Keys == t.Keys == P &&
    serving <= ticket &&
    (forall p :: p in P && cs[p] != Thinking ==> serving <= t[p] < ticket) &&
    (forall p,q ::
        p in P && q in P && p != q && cs[p] != Thinking && cs[q] != Thinking
        ==> t[p] != t[q]) &&
    (forall p :: p in P && cs[p] == Eating ==> t[p] == serving)
}
```

This does the trick! Dafny now verifies all proof obligations: the condition we defined Valid() to stand for holds initially, is maintained by all atomic events, and implies mutual exclusion.

6.2   Initialization Revisited

In the constructor, we initialized both ticket and serving to 0. This seems reasonable, but it is more specific than necessary. All we need to establish the invariant is that ticket and serving start off with the same value. We can therefore replace the second line of the constructor with

```
    ticket := serving;
```

This would set ticket to whatever arbitrary value serving happens to have on entry to the constructor. More to the point, it would make ticket and serving equal, which is enough to establish the invariant.

6.3   TLA+ Inspired Conjunctions

To improve readability, TLA+ allows conjunctions and disjunctions to be written as if they were bulleted lists. The "bullets" used are the operators for conjunction and disjunction, respectively, and the syntactic rules for grouping these pay attention to the level of indentation used in the program text. Inspired by these TLA+ expressions, Dafny allows conjunction and disjunction to be used as prefix operators instead of as infix operators. Stated differently, Dafny allows a conjunction to be preceded by && and allows a disjunction to be preceded by | |. Dafny does not pay attention to indentation, but even this simple allowance can let some formulas be formatted in a nice way. For example, we can write predicate Valid as follows:

```
predicate Valid()
  reads this
{
  && cs.Keys == t.Keys == P
  && serving <= ticket
  && (forall p :: p in P && cs[p] != Thinking ==> serving <= t[p] < ticket)
  && (forall p,q ::
        p in P && q in P && p != q &&
        cs[p] != Thinking && cs[q] != Thinking
        ==> t[p] != t[q])
  && (forall p :: p in P && cs[p] == Eating ==> t[p] == serving)
}
```

Note, the prefix allowance does not change the binding power of operators. This means that parentheses are still needed as before. In particular, note in this example that the forall quantifiers need parentheses—they do not end at the end of the line as the bullet syntax may lead you to believe. Another important operator to consider is implication, which binds more loosely than conjunction. Thus, if Valid contained a conjunct that was an implication, then it would need parentheses.

7   Event Scheduling

In what I have shown so far, the constructor and methods of class TicketSystem are never called. In other words, in the program text we have written, we have defined some atomic events, but we have not defined any scheduler that invokes the events and produces a particular interleaving. Instead, we have left it to our imagination that the events can be invoked at any time. This is typical. Models usually include only the initialization condition and the atomic events. The scheduler is tacit, and it is understood that the events can occur at any time, as long as the precondition that is guarding their execution holds.

For the tutorial purpose of seeing what this implicit scheduler that we are imagining looks like, let us write a scheduler explicitly. The scheduler will exhibit a high degree of nondeterminism, so we won't actually restrict the possible interleavings. The scheduler will still serve two purposes. One purpose is to demonstrate that it is always possible to schedule a process. If we accidentally had left out some event (say, method Leave), then our scheduler would not know what to do with a process in the Eating state. The second purpose is for us to warm up to issues of "fair" scheduling, which I will address in Sect. 8.1.

7.1   A Scheduler

We write a method Run that takes a nonempty set of processes and repeatedly calls these to perform an atomic event. The method looks like this:

```
method Run(processes: set<Process>)
  requires processes != {}
  decreases *
{
  var ts := new TicketSystem(processes);
  while true
    invariant ts.Valid()
    decreases *
  {
    var p :| p in ts.P;
    match ts.cs[p] {
      case Thinking => ts.Request(p);
      case Hungry => ts.Enter(p);
      case Eating => ts.Leave(p);
    }
  }
}
```

Here is an explanation of this code.

– Because the loop never terminates, it must be marked with `decreases *`.
This allows the loop to go on forever and it causes the verifier to omit termination checks. Similarly, a method that contains a nonterminating loop must
itself be declared with `decreases *`.
– Reasoning about loops is done via *loop invariants* [7,8,12]. These are conditions that hold at the very top of every loop iteration. Loop invariants
simplify the problem of reasoning about all possible iteration traces of the
loop to reasoning about just one, arbitrary iteration. The use of loop invariants bears resemblance to the use of an inductive hypothesis in mathematics.
In this example, the `invariant` declaration says that the invariant of the
ticket system is maintained by the loop.
– The assignment statement `x :| R` sets variable `x` to a value satisfying the
boolean expression `R`. The statement gives rise to a proof obligation that such
an `x` exists. As we have written our program so far, the verifier complains that
this proof obligation does not hold. That is because there is no connection
between `processes` (which is known to be nonempty) and `ts.P`. To correct
this problem, we add the postcondition

```
ensures P == processes
```

to the `TicketSystem` constructor. The `:|` assign-such-that statement in the
`Run` method is now proved to be legal. Its effect is to introduce a variable `p`
to stand for an arbitrary process from the set `ts.P`.
– The `match` statement continues execution with one of the given cases,
depending on the value of `ts.cs[p]`. The statement gives rise to a proof
obligation that there is a case for every possible value of the given expression. This is where the verifier would complain if we had forgotten to define
method `Leave` and left out the case for `Eating`. (Try commenting this line
out and you will see.)

Notice that it is the scheduler—that is, our `Run` method—that picks the process p to schedule next and controls which of the three events to invoke for process p. We have written the `Run` method so that p is picked arbitrarily among the processes, but having picked p, the choice of which event to invoke is determined by the control state of that process, `cs[p]`. This corresponds to what a scheduler really does: How a scheduler picks which process to schedule next may be more sophisticated than the arbitrary choice in our `Run` method, but once it has made that decision, the scheduler must be sure to start the process in (that is, set the program counter of the process to) the control state where the process last left off.

7.2 Guards of Events

Event `Enter` in our example models what in Sect. 4 I denoted by the pseudo-code statement **wait until**. You may think of the way we wrote method `Enter` as corresponding to a "busy waiting" (aka "spinning") implementation of **wait until**. If the scheduler picks a process in the `Hungry` state when its t value is not equal to `serving`, then that process just "skips" (see the `if` statement in method `Enter`). This is a common design for modeling a process that is suspended on a condition. Let me explain two alternative designs.

One alternative design is to replace our `Enter` method above with the following two methods:

```
method Enter0(p: Process)
  requires Valid() && p in P && cs[p] == Hungry && t[p] == serving
  modifies this
  ensures Valid()
{
  cs := cs[p := Eating];
}

method Enter1(p: Process)
  requires Valid() && p in P && cs[p] == Hungry && t[p] != serving
  modifies this
  ensures Valid()
{
}
```

Method `Enter0` corresponds to the then branch of the `if` statement in `Enter` and method `Enter1` corresponds to the else branch. Note that the guard of the `if` statement in `Enter` has become part of the preconditions of `Enter0` and (in negated form) `Enter1`. By breaking `Enter` into two methods in this design of the model, we are essentially thinking of transitioning from `Hungry` to `Eating` as one event (`Enter0`) and remaining hungry as another event (`Enter1`). This design is also common.

To see how the alternative design makes sense, it is instructive to look at how it impacts the scheduler. This is especially important since, as I have mentioned, the scheduler is usually left tacit. To deal with `Enter0` and `Enter1`, we change the `Hungry` case of method `Run` to:

```
case Hungry =>
   if ts.t[p] == ts.serving {
      ts.Enter0(p);
   } else {
      ts.Enter1(p);
   }
```

A second alternative design is to use only Enter0, not Enter1. In the original design, we thought of Enter as busy waiting—the process is scheduled, inspects t and serving, and may then find that it has nothing to do but wait further. By including only Enter0, our model reflects the thinking that a process in the Hungry state gets scheduled only when it can proceed. In other words, in this design, the scheduler understands and directly supports the **wait until** operation.

To accommodate this second alternative design, one possible way to rewrite the scheduler is to drop the else branch in the case for Hungry. If the scheduler happens to pick p to be a hungry process that is not yet being served, then the scheduler skips. In other words, an iteration of the scheduler loop that picks such a p ends up being an unproductive iteration.

We can make all of the scheduler's loop iterations productive if we make the selection of p more precise. We do that by strengthening the condition to this:

```
var p :| p in ts.P && (ts.cs[p] == Hungry ==> ts.t[p] == ts.serving);
```

With this condition, the verifier complains that it cannot always prove the existence of such a p. This is a valid complaint, because if the ticket system were coded incorrectly, we could end up in a situation where the scheduler cannot schedule any process. Such a situation reflects a deadlock.

We may be tempted to prove that a deadlock cannot occur and that the scheduler always has some process to schedule. However, I argue that the responsibility of avoiding deadlocks does not lie with the scheduler. Instead, if we want to model a scheduler that directly supports an **wait until** operation, then the scheduler is allowed to terminate if the processes get themselves into a deadlock situation. Thus, the scheduler in this second alternative design looks like:

```
var ts := new TicketSystem(processes);
while exists p :: p in ts.P &&
               (ts.cs[p] == Hungry ==> ts.t[p] == ts.serving)
   invariant ts.Valid()
   decreases *
{
   var p :| p in ts.P && (ts.cs[p] == Hungry ==> ts.t[p] == ts.serving);
   match ts.cs[p] {
      case Thinking => ts.Request(p);
      case Hungry => ts.Enter0(p);
      case Eating => ts.Leave(p);
   }
}
```

Note that the loop guard no longer uses the condition true and note that the Hungry case only calls Enter0.

7.3 Recording or Following a Schedule

Before moving on to a different representation of the model where we can prove that the ticket system does not exhibit deadlocks, let us consider one small change to the Run method. It is to add some code that records the scheduling choices that Run makes. We can easily do this by instrumenting Run with

```
var schedule := [];
```

before the loop and

```
schedule := schedule + [p];
```

inside the loop. Similarly, if we wish, we can also record the sequence of states, here as a sequence of 4-tuples, by instrumenting Run with

```
var trace := [(ts.ticket, ts.serving, ts.cs, ts.t)];
```

before the loop and

```
trace := trace + [(ts.ticket, ts.serving, ts.cs, ts.t)];
```

at the end of the loop.

Instead of recording the decisions that Run makes, we can change Run to free it from making any decisions at all. We accomplish this by letting Run take a predetermined schedule as a parameter. This schedule has the form of a function from times to processes.

```
method RunFromSchedule(processes: set<Process>, schedule: nat -> Process)
  requires processes != {}
  requires forall n :: schedule(n) in processes
  decreases *
{
  var ts := new TicketSystem(processes);
  var n := 0;
  while true
    // ...
  {
    var p := schedule(n);
    match // ...
    n := n + 1;
  }
}
```

The type nat -> Process denotes total functions from natural numbers to processes.

8 Liveness Properties

So far, I have covered the basics of modeling concurrency by breaking down a system into atomic events. Dafny's methods give a convenient representation of each atomic event, and I have shown how the system invariant can be captured in a predicate Valid() that is a pre- and postcondition of every method. To prove that the system can only reach "safe" states (for example, at most one philosopher is in the kitchen at any one time), we prove that the system invariant implies the safety property of interest.

There is another class of properties that you may want to prove about a concurrent system: liveness properties. Whereas a safety property says that the system remains in safe states, a liveness property says that the system eventually leaves anxious states. For example, in our ticket system, a desired liveness property is that a hungry philosopher eventually eats. In other words, this liveness property says that the system does not forever remain in a set of states where a particular philosopher is hungry; the system eventually leaves that set of "anxious" states.

8.1   Fair Scheduling

To prove any liveness property, we need to know more about the scheduler. For example, suppose a philosopher A enters the hungry state and that the scheduler, from that time onwards, decides to pick another philosopher B exclusively. Philosopher A will then remain hungry forever and our desired liveness property does not hold. In fact, in our ticket system, such a schedule will also eventually cause B to get stuck in the hungry state, skipping each time the scheduler gives it control.

When we reason about liveness properties, we work under the assumption that the scheduler is *fair*, meaning that it cannot ignore some process forever. In contrast, no fairness assumption is needed when reasoning about safety properties, since restricting our attention to fair schedules does not change the set of possibly reachable states.

8.2   State Tuple

When we were proving safety properties, it was convenient to formalize our model using methods. This let us make use of the program statements in Dafny. To prove liveness properties, we frequently have a need to refer to states that will eventually happen in the future. This is more conveniently done using a different formalization. So, we are going to start afresh.

Processes and control state are as before:

```
type Process(==)
const P: set<Process>
datatype CState = Thinking | Hungry | Eating
```

Instead of modeling the state using the fields of a class, we will model the state as a tuple. We define the tuple as an immutable record:

```
datatype TSState = TSState(ticket: int,
                           serving: int,
```

```
cs: map<Process, CState>,
 t: map<Process, int>)
```

The system invariant is like before, but speaks about the fields of a TSState record rather than the fields of an object. Not using objects, there are no issues of framing (like reads clauses) to worry about.

```
predicate Valid(s: TSState)
{
  s.cs.Keys == s.t.Keys == P &&
  s.serving <= s.ticket &&
  (forall p :: p in P && s.cs[p] != Thinking ==>
          s.serving <= s.t[p] < s.ticket) &&
  (forall p,q ::
     p in P && q in P && p != q &&
     s.cs[p] != Thinking && s.cs[q] != Thinking
     ==> s.t[p] != s.t[q]) &&
  (forall p :: p in P && s.cs[p] == Eating ==> s.t[p] == s.serving)
}
```

In Sect. 6.1, we did the hard work of strengthening the invariant to prove the mutual-exclusion safety property. This lets us simply restate the automatically proved theorem here.

```
lemma MutualExclusion(s: TSState, p: Process, q: Process)
  requires Valid(s) && p in P && q in P
  requires s.cs[p] == Eating && s.cs[q] == Eating
  ensures p == q
{
}
```

8.3   State Transitions

Following the format in TLA+, we define our model by a predicate Init that describes the possible initial states and a predicate Next that describes the possible transitions from one state to the next.

```
  predicate Init(s: TSState)
  {
    s.cs.Keys == s.t.Keys == P &&
    s.ticket == s.serving &&
    forall p :: p in P ==> s.cs[p] == Thinking
  }

  predicate Next(s: TSState, s': TSState)
  {
    Valid(s) &&
    exists p :: p in P && NextP(s, p, s')
  }
```

We define Next to hold only for pairs of states where the first state satisfies the system invariant, Valid, but we do not mention either Valid(s) in Init or

`Valid(s')` in `Next`. It is better to prove the invariance of `Valid` separately. Once we have defined `NextP`, you can do that by a lemma like:

```
lemma Invariance(s: TSState, s': TSState)
   ensures Init(s) ==> Valid(s)
   ensures Valid(s) && Next(s, s') ==> Valid(s')
```

We define predicate `NextP(s, p, s')` to say that a process p may take an atomic step from state s to state s'. As we have seen before, such an atomic step is `Request`, `Enter`, or `Leave`.

```
predicate NextP(s: TSState, p: Process, s': TSState)
  requires Valid(s) && p in P
{
   Request(s, p, s') || Enter(s, p, s') || Leave(s, p, s')
}
```

Predicate `NextP` is defined to have a precondition, which means it can be used only when its parameters satisfy the required condition. This is fitting for our purposes, since the call to `NextP` in `Next` is guarded by `Valid(s)` and `p in P`, and it means we can assume these conditions (rather than repeat them) in the body of `NextP`.

Finally, we write the predicates for the three atomic events:

```
predicate Request(s: TSState, p: Process, s': TSState)
   requires Valid(s) && p in P
{
   s.cs[p] == Thinking &&
   s'.ticket == s.ticket + 1 &&
   s'.serving == s.serving &&
   s'.t == s.t[p := s.ticket] &&
   s'.cs == s.cs[p := Hungry]
}
```

```
predicate Enter(s: TSState, p: Process, s': TSState)
   requires Valid(s) && p in P
{
   s.cs[p] == Hungry &&
   s'.ticket == s.ticket &&
   s'.serving == s.serving &&
   s'.t == s.t &&
   ((s.t[p] == s.serving && s'.cs == s.cs[p := Eating]) ||
    (s.t[p] != s.serving && s'.cs == s.cs))
}
```

```
predicate Leave(s: TSState, p: Process, s': TSState)
   requires Valid(s) && p in P
{
```

```
    s.cs[p] == Eating &&
    s'.ticket == s.ticket &&
    s'.serving == s.serving + 1 &&
    s'.t == s.t &&
    s'.cs == s.cs[p := Thinking]
}
```

8.4   Schedules and Traces

As we got a glimpse of in Sect. 7.3, a schedule is a function from times (represented by natural numbers) to processes.

```
type Schedule = nat -> Process

predicate IsSchedule(schedule: Schedule)
{
  forall i :: schedule(i) in P
}
```

A trace is a function from times to ticket-system states. Such a trace is possible for a given schedule if the trace starts in a state satisfying Init and every pair of consecutive states in the trace is allowed as an atomic event by the process scheduled at that time.

```
type Trace = nat -> TSState

predicate IsTrace(trace: Trace, schedule: Schedule)
  requires IsSchedule(schedule)
{
  Init(trace(0)) &&
  forall i: nat ::
    Valid(trace(i)) && NextP(trace(i), schedule(i), trace(i+1))
}
```

Finally, a schedule is fair if every process occurs infinitely often. That is, for any process p, no matter how many steps you have already taken—say, n steps—there is still a next time, n', where p will be scheduled.

```
predicate FairSchedule(schedule: Schedule)
{
  IsSchedule(schedule) &&
  forall p,n :: p in P ==> HasNext(schedule, p, n)
}
predicate HasNext(schedule: Schedule, p: Process, n: nat)
{
  exists n' :: n <= n' && schedule(n') == p
}
```

8.5   Currently Served Process

Leading up to proving the desired liveness property of our ticket system, I define two new ingredients. The first new ingredient is a function that tells us which process is being served, that is, which process is holding the ticket number shown on the "serving" display. Not every ticket-system state has a currently served process, but we expect that if *some* process is hungry or eating, then there is a currently served process. As it turns out, we will need the currently served process only when we know some process is hungry, so we attempt to define:

```
function CurrentlyServedProcess(s: TSState): Process
  requires Valid(s) && exists p :: p in P && s.cs[p] == Hungry
{
  var q :| q in P && s.cs[q] != Thinking && s.t[q] == s.serving;
  q
}
```

However, as we write this definition, the verifier complains that it cannot prove there is such a q (remember that the : | operator gives rise to a proof obligation that there exists such a q). The reason is that our system invariant is not strong enough. We need to strengthen it further to say that every ticket number from s.serving to s.ticket is being used.

We define a predicate

```
predicate TicketIsInUse(s: TSState, i: int)
  requires s.cs.Keys == s.t.Keys == P
{
  exists p :: p in P && s.cs[p] != Thinking && s.t[p] == i
}
```

and use it in the definition of Valid:

```
predicate Valid(s: TSState)
{
  ... &&
  (forall i :: s.serving <= i < s.ticket ==> TicketIsInUse(s, i))
}
```

Now, there does exist a q like we want in CurrentlyServedProcess, but the verifier needs help to do the proof. Adding an assert in the body of the function is enough of a hint for the verifier:

```
function CurrentlyServedProcess(s: TSState): Process
  requires Valid(s) && exists p :: p in P && s.cs[p] == Hungry
{
  assert TicketIsInUse(s, s.serving);
  var q :| q in P && s.cs[q] != Thinking && s.t[q] == s.serving;
  q
}
```

If you did the exercise of including lemma Invariance, you will find that the strengthened invariant causes the automatic proof of Invariance no longer to go through. Like CurrentlyServedProcess, it also needs a hint, but I will not go through the details here.

8.6   Next Step of a Process

Fairness tells us there exists some future time in a schedule where a process p is scheduled. Given HasNext(schedule, p, n), we can use a statement

```
var u :| n <= u && schedule(u) == p;
```

to obtain such a time, u. The second new ingredient we need for our liveness proof is a way to find a future time, n', where certain properties hold. To obtain n', we can iterate up from n, since u provides us with an upper bound for the iteration.

In our application, p is the currently served process, n is the current time, and n' is the next time that p is scheduled. We prove that serving is unchanged from time n to time n', that p remains in the same control state and holds the same ticket in n as in n', and that all hungry processes in n are still hungry in n' and hold the same ticket in n' as in n.

Brace yourself for two surprises. One surprise is that we can formulate this ingredient as a lemma that has an out-parameter! We usually think of a lemma as establishing some condition. In mathematics, it is common that a lemma would establish the existence of an n' with certain properties. In Dafny, a lemma is simply a method that isn't compiled into code, and therefore it is just as natural for a lemma to have out-parameters as it is for the lemma to have in-parameters. With an out-parameter, we might as well return the n' whose existence the lemma has established. The second surprise is that the proof uses a loop! In mathematics, lemmas tend to be recursive—that is, a lemma calls itself to obtain what is known as the induction hypothesis. In Dafny, where a lemma is just a method, the body of the lemma can use iteration as well as recursion. In this case, I find it natural to express the proof by iteration, since our strategy is to iterate up from n toward u until we find the n' we are looking for.

Here is the lemma:

```
lemma GetNextStep(trace: Trace, schedule: Schedule, p: Process, n: nat) returns (n': nat)
  requires FairSchedule(schedule) && IsTrace(trace, schedule) && p in P
  requires trace(n).cs[p] != Thinking && trace(n).t[p] == trace(n).serving
  ensures n <= n' && schedule(n') == p
  ensures trace(n').serving == trace(n).serving
  ensures trace(n').cs[p] == trace(n).cs[p]
  ensures trace(n').t[p] == trace(n).t[p]
  ensures forall q :: q in P && trace(n).cs[q] == Hungry ==>
          trace(n').cs[q] == Hungry && trace(n').t[q] == trace(n).t[q]
{
  assert HasNext(schedule, p, n);
  var u :| n <= u && schedule(u) == p;
  n' := n;
  while schedule(n') != p
    invariant n' <= u
    invariant trace(n').serving == trace(n).serving
    invariant trace(n').cs[p] == trace(n).cs[p]
    invariant trace(n').t[p] == trace(n).t[p]
    invariant forall q :: q in P && trace(n).cs[q] == Hungry ==>
              trace(n').cs[q] == Hungry && trace(n').t[q] == trace(n).t[q]
    decreases u - n'
  {
    n' := n' + 1;
  }
}
```

The loop invariant is the same as the postcondition of the lemma, except for the postcondition schedule(n') == p, which is obtained as the negation of the loop guard. The decreases clause is used to prove termination of the loop.

It gives a natural-number valued expression whose value decreases with every iteration [8].

8.7   Liveness Theorem

Finally, we are ready to state and prove the liveness theorem. It states that a hungry process eventually eats. Instead of just showing the existence of a future time when the process eats, the lemma returns that time, similarly to what we saw for the `GetNextStep` lemma. And as in the proof of `GetNextStep`, I find that the proof of the liveness theorem is naturally formulated as a loop. If you think like a programmer, this liveness-theorem proof is just an algorithm that finds (and returns) the next time the hungry process eats.

```
lemma Liveness(trace: Trace, schedule: Schedule, p: Process, n: nat) returns (n': nat)
  requires FairSchedule(schedule) && IsTrace(trace, schedule) && p in P
  requires trace(n).cs[p] == Hungry
  ensures n <= n' && trace(n').cs[p] == Eating
{
  n' := n;
  while true
    invariant n <= n' && trace(n').cs[p] == Hungry
    decreases trace(n').t[p] - trace(n').serving
  {
    // find the currently served process and follow it out of the kitchen
    var q := CurrentlyServedProcess(trace(n'));
    if trace(n').cs[q] == Hungry {
      n' := GetNextStep(trace, schedule, q, n');
      n' := n' + 1;  // take the step from Hungry to Eating
      if p == q {
        return;
      }
    }
    n' := GetNextStep(trace, schedule, q, n');
    n' := n' + 1;  // take the step from Eating to Thinking
  }
}
```

9   Conclusion

A central idea in reasoning about concurrency is to break up the behavior of each process into atomic events whose execution may be interleaved with the atomic events of other processes. I have shown how to go from the pseudo code of a simple mutual-exclusion protocol to two formalizations of atomic events. The atomic events can be verified to maintain some system invariant, and safety properties, like mutual exclusion, are proved as logical consequences of the system invariant. In the second formalization, I also expressed and proved a liveness property. The key here is to be able to reason about events that will eventually take place in the execution of the program. The liveness proofs I showed bear some resemblance to search algorithms.

When using Dafny to model concurrency, the Dafny language and verifier provide a logical foundation. The fact that Dafny is a programming language that can be compiled is not the central point. Indeed, we would not be interested in compiling and running the code that we wrote as part of our models. Nevertheless, the notation that Dafny borrows from other programming languages lowers the bar for entry into new formalization projects. The automation provided by the Dafny verifier and the rapid verification feedback provided in the Dafny IDEs also aid in the Dafny usage experience. For example, in the safety-property theorem, we only needed to supply the invariant and then all the proofs were carried out automatically.

Acknowledgments. Andreas Podelski brought up the problem of this ticket system at meeting 54 (Saint Petersburg, Russia, June 2013) of the IFIP Working Group 2.3, where several formalizations were subsequently presented. Xinhaoyuan on github proposed the prefix allowance of conjunctions and disjunctions in Dafny. I thank Shuo Chen for comments on an earlier draft of this article.

References

1. Abrial, J.-R.: Modeling in Event-B: System and Software Engineering. Cambridge University Press, Cambridge (2010)
2. Abrial, J.-R.: Mini-course around Event-B and Rodin, June 2011. https://www.microsoft.com/en-us/research/video/mini-course-around-event-b-and-rodin/
3. Abrial, J.-R., Butler, M., Hallerstede, S., Hoang, T.S., Mehta, F., Voisin, L.: Rodin: an open toolset for modelling and reasoning in Event-B. Softw. Tools Technol. Transf. **12**(6), 447–466 (2010)
4. Back, R.-J., Sere, K.: Action systems with synchronous communication. In: Olderog, E.-R. (ed.) Proceedings of the IFIP TC2/WG2.1/WG2.2/WG2.3 Working Conference on Programming Concepts, Methods and Calculi (PROCOMET 1994). IFIP Transactions, vol. A-56, pp. 107–126. North-Holland, June 1994
5. Chandy, K.M., Misra, J.: Parallel Program Design: A Foundation. Addison-Wesley, Boston (1988)
6. Dafny online (2017). http://rise4fun.com/dafny
7. Floyd, R.W.: Assigning meanings to programs. In: Proceedings of the Symposium on Applied Mathematics, vol. 19, pp. 19–32. American Mathematical Society (1967)
8. Gries, D.: The Science of Programming. MCS. Springer-Verlag, New York (1981). https://doi.org/10.1007/978-1-4612-5983-1
9. Hatcliff, J., Leavens, G.T., Leino, K.R.M., Müller, P., Parkinson, M.: Behavioral interface specification languages. ACM Comput. Surv. **44**(3), 16:1–16:58 (2012)
10. Hawblitzel, C., et al.: IronFleet: proving practical distributed systems correct. In: Miller, E.L., Hand, S. (eds.) Proceedings of the 25th Symposium on Operating Systems Principles, SOSP 2015, pp. 1–17. ACM, October 2015
11. Herbert, L., Leino, K.R.M., Quaresma, J.: Using Dafny, an automatic program verifier. In: Meyer, B., Nordio, M. (eds.) LASER 2011. LNCS, vol. 7682, pp. 156–181. Springer, Heidelberg (2012). https://doi.org/10.1007/978-3-642-35746-6_6
12. Hoare, C.A.R.: An axiomatic basis for computer programming. Commun. ACM **12**(10), 576–583 (1969)
13. Jackson, D.: Software Abstractions: Logic, Language, and Analysis. MIT Press, Cambridge (2006)
14. Koenig, J., Leino, K.R.M.: Getting started with Dafny: a guide. In: Nipkow, T., Grumberg, O., Hauptmann, B. (eds.) Software Safety and Security: Tools for Analysis and Verification. NATO Science for Peace and Security Series D: Information and Communication Security, vol. 33, pp. 152–181. IOS Press (2012). Summer School Marktoberdorf 2011 lecture notes

15. Lamport, L. (ed.): Specifying Systems: The TLA+ Language and Tools for Hardware and Software Engineers. Addison-Wesley Professional, Boston (2002)
16. Lamport, L.: The TLA+ video course, March 2017. http://lamport.azurewebsites.net/video/videos.html
17. Leino, K.R.M.: Specification and verification of object-oriented software. In: Broy, M., Sitou, W., Hoare, T. (eds.) Engineering Methods and Tools for Software Safety and Security. NATO Science for Peace and Security Series D: Information and Communication Security, vol. 22, pp. 231–266. IOS Press (2009). Summer School Marktoberdorf 2008 lecture notes
18. Leino, K.R.M.: Dafny: an automatic program verifier for functional correctness. In: Clarke, E.M., Voronkov, A. (eds.) LPAR 2010. LNCS (LNAI), vol. 6355, pp. 348–370. Springer, Heidelberg (2010). https://doi.org/10.1007/978-3-642-17511-4_20
19. Leino, K.R.M.: Developing verified programs with Dafny. In: Notkin, D., Cheng, B.H.C., Pohl, K. (eds.) 35th International Conference on Software Engineering, ICSE 2013, pp. 1488–1490. IEEE Computer Society (2013)
20. Leino, K.R.M.: Accessible software verification with Dafny. IEEE Software **34**(6), 94–97 (2017)

Software Is Not Soft
Challenges and Approaches to Dynamic Software Update

Xiaoxing Ma[1](✉) ⓘ, Tianxiao Gu[1], and Wei Song[2]

[1] State Key Laboratory for Novel Software Technology,
Institute of Computer Software, Nanjing University, Nanjing, China
xxm@nju.edu.cn, tianxiao.gu@gmail.com
[2] School of Computer Science and Engineering,
Nanjing University of Science and Technology, Nanjing, China
wsong@njust.edu.cn

Abstract. It is widely desired that running software systems can be updated on the fly in response to the changes in the environment they are situated in and in the requirements they must satisfy. Systematic support for dynamic software update must make it safe, efficient and easy to use. This chapter overviews related work and our efforts on dynamic software update at three different levels of granularity: code-level update of Java programs, component-level update of distributed systems, and process-level instance migration of workflow processes.

1 Introduction

Software, as its name suggests, is regarded as the *soft* or changeable part of a computing system. In practice, software systems are routinely revised to fix bugs, improve performance, or adapt to the changing environment and requirement. Moreover, recent popularization of Continuous Deployment [1] and Rapid Continuous Software Engineering[1] requires in-use software systems to evolve *"in very short rapid cycles, typically hours, days or very small numbers of weeks"*.

Normally, to update a running software system, one must first shut it down, redeploy the new version software, and then restart the system. However, for software used in application domains such as financial transaction processing, life-supporting systems, or transport control systems, non-stop services are mandatory, and interruptions caused by updating software are unacceptable. Even for everyday software such as desktop operating systems and word processors, frequent restarts for updating could be distracting and annoying.

Dynamic Software Update (DSU) adapts a running software system to a new version without shutting it down [2–4]. This technique can greatly reduce the disruption to system services caused by software updates. At first glance DSU does not look challenging, because software can be treated as data in both the Universal Turing Machine model and the von Neumann Architecture. However,

---

[1] http://continuous-se.org.

ⓒ Springer Nature Switzerland AG 2018
J. P. Bowen et al. (Eds.): SETSS 2017, LNCS 11174, pp. 143–175, 2018.
https://doi.org/10.1007/978-3-030-02928-9_5

the real challenge of DSU is not how to modify the running software, but how to do it *safely, efficiently* and *automatically.*

Regarding the difficulty of evolving software systems, especially doing it at runtime, we would claim that software is *not soft.* A software system is a *logical* artifact that lacks the inherent flexibility of any *physical* object. A small change in the environment or the requirement of a software system, which is often unforeseen, may cause a significant change to the software system [5]. Moreover, even though a new version of the software system is successfully developed, to update the running software system to this new version on the fly needs sophisticated enabling techniques. While offline software evolution has been a central topic in software engineering for a long time [5,6], the challenges and approaches to dynamic software update are the topic of the current chapter.

The idea of changing running software systems on the fly is not new [2], which at least can be traced back to dynamic linking that was systematically implemented in MULTICS [7]. However, general-purpose DSU, which aims at dynamically upgrading arbitrary running programs, is still a dream not fully realized and has attracted a lot of research in multiple fields including software engineering [2,3,8–12] programming languages [4,13–18], and operating systems [19–22].

Modern application systems generally have a multi-layer software stack. For example, from bottom to top, there could be hypervisors, operating systems, program language virtual machines, component containers, service orchestration or workflow management systems. In principle, DSU support can be provided at any of these layers. Intuitively, the lower layer DSU is implemented, the more general its support can be, but the less guarantee can be provided and the more tedious the technique is. So it is important to provide DSU at different layers[2], so that users can choose a proper granularity to update their software, and strike a balance among the requirements of safety, efficiency, and ease-of-use.

In this chapter, we will discuss how our work builds upon previous researches to provide safe, efficient, and easy-to-use DSU support at the code level [18,24–26], the component level [10,27,28], and the workflow process level [29,30].

To pave the way for presenting the solutions in the following sections, in the rest of this section, we will first give a generic DSU scenario and then discuss the technical challenges of DSU supporting systems.

1.1   A Scenario of Dynamic Software Update

Figure 1 illustrates a generic scenario of DSU. At the beginning, a software vendor released a version of some software system SW_{old}. The software system can be released in different forms. It can be a bundle of Java classes in the form of bytecode and to be executed on a JVM. It can be a set of components to be

---

[2] Continuous deployment techniques such as Blue-Green Deployment [23] will not be discussed because they do not actually update running software but gradually redirect clients from the service provided by old version software to that of the new version, with the assumption that clients are independent with each other.

deployed on a distributed enterprise middleware platform. It can also be a work-flow process definition to be interpreted by a Workflow Management System (WfMS).

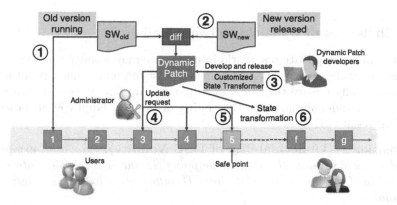

Fig. 1. Scenario of updating running software

The old version was deployed and started in a client organization (① in Fig. 1), and users had been relying on its non-stopping service. After some time, the vendor released a new version SW_{new} (②), in response to, for example, an emergent security vulnerability reported or a new functionality requested. Here we assume that both the old and the new versions are correct by themselves.

Being aware that its clients were reluctant to offend their users by stopping the systems to apply the update, the vendor (or some third-party developer) also managed to provide a *dynamic patch* (③) so that clients' running systems can be updated on-the-fly. Depending on the concrete forms of the software, dynamic patches also take different forms. However the common purpose is to specify the condition under which the update can be applied and how to transform the runtime state left by the old version software to a proper state of the new version, in addition to the static difference between the two versions.

Upon receiving the dynamic patch, the administrator of the client organization requests the DSU system to apply the patch without the notice of users (④). The DSU system (*e.g.*, a DSU-enhanced JVM, a dynamic component middleware system, or a WfMS with instance migration capability) loads in the dynamic patch together with the new software version, and introspects on the current state of the running software to determine if it is a *safe point* for update. The condition for safe points is specified by the dynamic patch, or defined by default in the DSU system.

If the current state (③) is not safe for applying the update, the DSU system will wait for a while till the running software enters a safe point (⑤), or it may drive the running software into such a state.

Then DSU system suspends the running software system, or only a part that is affected by the update, to apply the patch. If necessary, the state left by the old version software will be transformed to a corresponding state of the new version, with the state transformers included in the dynamic patch, or according to some default transformation rules (⑤). Finally, the program is resumed to execute under the new version SW_{new} (⑥).

1.2 Challenges of Dynamic Software Update

With the above application scenario in mind, one may wonder why DSU is difficult and not widely adopted as desired. The first reason is that it is not possible to automatically ensure the safety of a dynamic update without limitations on the program-under-update and the timing of update. Gupta *et al.* proved the following result[3] [31]:

Proposition 1 (Undecidability of DSU Validity). *For arbitrary program Π and its new version Π', a state mapping S, and a reachable state s of Π, the validity of the dynamic update from Π with state s to Π' with state $S(s)$ is undecidable.*

Here the validity means that from $S(s)$ the updated program will eventually reach a state that is reachable from the initial state in Π'.

This result implies that there is no free lunch. To develop a DSU system, we have to make trade-offs among the generality of software and their updates, the flexibility in the timing of update, the automation of the state transformation, and the safety of the dynamic update. And this turns out to be a challenging software engineering task.

Elaborately, a general-purpose DSU-system are expected to meet the following requirements:

Safety. Ideally, a dynamic software update should not cause any error that would not happen in a traditional shutdown-redeploy-restart update. However, as discussed above, this cannot be automatically guaranteed without imposing limitations on the update. There can be different trade-offs in different settings. For example,

- A DSU-enhanced JVM should guarantee at least the type safety of the updated program, but may leave the semantic correctness for dynamic patch developers.
- A dynamic component middleware may ensure the safety of dynamic update of a component by putting it in quarantine during the update.
- A WfMS must prevent running workflow instances from errors caused by schema evolution, but may leave the business integrity to the judgement of administrators.

---

[3] For ease of reading and to focus on the software engineering issues of DSU, in this chapter definitions and propositions are often presented informally or semi-formally, and intuitive concepts are used without definitions. Interested readers are referred to the original publications for complete and rigorous treatment of the subjects.

Efficiency. The efficiency of DSU can be measured in different aspects.

    Timeliness Dynamic updates are expected to be applied as soon as possible. Timeliness is measured as the time span between when an update request is received and when it is applied (the duration between state ③ and state ⑤ in Fig. 1).

    Disruption An efficient DSU approach should minimize the time span during which the software system is paused for carrying out dynamic update. In cases that the DSU system only freezes a part of the running system, the disruption can be measured as the loss of serving capability caused by the dynamic update.

    Overhead The DSU system should not introduce significant overhead to software execution before and after the update.

Ease-of-use. Ideally the dynamic update support should be transparent to the development and revision of software systems. More challengingly, the need for human-specified state transformers, which are often tedious and error-prone to develop, should be avoided or reduced to a minimum.

Needless to say that these requirements often conflict with each other. The challenge is how to strike a proper balance between them in a given context.

The rest of the chapter is organized as follows. In Sect. 2, we present the Javelus system that supports code-level dynamic update of Java programs. Sections 3 and 4 are devoted to dynamic update of component-based systems and instance migration of workflow processes, respectively. Finally Sect. 5 concludes the chapter.

2 Dynamic Update of Java Programs

In this section, we focus on general-purpose DSU support for managed programming languages, or more specifically, Java [14,16–18]. Java is the most widely used programming language for long-running server-side programs. These programs are often required to provide non-stopping services, and thus have a particularly strong demand for DSU support. Moreover, modern Java Virtual Machines (JVMs) provide rich runtime type information and powerful runtime manipulation facilities such as dynamic class loading, just-in-time compiling and hot swapping, which make it easier to implement practical DSU support. There are also systems supporting DSU for C programs, *e.g.*, Ginseng [4,13] and Kitsune [15]. However, these DSU systems require programs be compiled with special compilers ahead-of-time and are hard to be widely adopted.

Javelus[4] is a DSU supporting system developed on top of the industry-strength HotSpot JVM[5]. In the rest of this section, we will first give an example of a dynamic update of a server program, and then discuss how Javelus makes the dynamic update of Java programs efficient, easy to use, and reliable [18,24–26,32].

---

[4] http://moon.nju.edu.cn/dse/javelus/.
[5] http://openjdk.java.net/groups/hotspot/.

2.1   An Example of Program Update

Let's consider a simplified version of a real update of a well-known open source program, *viz.*, Apache SSHD Server[6]. In its rev. b98697, class `DefaultSshFuture` is updated for better space efficiency. The class provides a method `addListener` to add listeners (Fig. 2a). For most cases, there is only one or two listeners but apparently the implementation should support adding more. In the original version, the first-added listener is referenced by field variable `firstListener`, and other listeners, if there are any, are stored into `otherListeners`, which is an auto-expanding list container (`ArrayList`).

```
1  class DefaultSshFuture {
2    SshFutureListener firstListener;
3    List otherListeners;
4    void addListener(SshFutureListener listener) {
5      if (firstListener == null) {
6        firstListener = listener;
7      } else {
8        if (otherListeners == null) {
9          otherListeners = new ArrayList(1);
10       }
11       otherListeners.add(listener);
12     }
13   }
14   void removeListener(SshFutureListener listener) {...}
15 }
```

(a) The old version of `DefaultSshFuture`

```
1  class DefaultSshFuture {
2    Object listeners;
3    void addListener(SshFutureListener listener) {
4      if (listeners == null) {
5        listeners = listener;
6      } else if (listeners instanceof SshFutureListener) {
7        listeners = new Object[]{listeners,listener};
8      } else {
9        // expand the array and append
10       // the listener at the end
11     }
12   }
13   void removeListener(SshFutureListener listener) {...}
14 }
```

(b) The new version of `DefaultSshFuture`

Fig. 2. An update (rev. b98697) of class `DefaultSshFuture` in Apache SSHD.

Contrastingly, in the new version (Fig. 2b), to save a little memory, only a single polymorphic field variable `listeners` is employed. The variable is typed

---

[6] http://mina.apache.org/sshd-project/index.html.

in `Object`, and at runtime it will refer to a `SshFutureListener` object if there
is only one listener, but to an array of listeners if more than one listeners are
added in.

Assume that we are going to apply this update at runtime without shutting
down the running SSHD server. Although the change seems quite simple, it is
very difficult, if not impossible, for the DSU system to figure out how to make
it without a manually specified state transformer. By default, the DSU system
can only initialize `listeners` to `null` because it has no clue about the semantic
correspondence between the different data structures used in the two versions.

```
1 public void updateObject(
2     @OldField(clazz="DefaultSshFuture", name="firstListener",
3                     signature="LSshFutureListener;")
4     SshFutureListener firstListener,
5     @OldField(clazz="DefaultSshFuture", name="otherListeners",
6                     signature="Ljava/util/List;")
7     java.util.List otherListeners){
8
9   if (firstListener != null) {
10     listeners = firstListener;
11     if (otherListeners != null) {
12         int size = otherListeners.size();
13         Object[] array = new Object[size + 1];
14         array[0] = firstListener;
15         for (int i = 0; i < size; i++) {
16             array[i + 1] = otherListeners.get(i);
17         }
18         listeners = array;
19     }
20   }
21 }
```

Fig. 3. State transformer for `DefaultSshFuture`

Figure 3 presents the state transformer for the dynamic update of `Default-`
`SshFuture`. Javelus will analyze the difference between the two versions and
generate a transformer template for each updated class. One just need to provide the transformation logic, and with the tricks played by the template the
transformer can be compiled as usual Java code without accessing violations.[7]

2.2 To Be Efficient: Lazy Update

A key benefit of DSU is the non-stopping services of programs, despite of software
updates applied during the course. However, a naively designed DSU support
could impose a notable pause (from [5] to [6] in Fig. 1) of program execution to
apply the update, or it could introduce significant overhead after, and even before

---

[7] A more complete description of the procedure can be found at http://moon.nju.edu.
cn/dse/javelus/a-tutorial-of-javelus.

the dynamic update. The latter is especially unacceptable because performance would be degraded even if there were no dynamic update around.

Unfortunately, in implementing the DSU support for Java, there is an unavoidable trade-off between shortening the pause time during dynamic updating and eliminating the overhead during normal program execution. To understand the challenges and set the context for discussing how Javelus realizes efficient updating with a short pause time, let's briefly overview how dynamic updating of Java programs is generally realized.

Overview of Dynamic Program Update. As shown in Fig. 4a, the runtime representation of a program consists of three parts: the code, the stacks of frames, and the heap of objects.

Code The update of code is the easiest part because HotSpot JVM has already provided facilities such as dynamic class loading, just-in-time compilation, and de-optimization to do this job.

Stacks The update of stack frames is possible [21] but difficult to get right. A cost-effective approach adopted by most code-level DSU systems, including Javelus, is to avoid updating them by postponing updates until no active changed method appears on any stack (Fig. 4b).

Heap In the heap, the stale objects (*i.e.*, objects whose classes are changed) must be updated to be consistent with their new classes in the code part. Type safety must be guaranteed after the update.

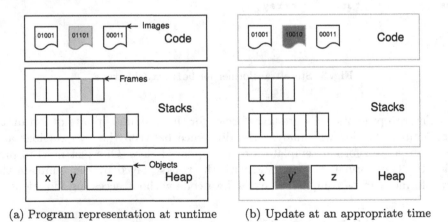

(a) Program representation at runtime   (b) Update at an appropriate time

Fig. 4. How to update running program: an overview.

The memory space of the heap is usually significantly larger than those of code and stack frames. The long pausing time of dynamic update is mostly caused by the update of objects in the heap. To update the heap, we need to (1) traverse the entire heap to locate all stale objects, (2) re-allocate the objects in new size to avoid memory corruption, (3) adjust all references pointing to the objects being updated if they are re-allocated at different addresses. and (4) apply state transformation to the object.

Updating Stale Objects: Eager vs. Lazy. There can be two tactics for updating stale objects in the heap. One tactic, as depicted by Fig. 5a, is to find all stale objects, update these objects to their new class schema, and fix the references to them all at once during the pause of program execution. The benefits of this tactic are the conceptual cleanness of having a consistent state when the program is resumed to execute in the new version, and the fact that there should be no overhead after the update. However, it may take a long time to update everything all at once, especially when there are many objects to check and update. The long pause time betrays the aim of dynamic update and is unacceptable for programs with real-time response requirements.

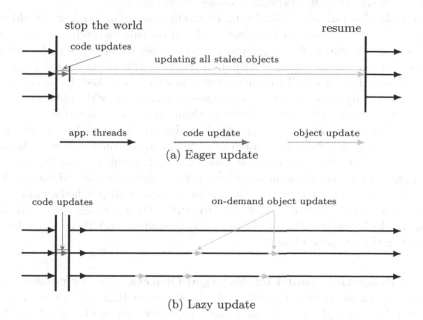

Fig. 5. Dynamic update: eager vs. lazy

The other tactic, as shown in Fig. 5b, is to update only the code during the pause time, and then resume program execution immediately. Stale objects in the heap are left as is, and they will be updated on-demand, *i.e.*, when they are accessed in the first time thereafter. With this tactic the program is updated smoothly, as it reduces the pause of program execution to minimum, and the cost of updating stale objects is distributed over the later execution of the program. The on-demand update has an extra advantage that, as we observed, many stale objects will not be used anymore and thus no update is needed.

However, a naive implementation of the lazy tactic could cause significant overhead to program execution after, and even before, dynamic update. First, because every object in the heap is potentially stale, a staleness check before every object access is needed, which is prohibitively expensive. Second, when a stale object is detected and updated to a larger one, we cannot manipulate the layout of heap to accommodate the enlarged object. Thus inefficient indirections have to be employed. Next let's see how Javelus addresses these two problems and makes the lazy update efficient.

Reducing Unnecessary Staleness Checking. Java is a statically typed language that guarantees type safety at runtime, which means a reference will never point to an object not belonging to the statically declared type of the reference. Taking staleness checking as type checking against type errors caused by dynamic update, it is natural to leverage the type system and runtime type information provided by the JVM to optimize staleness checking.

First, Javelus builds a unified type hierarchy containing both of the old version and the new version of the classes. Based on this hierarchy, it can safely eliminate the checking of any reference whose type, super-types and subtypes are not involved in the update. Although effective, this optimization is insufficient because there are still too many references to be checked. In fact, a lot of objects, especially those stored in containers, are accessed with references typed in Object. However, the vast majority of them are actually not stale.

A further optimization implemented in Javelus is to make the checking implicit, leveraging the dynamic binding mechanism. Javelus rewrites methods in the dynamic dispatching table of the stale class with a stub method for staleness checking, and removes the staleness check prior to dynamic method dispatching. If the object is fresh, the correct version of the method is dispatched and invoked, and no unnecessary checking happens. Otherwise, the rewritten stub method is invoked, which triggers the on-demand object update and then re-invoke the method on the updated object.

Partial Delegation Model for Enlarged Objects. Another problem faced by the lazy tactic is how to deal with the situation that objects need to be enlarged. For example, the updated class may have new fields added in. With the eager tactic, enlarged objects are relatively easy to handle because they can be allocated in any free space, and then all references to the stale objects are updated accordingly all at once. However, with a lazy approach, stale objects are updated on-demand from time to time and must be done very quickly, so it is unacceptable to scan the heap to find out all references to the object being updated.

For example, Fig. 6a shows the heap snapshot before update. Suppose that object y is enlarged in the new version. We cannot simply allocate the updated object y' in an other place, because references to y would be inconsistent (Fig. 6b). A common solution is leaving a forward pointer at the expired object y (Fig. 6c), but it is inefficient to use indirection in memory accessing.

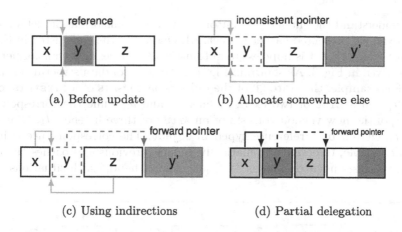

(a) Before update   (b) Allocate somewhere else

(c) Using indirections   (d) Partial delegation

Fig. 6. How to allocate an enlarged object

Javelus solves the problem with a partial delegation model (Fig. 6d). With this model, the new object y' is implemented with two physical objects. The first one reuses the space of the old object y, which contains all the unchanged fields. The other one is the newly allocated y', but only used for those changed fields. In this way only those accesses to the changed fields need to be redirected. The two physical objects will be merged as a normal object in the next round of garbage collection. Javelus also uses the existing shared field defined by HotSpot JVM to store forward pointers, thus having no extra space overhead when there is no dynamic update.

With the reduced staleness checking, partial delegation for enlarged objects and various other optimizations, Javelus implements an efficient lazy approach to dynamic update of Java programs. Compared to the eager approach, Javelus reduces the pause time by tens, or even hundreds times, while only introducing negligible overhead (for on-demand object update) after update. More details of the implementation and efficiency evaluation of Javelus can be found in [18].

2.3   To Be Easy to Use: Automated State Transformation

Manual craft of state transformers is often tedious and error-prone, because the developer must understand the implementation details of both the old and the new version. The developer also has to violate the principle of encapsulation when manipulating objects' low-level state representation, as exemplified by the code in Fig. 3. In addition, since the timing of dynamic update cannot be known beforehand, the transformers must be able to deal with all the possible states left by the old version.

Automated transformation of object state for dynamic update is highly desirable [33], although generally its correctness cannot be fully guaranteed (*cf.* Proposition 1). An experimental approach to automated state transformation, called AOTES, is developed to relieve DSU users of state transformers [26].

To understand the challenge of automating state transformation, let's return to our example presented earlier in Sect. 2.1. Observing the code listed in Fig. 2, one must admit that it is hopeless to automatically synthesize a transformer like the one given in Fig. 3. As shown in Fig. 7, the change of data structures is arbitrary. For example, the state ③ of the old version consists of a `firstListener` object l_1 and a `List` of two extra listeners l_2 and l_3, while the corresponding state ③ of the new version consists of an `Array` of three listeners l_1, l_2 and l_3, which is referred by a reference typed in `Object`. The correspondence is hard, if not impossible, to derive automatically. In fact, previous approaches based on guessing correspondence, such as TOS [33], cannot handle such situations.

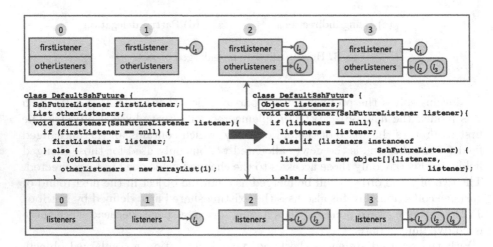

Fig. 7. Data structures of two versions of `DefaultSshFuture`

Fortunately, with a closer look at the example, we can find that there does exist a correspondence, not between the concrete states, but between the behaviors (*i.e.*, the histories of methods invoked) leading to the states. As shown in Fig. 8, although the state ③ of the old version looks completely different from the state ③ of the new version, both of them can be achieved with a method history of `addListener(`l_1`)`, `addListener(`l_2`)`, `addListener(`l_3`)`, starting from their corresponding initial states.

This observation inspired the basic idea of AOTES. Specifically, AOTES first tries to synthesize a method history that can produce the current state from the initial state in the old version. Then it replays the synthesized method history in the new version to get the target state.

The difficulty is how to figure out such a method history. A naive attempt is searching from the initial state by tentatively applying methods of the object until the current state is achieved. This is infeasible because we do not have the actual arguments needed by the methods. In AOTES the searching is on the reversed direction, starting from the current state and aiming at the initial state.

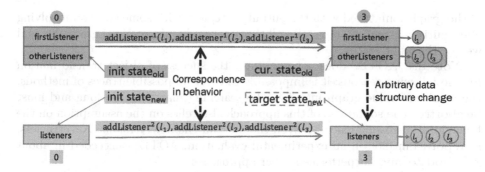

Fig. 8. Behavior correspondence of two versions of `DefaultSshFuture`

At each step of the searching, for the method considered, we have the output state, and try to figure out the input state, *i.e.*, the object state before applying the method and the actual arguments provided for the method, which will be used to replay the method history in the new version.

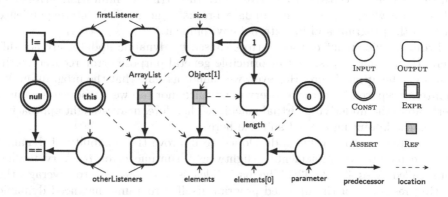

Fig. 9. A value graph of `DefaultSshFuture` (lines 5, 8, 9 and 11 executed)

The technique used to simulate the "reverse" execution of methods is based on symbolic execution and constraint solving. It is difficult to reverse every statement/bytecode instruction to infer the input state from the output state. Instead, AOTES employs a hybrid execution mode consisting forward execution, backward execution and symbolic execution. Specifically, AOTES first transforms an execution trace of a method into a directed *value graph* by offline symbolic execution. Then, AOTES realizes forward and backward execution by forward and backward traversing of the value graph to resolve the value of each value node. For value nodes that cannot be resolved by forward and backward execution, AOTES also conducts an online symbolic execution and leverages constraint solving to infer their values. For example, the graph shown in Fig. 9 symbolically encodes the logic of a trace of `DefaultSshFuture` in Fig. 2a. The output nodes of the graph is matched with the output state, and with some constraint solving and heuristic attempts, hopefully all the other nodes are resolved gradually, and we get the input state.

Note that AOTES does not guarantee the success of object transformation for the following reasons: it is impossible to cover all possible traces of methods; the resolve of value graph may fail; the searching may take too long and must be aborted. The soundness of this approach also relies on the assumption on the behavioral correspondence between the old and the new versions. Nevertheless, as reported in [26], in an experimental evaluation, AOTES succeeded in about 80% updates and outperformed other approaches.

2.4   To Be Reliable: Recovery from Dynamic Update Errors

It is hard to completely avoid errors caused by dynamic updates where state transformation is involved. As discussed above, human errors can occur in manually crafted state transformers. Aggressive automated approaches based on predefined rules [16] or program synthesis [26,33] may also lead to runtime errors.

In practice, dynamic updates are often restricted to cases where no state transformation is needed [34,35]. Even with this stringent limitation, errors can still happen when the dynamic update breaks some implicit interdependence between the program and its external environment.

From the viewpoint of users, errors caused by dynamic updates are not different from other errors, and in principle general-purpose error recovery techniques can be applied here. However, we cannot assume that the program under update is prepared for error recovery in advance, nor can we introduce too much overhead to the underlying virtual machine. Therefore, heavy-weight approaches such as checkpointing are not suitable here.

An extension to Javelus is developed to improve the reliability of dynamic software update. It implements a lightweight runtime error recovery mechanism called Ares [24,25,32]. The basic idea is very simple—to leverage the existing resilience of the updated program itself. Programs that need dynamic update, especially those long-running server programs, often provide comprehensive exception handing and error tolerance capabilities, although not intended for dynamic update errors.

For example, Fig. 10 lists the code of a Java method that retrieves the password of a user from a database. Java language forces its programmer to handle all potential *checked* exceptions with `try-catch` clauses, if not to throw them to the caller of the method. Let's suppose that a dynamic update erroneously assigns `null` to the variable `dbConnection` at line 5, and consequently method `credentials` throws a `NullPointerException`. This *unchecked* exception indicates a runtime error, and will crash the program, because `getPassword` and its callers did not expect such an exception.

However, the method does consider the situation that something is wrong with the database querying (line 14), and `null` is returned in this case (line 17). To rescue the program from crashing, Ares synthesizes an error handler at runtime. The handler will catch the unchecked exception, and transform it to a

```
1 String getPassword(String username) {
2   try {
3     PreparedStatement stmt = null;
4     try {
5       stmt = credentials(dbConnection, username);
6     } catch (SQLException e) {
7       throw new SQLException(e);
8     }
9     ResultSet rs = stmt.executeQuery();
10    if (rs.next()) {
11      return rs.getString(1);
12    }
13    return null;
14  } catch (SQLException e) {
15    containerLog.error(sm.getString("jdbcRealm.exception"),e);
16  }
17  return (null);
18 }
```

Fig. 10. A method with resilience

checked exception that has an effective handler in the context. In our case the NullPointerException can be transformed to SQLException.

Another aggressive recovery tactic is to abort the execution of the current method and make a premature return. For our example, Ares may choose to directly return a null at line 5.

The question here is how to choose the "best" way to handle the error. With exception transformation one needs to choose from multiple checked exception handlers available in the context. With premature return one may abort one or more method frames in the stack. Ares performs an in-vivo testing to evaluate each handler and chooses the one that will neither cause other errors soon nor do too much harm to the application logic.

The actual design and implementation of Ares is more complex than described above, and readers are referred to [24] for details. Experimental evaluation shows that Ares can recover from 11 of 16 errors caused by inappropriate state transformation in dynamic updates [25,32].

3   Dynamic Update of Distributed Components

A component-based distributed software system consists of a set of self-contained distributed components interacting with each other through well-defined interfaces. Compared to dynamic program update at code level and instance migration of workflow processes, dynamic update of software components is more mature and more widely used in practice, thanks to the loose coupling between components. Mainstream component frameworks such as Java EE[8] or OSGi[9] all provide some support for hot deployment of components.

---

[8] http://www.oracle.com/technetwork/java/javaee/.
[9] http://www.osgi.org/.

However, the state of practice is far from satisfactory because the hot deployment of a component does not guarantee the consistency of the whole component-based system. It is not rare that a careless hot deployment of a revised component messes up the whole running application system. Conscientious administrators always tend to avoid hot deployment in production systems.

The basic means of ensuring the consistency of a system when updating one of its components is to passivate *all* components that potentially depend on the to-be-updated component. Nevertheless, this means may introduce too much disruption to the normal service of the system, because the component platform is oblivious to the business logic encapsulated in components, and has to be very conservative in deciding the scope of depending components. So the challenge of DSU at component level is to solve the dilemma of safety (*i.e.*, guaranteeing consistency) and efficiency (*i.e.*, minimizing disruption).

In the rest of this section, we first present our system model and a running example, and then discuss different criteria for safe dynamic update of components.

3.1   System Model and Running Example

Component-based distributed system (CBDS) is a general abstraction of systems that are "discrete" in both the structural aspect and the behavioral aspect. Structurally, the *static configuration* of a CBDS is modeled as a directed graph whose nodes represent components, and directed edges represent *static dependencies*. A component can only use services provided by its depended components.

For example, Fig. 11 shows an example CBDS, which is borrowed from previous work [10,28]. In this system a portal component (Portal) depends on an authentication component (Auth) and a business processing component (Proc), while Proc depends on both Auth and a database component (DB).

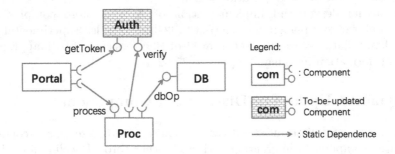

Fig. 11. An example component-based distributed system

Behaviorally, the execution of a CBDS is divided into independent transactions. A (local) transaction[10] hosted by a component is a sequence of actions

---
[10]   Here the notion of transaction is weaker than the ACID transaction of database systems. It is only assumed that all local transactions are consistent and isolated.

that accomplishes a given task and completes in bounded time. Actions include local computations and message exchanges.

A transaction T hosted by component h_T can initiate a sub-transaction T' hosted by $h_{T'}$ if h_T statically depends on $h_{T'}$. A transaction is called a *root* transaction if it is not a sub-transaction of any transaction. The extended transaction set of a root transaction T, denoted as $ext(T)$, is the set of T and all its direct or indirect sub-transactions. The extended transaction set of a root transaction models a *distributed* transaction running on the CBDS.

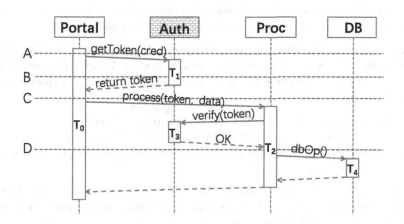

Fig. 12. A concrete scenario of the CBDS in Fig. 11

A concrete usage scenario of the system is depicted in Fig. 12. Upon receiving a request from an outside client, the Portal initiates a transaction T_0 to serve the request. T_0 first gets an authentication token from Auth (initiating T_1), and then uses it to require the service from Proc (T_2). Proc verifies the token through Auth (T_3) and then starts computing, and interacts with DB for database operations (T_4). The whole distributed transaction is the extended transaction $ext(T_0) = \{T_0, T_1, T_2, T_3, T_4\}$.

Let's assume that component Auth is going to be updated to exploit a stronger encryption algorithm. If this update is applied offline, there will be no problem because the change is transparent to other components in the system— although the new algorithm is incompatible with the old one, all encryption and decryption are done within Auth. The problem is whether we can safely update the component at runtime.

Before discussing criteria for safe dynamic update, we first need to consider what the safety means. Classic software correctness refers to the property of a program that all executions of this program satisfy its specification. However, in the context of dynamic update, we have two versions of a program, with two potentially different specifications. Moreover, besides the executions of the old and the new program versions, we may have executions that begin in the old version and end in the new version. The notion of correctness in this situation can be tricky and application dependent [11, 12].

For CBDS, we need a generic notion of safety instead of application-specific correctness. On one hand, it is often the case that application specifications are not explicitly given, and what we know is that each version is correct with respect to its own specification. So directly reasoning about application-specific correctness is often infeasible. On the other hand, the structural and behavioral "discreteness" makes it possible to reason at an abstract level concerning the isolation and consistency of transactions, which indirectly ensure the well-behavedness of the whole system under dynamic update.

To this end, we use following notion of safety of dynamic update.

Definition 1 (Safety of dynamic component update). *Given a CBDS S satisfying the old specification $Spec_{old}$, and a revision C' of a component C in S such that $S[C'/C]$ satisfies the new specification $Spec_{new}$, a dynamic update of C to C' in S is safe iff*

- *The transactions that end before the update satisfy $Spec_{old}$;*
- *The transactions that begin after the update satisfy $Spec_{new}$;*
- *The transactions that begin before the update, and end after it, satisfy either $Spec_{old}$ or $Spec_{new}$.*

The first condition is guaranteed by the correctness of S, while the last two conditions must be ensured through some restriction on the state of S under which the dynamic update happens.

3.2   Quiescence and Tranquility

According to Proposition 1, if a dynamic update of a component is allowed to happen at any time, its safety cannot be guaranteed. An obvious restriction is to require that the to-be-updated component is *idle* when the update happens. Unfortunately, the following proposition [28] indicates that idleness is insufficient for the safety of dynamic component update.

Proposition 2. *For an arbitrary component C in an CBDS, and a new version C' of the component, such that both S and $S[C'/C]$ are correct by themselves, the safety of the dynamic update of C to C' is undecidable, even under the condition that C is idle when the update happens.*

For our example scenario in Fig. 12, component Auth is idle at time A, C, and D. However, if we update Auth at time C, T_0 on Portal would get a token issued by the old Auth and send it to Proc, then Proc would verify it with the new Auth for authentication. The authentication would fail because of the incompatibility between the algorithms used in the two versions of Auth. Note that, if the update is applied offline, such a problem will never appear in either the original system or the updated system.

To avoid this kind of dynamic update errors, Kramer and Magee proposed a criterion called *quiescence* as a sufficient condition for a node to be safely manipulated in dynamic reconfigurations [3].

Definition 2 (Quiescence). *A node is quiescent if:*

1. *It is not currently engaged in an interaction*[11] *that it initiated;*
2. *It will not initiate new interactions;*
3. *It is not currently engaged in servicing an interaction;*
4. *No interaction has been or will be initiated by other nodes which require service from this node.*

A node is *passive* if it satisfies the first two conditions. The last two conditions further require the node independent of all existing and future interactions. As explained by the authors, the state of a quiescent node is both *consistent* and *frozen*. It is consistent because it does not contain the results of partially completed interactions, and is frozen because its state will not change as a result of new interactions.

Proposition 3 (Sufficiency of quiescence). *A dynamic update of component C in a CBDS is safe if it is carried out in the state that C is quiescent.*

The quiescence condition is quite conservative. For our example in Fig. 12, at none of the four time points is Auth quiescent. At time B it is engaged in the interaction between T_0 and T_1. For other time points, it either will be (A), or has been (D), engaged in an interaction, or both are the cases (C).

Kramer and Magee also proposed a management protocol to drive a component to-be-updated into a quiescent state. The basic idea is to passivate all components that directly or indirectly depend on it. For our example, to make Auth quiescent, we have to passivate both Portal and Proc, in addition to Auth itself.

This approach is relatively easy to implement and thus widely adopted, because the dependence relation between components is defined by the static configuration of the system. However using quiescence as the criterion for safe dynamic update may cause significant disruption to the normal service of the system under update, especially when indirect dependences between interactions are considered.

A closer look at our example can reveal that, at time A, it is actually safe to update Auth. This is because the old Auth has not been used yet and T_0 does not mind to use the new Auth. Similarly it should also be safe to update Auth at time D. This indicates there is large room to relax the quiescence criterion to reduce disruption.

To this end, Vandewoude *et al.* proposed the concept of *tranquillity* [9], as a low-disruptive alternative to quiescence.

Definition 3 (Tranquillity). *A node is tranquil if:*

1. *It is not currently engaged in an interaction that it initiated;*

---

[11] In their paper [3], Kramer and Magee used the term *transaction* to mean "an exchange of information between *two* and *only two* nodes", which was different from our use of the term. To avoid confusion, we rename it to *interaction* in Definition 2. This also applies for Definition 3 below.

2. It will not initiate new interactions;

3. It is not actively processing a request;

4. None of its adjacent nodes are engaged in an interaction in which it has both already participated and might still participate in the future.

For our example, Auth is tranquil at both time A and time D. Note that, according to Definition 3 Auth is also tranquil at time C, because for its adjacent node Portal the interaction has already finished, and for Proc the interaction has not begun yet. The criterion does not consider the indirect relation between the two interactions.

Vandewoude *et al.* proposed to use tranquility as a sufficient condition for safe dynamic update. However, this is based on the assumption that there exists no dependence between nonadjacent nodes. The authors justified this assumption with the black-box principle of components that the behavior of a nonadjacent node should be transparent to the current node. That is, in our term, a sub-transaction of a sub-transaction would not be considered as a part of the whole distributed transaction.

However, as evidenced by our example, this assumption may not hold in many cases. In our example, Auth does satisfy the black-box principle as the encryption and decryption algorithms are completely transparent to other components. Nevertheless, when dynamic updates are taken into account, potential indirect dependences must be considered. In fact, as discussed above, dynamic update of Auth at time C is unsafe.

Having said that, the idea of tranquility did contribute an important insight for lowering disruption. When deciding the part of the system that could be affected by the dynamic update, the dynamic progress of transactions need to be taken into account to reduce the conservativeness of static dependences. Next we leverage this observation to develop a new criterion that is low-disruptive but safe.

3.3   Version Consistency

Aforementioned criteria are directly specified on the status of the component to-be-updated. To reduce the unnecessary conservativeness without sacrificing safety, we need to work at a finer-grained level, *i.e.*, to consider the well-behavedness of transactions, instead of components. This leads to the notion of version consistency [10, 28].

Definition 4 (Version Consistency). *In a CBDS a transaction T is version consistent with respect to a dynamic update of component C to its new version C', if there do not exist two transactions $T_1, T_2 \in ext(T)$ such that T_1 is hosted by C and T_2 is hosted by C'. A dynamic update of component C is version consistent if it happens when C is idle and all the transactions in the system are kept version consistent.*

Version consistency is stronger than tranquility in that it takes indirect dependences between transactions into account. Given the consistency and isolation of transactions that a reasonable CBDS must provide, version consistency is sufficient for the safety of dynamic update as defined in Definition 1.

Proposition 4 (Sufficiency of version consistency). *A dynamic update of component C in a CBDS is safe if it is version consistent.*

For our example, the update of Auth at time A is version consistent, although at this time transaction T_0 has already begun on Portal. This is because all transactions in $ext(T_0)$ will be served as if the update happened before they all began. Similarly, the update at time D is also version consistent, because all transactions in $ext(T_0)$ will be served as if the update happened after they all ended. However, the update at time C is not version consistent, because T_1 is served by the old version Auth but T_3 by the new version, and both T_1 and T_3 belong to $ext(T_0)$.

This example illustrates that version consistency is more accurate than quiescence and tranquility. However, unlike quiescence and tranquility, version consistency cannot be directly checked at the to-be-updated component because it is a non-local property that depends on the progressing of distributed transactions in the system. Further means of identifying some locally checkable condition that can ensure the version consistency of dynamic updates is needed.

3.4   Dynamic Dependences

The static edge from component Portal to Auth in Fig. 11 indicates the *possibility* that a transaction running on the former may depend on the service of the latter. However, this possibility is not necessarily the reality at all time. A more accurate characterization of the dependence at runtime with consideration of the actual transactions is needed. The challenge here is that how can we know when the possible dependence becomes real—after all the behavior of transactions cannot be fully predicted.

To this end, future edges and past edges are introduced to represent *dynamic dependences* between components at runtime. A *future edge* from component C_1 to component C_2, labelled with the identifier of a root transaction T, represents that, due to the task of T, C_1 *may* initiate a sub-transaction on C_2 in the future. Symmetrically, a *past edge* from C_1 to C_2, labelled with T, represents that, due to the task of T, C_1 *might* have initiated a sub-transaction on C_2 in the past. A double loop edge on a component C, also labelled with the identifier of a root transaction T, represents that there is a transaction $T' \in ext(T)$ currently hosted by C. It should be understood as both a future edge and a past edge entering the node itself.

For example, in Fig. 13a, the future edge 1 from Portal to Auth, whose label T_0 is omitted, indicates that Portal may use Auth in the future to serve T_0. The past edge 5 in Fig. 13c says that Portal might have used Auth before. The double loop edge on Auth in Fig. 13b means that at this time there is a transaction belonging to $ext(T_0)$ running on it.

Note that future and past edges are actually conservative estimations of dynamic dependences. For our example, it is allowed that Portal will never use

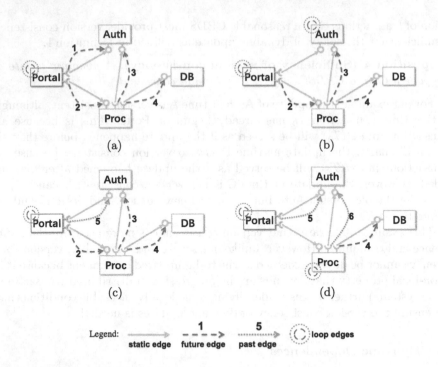

Fig. 13. Dynamic dependence management

Auth in the future although the above-mentioned future edge 1 exists. However, the absence of such an edge, as depicted in Fig. 13b says that definitely Portal will not initiate sub-transaction on Auth for T_0 any more in the future. Similarly, it is allowed that Portal didn't use Auth in reality although past edge 5 exists in Fig. 13c, but the absence of such an edge in Fig. 13a guarantees that Portal has never used Auth before. The same conservativeness also applies to double loop edges.

With these edges properly maintained according to the above constraints at runtime, we can identify a locally checkable condition that is sufficient for version consistency.

Definition 5 (Freeness). *A component C is said to be free of dependences with respect to a root transaction T if there does not exist a pair of T-labelled future/past edges entering C. C is said to be free in a system if it is free with respect to all the transactions in the system.*

For our example, the four configurations (a)–(d) shown in Fig. 13 correspond to the four time points A-D in Fig. 12, respectively. Auth is free in Fig. 13a as there is no past edge entering it. This means that, with respect to T_0, Auth can be safely updated at time A because it has not been used by T_0 yet. Similarly, Auth is free and can be safely updated at time D, because it will not be used by T_0 any more. However, Fig. 13c shows that Auth is not free at time C, as there exist both a future edge and a past edge entering it. This means Auth has been used by $ext(T_0)$ in the past *and* will be used in the future. The double loop edge on Auth in Fig. 13b trivially falsify its freeness.

This example demonstrates the intuition behind the sufficiency of freeness as a condition for version consistent update, for which a proof is given in [10].

Proposition 5 (Sufficiency of freeness). *A dynamic update of a component C in a CBDS is version consistent if it happens when C is free in the system.*

3.5   ConUp: Efficient Implementation of Version Consistency

Compared to the criterion of quiescence, version consistency, supported by the dynamic dependence management framework, allows for more timely and less disruptive dynamic update without sacrificing its safety. However, the real gain of efficiency is largely determined by the accuracy of dynamic dependence estimation and the overhead introduced to maintain the dynamic edges.

ConUp provides an efficient implementation of the version consistency approach [28]. It is a distributed component platform built on top of the Apache Tuscany[12] reference implementation for Service Component Architecture[13] component model.

First, ConUp implements the distributed algorithm given in [10] to establish and remove future and past edges at runtime. To make dynamic updates timely and low-disruptive, ConUp tries to minimize the conservativeness of the estimation of dependence embodied in the dynamic edges. The earlier the future edges are removed, the less dependences estimated. Similarly, the later the better past edges are added. ConUp only sets up a past edge at the end of a sub-transaction. For future edges, they can be set up at the beginning of the first sub-transaction of the root transaction. However, the more important problem is when they can be safely removed. To this end, ConUp automates the estimation of future behavior of transactions through some control-flow analysis and load-time instrumentation [27]. Experiments showed that this lightweight technique provided satisfactory accuracy [27,28].

Second, ConUp supports different strategies to achieve the freeness of to-be-updated component. In addition to waiting for freeness to manifest itself (WF), ConUp can also drive the to-be-updated component into a free state by temporally blocking the progress of some transactions (BF), or by letting the new version component running concurrently with the old version (CV). The WF strategy does not introduce disruption other than the overhead of maintaining dynamic edges, but it cannot guarantee to achieve freeness timely. On the contrary, the BF strategy normally achieves freeness timely, but may have some disruption due to the temporal blocking of some transactions. The CV strategy, when applicable, is the best choice because it provides both timeliness and low-disruption.

---

[12] http://tuscany.apache.org/.
[13] http://www.oasis-opencsa.org/sca.

Finally, ConUp realizes an on-demand mechanism for the management of dynamic edges. The dynamic edges are not maintained at normal execution of the system. Once a dynamic update request is received, ConUp starts to set up future and past edges and makes the configuration valid in a short time. With this mechanism ConUp introduces no overhead when there is no request for dynamic update.

Evaluation experiments with a third-party application running on ConUp showed that [28], with the criterion of tranquility, a significant portion (5–10%) of dynamic component updates could be inconsistent, while both the quiescence and the version consistency criteria were safe. Nevertheless, version consistency significantly outperformed quiescence in terms of timeliness and disruption [28].

4   Instance Migration of Workflow Processes

Workflow processes, or simply processes, are flow-oriented high-level software artifacts widely used in business process management, service-oriented applications and scientific computing/cloud computing applications [36]. To implement a business procedure, a process orchestrates services of self-contained components by specifying the control-flow and data-flow between them. Just like other software artifacts, processes are prone to revisions caused by requirement evolutions and environment changes.

The need for dynamic update support can be more evident for workflow processes than other software applications. The reason is that, process instances are often long-running and may involve significant amount of human effort and computing resources. So, naively withdrawing running instances and restarting them in the new process version would be expensive or even unacceptable. At the same time, letting running instances untouched and only applying changes to newly started instances would also be undesirable, because the existing instances could not enjoy the benefits of the new version. More importantly, sometimes the regulations will force the update of running instances to comply with the updated policies. In practice it is not rare that workflow administrators are forced to handle the issue manually in a case-by-case way, *i.e.*, to specify an *ad hoc* process definition for each of the running instances.

Automatic support for flexible and safe instance migration has been extensively studied in the literature [37–40]. However, existing approaches are often too conservative to allow many actually safe instances to migrate. In this section we will briefly review the representative ideas of these approaches and discuss our recent work on a more relaxed criterion for safe instance migration [30].

4.1   The Problem of Instance Migration

Let's first define workflow process and instance migration for process update, following the notations used in [30].

Definition 6 (Workflow process). *A data-aware workflow process*[14] *is defined with a five-tuple* $P = (N, F, D, I, O)$, *where*

- *N is the set of activities, including structured activities such as XOR-split, XOR-join, AND-split, and AND-join.*
- *F is the flow relation representing activity orders.*
- *D is the set of variables defined or used in P.*
- *I and O are functions assigning input and output variables to each activity in N.*

Definition 7 (Process instance and instance migration).

- *A running instance I of process P is defined by P and a runtime state* s_I. s_I *not only represents the current control-flow state that specifies the next activities to be executed, but also assigns values to the variables in P.*
- *A migration of a running instance I from the old process version P to a new version* P' *is defined as a quadruple* (P, P', s_I, S) *where S is a state mapping such that* $S(s_I)$ *is a well-formed state of* P'.

Definition 6 abstracts executable workflow process languages such as YAWL [41], WS-BPEL [42] and BPMN 2.0 [43], which are Turing-complete, as they all provide general-purpose programming constructs such as loops and conditions. So the undecidability result of Proposition 1 also applies to the validity of dynamic update of processes.

Proposition 6 (Undecidability of instance migration validity). *The validity of an arbitrary instance migration* (P, P', s_I, S), *which means whether* $S(s_I)$ *is a reachable state of* P', *is undecidable.*

Note that even a valid migration cannot guarantee the correctness of the instance after update. It just ensures that the migrated instance can continue with the updated process definition. At the same time, reasonable constraints on the state s_I and the state mapping S are often needed—after all, not all states of running instance I are suitable for migration, and not all reachable states of P' are appropriate target states.

The crux of supporting instance migration is to strike a balance between allowing as many as possible running instances to be migrated and providing as strong as possible guarantees, so that users can be confident that their business is properly handled during and after the update.

---

[14] The meaning of *process* in the community of business process management and workflow management is different from its use in programming language and operating system communities. The former is a static concept just like a program or a schema, whose runtime instance is corresponding to the latter use of the term.

4.2   An Example Scenario of Process Update

Before discussing different approaches to instance migration, we first introduce an illustrative example of process update. The UML activity diagram depicted in Fig. 14a shows a WS-BPEL process of Indonesian tour booking used in a tour agency in China. The input and output of each activity of the process are also depicted in the figure[15]. Upon receiving a tour request from the customer (A_1 in Fig. 14a), an execution instance of the process is created. It first invokes the passport service to apply a passport for the customer (A_2). Based on the passport information and the customer's tour request, the WS-BPEL process then invokes the visa service to apply a visa for the customer (A_3). Next, it concurrently books a flight (A_4) and a hotel (A_5) for the customer. After all these steps are done, it combines these results together (A_6) which are finally sent back to the customer (A_7).

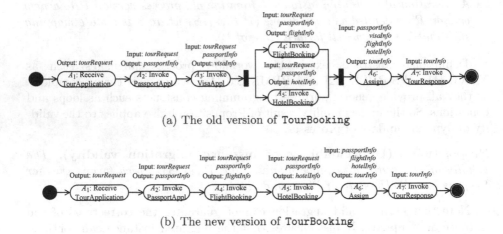

(a) The old version of `TourBooking`

(b) The new version of `TourBooking`

Fig. 14. An update of WS-BPEL process `TourBooking`

Since Jan 1, 2015, the Indonesia government allows Chinese tourists to travel to the county free of visa. In addition, the tour agency finds that hotel services are often correlated with flight services in the aspect of QoS (i.e., cost). For example, if a customer chooses the Lion Air, there will be a discount if she or he books certain hotels in Indonesia. Taking these issues into account, the tour agency revises the WS-BPEL process for booking the tour. Figure 14b depicts the revised process.

The old version process in Fig. 14a and the new version in Fig. 14b are referred to as P_1 and P_2, respectively. Suppose that there is an instance I of P_1. Its trace, *i.e.*, the sequence of completed activities, and the current state are denoted by

---

[15] This is a simplified version of the running example used in [30], to which interested readers are referred for more comprehensive process definition and explanations.

$\sigma = A_1 A_2 A_3 A_5 A_4$ and s, respectively. Suppose that at this moment, the new version of the process is deployed. The customer served by I could be annoyed if she or he was forced to redo the booking process. Appropriate instance migration is needed to cope with the dynamic process evolution. The question here is how to decide whether the migration of I from P_1 to P_2 is valid or not.

4.3   Criteria for Instance Migration

In the literature, there is abundant research work on process evolution and instance migration, and comprehensive surveys such as [44] and [37] also exist. Here we are not going to review them systematically, but discuss several representative criteria for instance migration and their limitations, to pave the way for introducing the dependence analysis-based approach later in Sect. 4.4.

Existing approaches to instance migration can be roughly classified into two categories: process-based and instance-based. Process-based approaches define the migration criteria from the perspective of process structures before and after change, while instance-based approaches define their criteria based on execution traces of running instances.

A classic process-based approach proposed by van der Aalst and Basten is based on the concept of workflow inheritance [38]. By restricting process changes to inheritance-preserving ones, this approach guarantees that instance migrations can be carried out without anomalies from the control-flow perspective.

Definition 8 (Inheritance of workflow). *Process P is considered a subclass of process Q if it is not possible to distinguish the behaviors of P and Q when*

(protocol inheritance) *only activities of P that are also present in Q are executed; or*

(projection inheritance) *arbitrary activities of P are executed, but only the effects of activities that are also present in Q are taken into account.*

For our example, unfortunately, there is no inheritance relation between P_1 and P_2 in Fig. 14, because A_3 cannot be hidden, and, the control-flow relation between A_4 and A_5 has been changed.

It is not difficult to see that process-based approaches tend to be over conservative because they restrict the change of process. It is often the case that, although the change of process definition is wild, the instance to-be-migrated happens to be acceptable for the new process version because, for example, the trace of the instance has not involved any changed part of the process yet.

This observation underpins the instance-based approaches. Casati *et al.* proposed a notion of compatibility [40] between the trace of the instance to be migrated and the new process version.

Definition 9 (Compatibility of trace replaying). *A trace σ of an instance I of process P is compatible with a new process version P' if there exists an execution of P' such that σ is a prefix of the execution.*

Intuitively, if σ is compatible with P', I can also be seen as an instance of P', and thus can naturally continue in P'.

For our example, if only instances with compatible traces are allowed to migrate, I will be unqualified because $\sigma = A_1 A_2 A_3 A_5 A_4$ cannot be replayed in P_2. Obviously this criterion is too stringent. To mitigate this problem, Casati *et al.* also proposed that I undergone some modifications to make it suitable for migration. For instance, one can rollback or compensate some activities to make the trace compatible with the new process version. In the worst case the instance would be rolled back to the beginning. In our example, one needs to roll back A_4, A_5 and A_3 to make σ compatible with P_2.

The approach proposed by Ryu *et al.* [39] is even more restrictive. In addition to requiring the above (backward) compatibility, the approach also requires that all possible *future* executions from current state to the final state in the old process P are also supported by the new process P'. The rationale is to guarantee the success of interactions with external clients.

An improvement of the trace replaying approach is to tolerate the deletion of activities from the old process definition, and to ignore past loop iterations [45]. With this improvement, the trace σ in our example will be reduced to $\sigma' = A_1 A_2 A_5 A_4$. Unfortunately it still cannot be replayed in P_2, and I will also fail to be migrated.

On the other hand, we observe that the projection of the I's state s to D_2 corresponds to a reachable state of P_2. Therefore, the migration of I from P_1 to P_2 should be allowed. This indicates that we need a more relaxed criterion.

4.4   Instance Migration Based on Dependence Analysis

Trace replaying requires that activities executed in a trace σ must be able to appear in the same order in the new process version. This is often unnecessarily conservative because activities can be freely re-ordered if there is neither control dependence nor data dependence between them. With this observation, Song *et al.* relaxed the criterion and proposed a dependence analysis-based technique to decide the migratability of running instances [30].

In this approach, an instance dependence graph (IDG) is first constructed to capture the control dependences and data dependences between the activities appearing in the trace of the to-be-migrated instance. This is done with standard control-flow and data-flow analysis methods [46], and the result is a directed acyclic graph[16].

Figure 15a presents the IDG of an instance of the TourBooking process P_1, with a trace $\sigma = A_1 A_2 A_3 A_5 A_4$. We can see from the graph that A_3 depends on A_2, which in turn depends on A_1, and both A_5 and A_4 depend on A_1 and A_2 because of the data dependences caused by the relations between the input and output variables of these activities.

---

[16] It must be acyclic because multiple occurrences of a same activity in σ are modeled as different nodes in the graph.

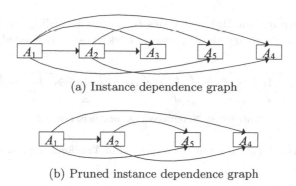

(a) Instance dependence graph

(b) Pruned instance dependence graph

Fig. 15. IDG and PIDG of process `TourBooking`

The second step is to remove from the IDG those activities that do not affect the state mapping of the migration. The idea is that, for each variable effective at the the end of σ in P_1 and also used in P_2, a backward slicing is carried out to find out all activities in σ that have direct or indirect impact on the value of the variable. An activity can be removed if it does not appear in any such slice. The result is called a pruned instance dependence graph (PIDG). With this step, the approach can reasonably handle cases that some activities appears in P_1 but are removed from P_2. Note that the pruning carefully preserves the integrity of the instance state (variables).

For our example, Fig. 15b is the pruned version of the IDG in Fig. 15a. Activity A_3 is not present in P_2, but this fact does not directly lead to its removal from the IDG. It is removed because it contributes nothing to the state at the end of σ from the perspective of P_2 – the variable *visaInfo* produced by A_3 is not used in P_2 any longer. Other activities are preserved because they all contribute to the state encoded by the variables *passportInfo*, *flightInfo* and *hotelInfo*, directly or indirectly.

The final step is to replay the PIDG on the new process version. Activities can be replayed in any order consistent with the partial order defined by the PIDG. Different from trace replaying, activities without direct or indirect edges between them are allowed to be in arbitrary order. Once the replay is successful, the instance is considered migratable, and the target state is also obtained.

Proposition 7 states the soundness of this criterion.

Proposition 7 (Validity of dependence-based migration). *Given two process versions P, P', and an instance I of P, whose current state and completed trace are s and σ, respectively, if there exists a topological ordering ρ of the activities in the PIDG of σ such that ρ can be replayed in P', then the migration of I from P to P' is valid.*

In implementation, it is unnecessary to exhaust all topological orderings of the PIDG of an instance to deny its migratability. The reason is that the order of independent activities does not affect the result state. In the procedure of replaying, if there are multiple activities to choose according to the PIDG and P_2, one can make arbitrary choice, and no backtracking is needed.

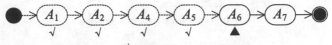

Activity status: √: replayed; ▲: next to be executed

Fig. 16. Target state of the migration of `TourBooking` instance

Returning to our example, Fig. 16 shows the result of replaying the PIDG in Fig. 15b on the process P_2 depicted in Fig. 14b. A_1 and A_2 are first replayed according to the PIDG and P_2. Then A_4 is chosen before A_5 according to P_2, although they are independent with each other in the PIDG. Finally we arrive at A_6, the target state after migration.

This simple example indicates that the dependence analysis-based approach is more relaxed than trace replaying as it allows more instance to migrate. Comprehensive experimental evaluations and case studies presented in [30] further confirmed this.

5 Conclusion

Situated in increasingly open and dynamic environment, and evolving at an accelerating pace, software needs to be *softer* and can be updated on the fly. This chapter gives a tutorial overview of several DSU approaches at the code level, the component level, and the workflow process level. The common theme of these approaches is the balance between the requirements of safety, efficiency and ease-of-use.

Although DSU is widely desired and has attracted a lot of research, its adoption is still limited in practice. The biggest obstacle, we believe, is still the risk that a dynamic update needs to take. Existing DSU approaches do provide some generic safety guarantees such as type safety and workflow validity, but they are often insufficient to ensure the application-level correctness of the ongoing business, especially when the environment and users are taken into account. Further research efforts on the verification and validation of DSU are needed. Notably, recent work on systematic testing for DSU safety [47] and controller synthesis according to formal specifications [12] provides a start point for the research.

Acknowledgement. We are grateful to Luciano Baresi, Carlo Ghezzi, Hans-Arno Jacobsen, Jian Lü, Valerio Panzica La Manna and other co-authors for their collaboration in previous work on dynamic software update. In addition, Xiaoxing Ma would like to thank his colleagues Yu Huang and Chang Xu whose work on environment perception were also discussed at SETSS 2017. Our work on DSU was supported by the National 973 Program of China (Grant No. 2015CB352202), the National Natural Science Foundation of China (Grant Nos. 61690204, 61761136003, 61472177), and the Collaborative Innovation Center of Novel Software Technology and Industrialization.

References

1. Olsson, H.H., Alahyari, H., Bosch, J.: Climbing the "stairway to heaven" - a multiple-case study exploring barriers in the transition from agile development towards continuous deployment of software. In: Proceedings of the 38th Euromicro Conference on Software Engineering and Advanced Applications (SEAA 2012), pp. 392–399, September 2012
2. Fabry, R.S.: How to design a system in which modules can be changed on the fly. In: Proceedings of the 2nd International Conference on Software Engineering, pp. 470–476 (1976)
3. Kramer, J., Magee, J.: The evolving philosophers problem: dynamic change management. IEEE Trans. Softw. Eng. 16(11), 1293–1306 (1990)
4. Hicks, M., Nettles, S.: Dynamic software updating. ACM Trans. Program. Lang. Syst. 27(6), 1049–1096 (2005)
5. Bennett, K.H., Rajlich, V.T.: Software maintenance and evolution: a roadmap. In: Proceedings of the Conference on the Future of Software Engineering. ICSE 2000, pp. 73–87. ACM, New York (2000)
6. Rajlich, V.: Software evolution and maintenance. In: Proceedings of the on Future of Software Engineering. FOSE 2014, pp. 133–144. ACM, New York (2014)
7. Daley, R.C., Dennis, J.B.: Virtual memory, processes, and sharing in MULTICS. Commun. ACM 11(5), 306–312 (1968)
8. Ajmani, S., Liskov, B., Shrira, L.: Modular software upgrades for distributed systems. In: Thomas, D. (ed.) ECOOP 2006, vol. 4067, pp. 452–476. Springer, Heidelberg (2006). https://doi.org/10.1007/11785477_26
9. Vandewoude, Y., Ebraert, P., Berbers, Y., D'Hondt, T.: Tranquility: a low disruptive alternative to quiescence for ensuring safe dynamic updates. IEEE Trans. Softw. Eng. 33(12), 856–868 (2007)
10. Ma, X., Baresi, L., Ghezzi, C., Panzica La Manna, V., Lu, J.: Version-consistent dynamic reconfiguration of component-based distributed systems. In: Proceedings of the 19th ACM SIGSOFT Symposium and the 13th European Conference on Foundations of Software Engineering. ESEC/FSE 2011, pp. 245–255. ACM, New York (2011)
11. Ghezzi, C., Greenyer, J., La Manna, V.P.: Synthesizing dynamically updating controllers from changes in scenario-based specifications. In: Proceedings of the 7th International Symposium on Software Engineering for Adaptive and Self-Managing Systems. SEAMS 2012, pp. 145–154. IEEE Press, Piscataway (2012)
12. Nahabedian, L., et al.: Assured and correct dynamic update of controllers. In: Proceedings of the 11th International Symposium on Software Engineering for Adaptive and Self-Managing Systems. SEAMS 2016, pp. 96–107. ACM, New York(2016)
13. Neamtiu, I., Hicks, M.: Safe and timely updates to multi-threaded programs. In: Proceedings of the ACM SIGPLAN Conference on Programming Language Design and Implementation, pp. 13–24 (2009)
14. Subramanian, S., Hicks, M., McKinley, K.S.: Dynamic software updates: a VM-centric approach. In: Proceedings of the ACM SIGPLAN Conference on Programming Language Design and Implementation, pp. 1–12 (2009)
15. Hayden, C.M., Smith, E.K., Denchev, M., Hicks, M., Foster, J.S.: Kitsune: efficient, general-purpose dynamic software updating for C. In: Proceedings of the ACM International Conference on Object Oriented Programming Systems Languages and Applications, pp. 249–264 (2012)

16. Würthinger, T., Wimmer, C., Stadler, L.: Unrestricted and safe dynamic code evolution for Java. Sci. Comput. Program. **78**(5), 481–498 (2013)
17. Pina, L., Veiga, L., Hicks, M.: Rubah: DSU for Java on a stock JVM. In: Proceedings of the 2014 International Conference on Object Oriented Programming Systems Languages Applications, pp. 103–119 (2014)
18. Gu, T., et al.: Low-disruptive dynamic updating of Java applications. Inf. Softw. Technol. **56**(9), 1086–1098 (2014). Special Sections from "Asia-Pacific Software Engineering Conference (APSEC), 2012" and "Software Product Line conference (SPLC), 2012"
19. Baumann, A., et al.: Providing dynamic update in an operating system. In: ATEC 2005: Proceedings of the Annual Conference on USENIX Annual Technical Conference, p. 32. USENIX Association, Berkeley (2005)
20. Arnold, J., Kaashoek, M.F.: Ksplice: automatic rebootless kernel updates. In: Proceedings of the 4th ACM European Conference on Computer Systems. EuroSys 2009, pp. 187–198. ACM, New York (2009)
21. Makris, K., Bazzi, R.A.: Immediate multi-threaded dynamic software updates using stack reconstruction. In: Proceedings of the 2009 Conference on USENIX Annual Technical Conference. USENIX 2009, p. 31. USENIX Association, Berkeley (2009)
22. Kashyap, S., Min, C., Lee, B., Kim, T., Emelyanov, P.: Instant OS updates via userspace checkpoint-and-restart. In: USENIX Annual Technical Conference (USENIX ATC 16), Denver, CO, pp. 605–619. USENIX Association (2016)
23. Fowler, M.: Blue-green deployment, March 2010. https://martinfowler.com/bliki/BlueGreenDeployment.html. Accessed 1 Feb 2018
24. Gu, T., Sun, C., Ma, X., Lü, J., Su, Z.: Automatic runtime recovery via error handler synthesis. In: Proceedings of the 31st IEEE/ACM International Conference on Automated Software Engineering. ASE 2016, pp. 684–695. ACM, New York (2016)
25. Gu, T., Zhao, Z., Ma, X., Xu, C., Cao, C., Lü, J.: Improving reliability of dynamic software updating using runtime recovery. In: 23rd Asia-Pacific Software Engineering Conference (APSEC 2016), pp. 257–264, December 2016
26. Gu, T., Ma, X., Xu, C., Jiang, Y., Cao, C., Lü, J.: Synthesizing object transformation for dynamic software updating. In: Proceedings of the 39th International Conference on Software Engineering Companion. ICSE-C 2017, pp. 336–338. IEEE Press, Piscataway (2017)
27. Su, P., Cao, C., Ma, X., Lü, J.: Automated management of dynamic component dependency for runtime system reconfiguration. In: Proceedings of the 20th Asia-Pacific Software Engineering Conference (APSEC 2013) (2013)
28. Baresi, L., Ghezzi, C., Ma, X., Panzica La Manna, V.: Efficient dynamic updates of distributed components through version consistency. IEEE Trans. Softw. Eng. **43**(4), 340–358 (2017)
29. Song, W., Ma, X., Hu, H., Zou, Y., Zhang, G.: Migration validity of WS-BPEL instances revisited. In: 2013 IEEE 16th International Conference on Computational Science and Engineering, pp. 1013–1020, December 2013
30. Song, W., Ma, X., Jacobsen, H.A.: Instance migration validity for dynamic evolution of data-aware processes. IEEE Trans. Softw. Eng. (2018, accepted, to appear)
31. Gupta, D., Jalote, P., Barua, G.: A formal framework for on-line software version change. IEEE Trans. Softw. Eng. **22**(2), 120–131 (1996)
32. Gu, T.: On dynamic updating of Java programs. Ph.D. thesis, Nanjing University, China (2017)

33. Magill, S., Hicks, M., Subramanian, S., McKinley, K.S.: Automating object transformations for dynamic software updating. In: Proceedings of the ACM International Conference on Object Oriented Programming Systems Languages and Applications, pp. 265–280 (2012)

34. Buban, G., et al.: Patching of in-use functions on a running computer system, US Patent App. 10/307,902, 3 June 2004

35. Open Source Software Project: kpatch: dynamic kernel patching. https://github.com/dynup/kpatch (2016). Accessed 07 July 2016

36. Dumas, M., van der Aalst, W.M., ter Hofstede, A.H.: Process-Aware Information Systems: Bridging People and Software Through Process Technology. Wiley, New York (2005)

37. Rinderle, S., Reichert, M., Dadam, P.: Correctness criteria for dynamic changes in workflow systems: a survey. Data Knowl. Eng. **50**(1), 9–34 (2004)

38. van der Aalst, W., Basten, T.: Inheritance of workflows: an approach to tackling problems related to change. Theor. Comput. Sci. **270**(1), 125–203 (2002)

39. Ryu, S.H., Casati, F., Skogsrud, H., Benatallah, B., Saint-Paul, R.: Supporting the dynamic evolution of web service protocols in service-oriented architectures. ACM Trans. Web **2**(2), 13:1–13:46 (2008)

40. Casati, F., Ceri, S., Pernici, B., Pozzi, G.: Workflow evolution. Data Knowl. Eng. **24**(3), 211–238 (1998)

41. van der Aalst, W., ter Hofstede, A.: YAWL: yet another workflow language. Inf. Syst. **30**(4), 245–275 (2005)

42. Alves, A., et al.: Web services business process execution language version 2.0. OASIS Standard, April 2007

43. Rademakers, T.: Activiti in action: executable business processes in BPMN 2.0. Manning Publications Co., Greenwich (2012)

44. Song, W., Jacobsen, H.A.: Static and dynamic process change. IEEE Trans. Serv. Comput. **11**(1), 215–231 (2018)

45. Rinderle-Ma, S., Reichert, M., Weber, B.: Relaxed compliance notions in adaptive process management systems. In: Li, Q., Spaccapietra, S., Yu, E., Olivé, A. (eds.) ER 2008, vol. 5231, pp. 232–247. Springer, Heidelberg (2008). https://doi.org/10.1007/978-3-540-87877-3_18

46. Ferrante, J., Ottenstein, K.J., Warren, J.D.: The program dependence graph and its use in optimization. ACM Trans. Program. Lang. Syst. **9**(3), 319–349 (1987)

47. Hayden, C., Smith, E., Hardisty, E., Hicks, M., Foster, J.: Evaluating dynamic software update safety using systematic testing. IEEE Trans. Softw. Eng. **38**(6), 1340–1354 (2012)

Challenges for Formal Semantic Description: Responses from the Main Approaches

Cliff B. Jones[✉][iD] and Troy K. Astarte[iD]

School of Computing, Newcastle University, Newcastle upon Tyne NE4 5TG, UK
cliff.jones@ncl.ac.uk

Abstract. Although there are thousands of programming languages, most of them share common features. This paper reviews some key underlying language concepts and the challenges they present to the task of formally describing language semantics. The responses to these challenges in operational, axiomatic and denotational approaches to semantic description are reviewed. There are interesting overlaps between these responses; similarities are exposed even where accidental notational conventions disguise them so that essential differences can be pinpointed. Depending on the objectives of writing a formal semantic description of a language, one or other approach might be considered the best choice. An argument is made for increasing the use of formal semantics in language design and here it is suggested that the operational approach is the most viable for a complete language description.

1 Introduction

There are a number of different approaches to recording formal descriptions of the semantics of programming languages, but most can be placed into one of three styles: operational, denotational, or axiomatic. Any approach to describing semantics formally must find ways to tackle a set of challenges derived from common features in programming languages, such as nested blocks or concurrency. In this paper, an initially simple illustrative language is described using all three approaches and remarks are made about how they address the particular challenges. It is interesting to note the degrees of similarity present given the apparent conceptual differences between approaches.

The paper begins by setting out some reasons for considering semantics and introducing the kernel of the example language. Simple applicative languages are considered first and some conclusions are drawn that are relevant to imperative languages. Throughout the paper, new features for the example language are considered and the formal semantic descriptions of these features are discussed. Finally, a concurrent, object-oriented language is introduced as a vehicle to illustrate the combination of all the features covered; an operational semantics for such a language is outlined.

© Springer Nature Switzerland AG 2018
J. P. Bowen et al. (Eds.): SETSS 2017, LNCS 11174, pp. 176–217, 2018.
https://doi.org/10.1007/978-3-030-02928-9_6

This is not primarily intended to be a historical paper; readers interested in such a view of formal semantics could read [AJ18] which examines four early semantic descriptions of ALGOL 60 and draws some conclusions. A more complete treatment of the history of programming language semantics is presented in Astarte's PhD thesis [Ast19]. Nor is the objective here to provide a tutorial on semantic description formalisms; the reader is assumed to have some previous contact with the subject. The aim here is to look beyond the trivial language features that are easily handled by any formal approach.

1.1   Why Describe Semantics Formally

It is worth beginning by reviewing the reasons for describing the semantics of programming languages. Unlike natural languages, programming languages are formal objects which means they follow a fixed (and relatively small) set of rules that govern their structure and behaviour.

It is essential that the different users of a language, from programmers through standard writers to compiler creators, all share a precise understanding of these rules.[1] Natural language can be (and is) used for this purpose, but words are always ambiguous and can all too easily lead to contradictions or omissions. Therefore, formality is frequently utilised—and even in natural language descriptions, the careful wording required ultimately results in formality of approach regardless of notation [Tur09]. Another advantage to the use of formalism is that it can help ensure completeness: if there is a form to be followed for every language construct, the chances of accidentally omitting part of a language is significantly lowered.

This is not to suggest that a formal description always defines one unique result for a program in a language: it is often necessary to leave certain parts of the description undefined in order to allow for implementation specifics and non-determinism at run time. Carefully delineating these areas of non-definition is, however, essential.

In addition to being formal, a useful programming language semantics must also be *tractable*—it must enable proofs to be made about the language itself, about the correctness of implementations of the language and about programs written in the language [Bur66]. Ideally, a good semantics allows the proof of deep properties, some of which are relied upon in compiler optimisation. Different approaches to semantics tend to make different properties easier to prove than others [Gor75].

Arguably an even more important use of formal semantics is in the design of programming languages: there exist thousands of programming languages, most of which are sadly lamentable;[2] even the best often exhibit *feature interaction*

---

[1] See, for example, the work of the IBM Laboratory Vienna on producing formal definitions of PL/I for use in compiler writing, such as [BBH+74, Jon76].

[2] In the paper 'Hints of Programming Language Design', Tony Hoare had the following to say in conclusion: "This paper has given many practical hints on how *not* to design a programming language. It has even suggested that many recent languages have followed these hints" [Hoa73].

where features that are useful and straightforward when taken separately lead to incomprehensible behaviour when combined. The use of a formal semantics during the creation of a language—ideally, before even any syntax is created—can contribute greatly to the simplicity and clarity of the resultant language. Unfortunately, formal semantics has typically been applied *post facto* to extant languages.[3] Arguments for the use of semantics in the design of languages are given in Sect. 7.

The choice of semantic description approach is often motivated by the intended use of the semantics. Received wisdom generally holds that operational semantics is most useful to compiler writers, denotational to the language designer and axiomatic semantics in program verification. However, some writers have pointed out that the distinction is not always as clear cut as this [Ame89].

Of course, the challenge of describing the semantics of a modern programming language is far greater than for, say, first-order predicate calculus. Researchers have learnt what they can from previous work by logicians and carried these lessons forward: the extensions involved are challenging and interesting.

1.2   Main Approaches

The main focus in this paper is on operational, axiomatic and denotational semantics; Sect. 2 illustrates the differences in these approaches on a core language but it is worth briefly characterising the approaches here.

An operational semantics describes the meaning of a language in terms of an *abstract interpreter* that takes a program and a starting state and computes allowed final states. Typically, the interpreter will be defined in terms of sub-functions for each construct in the language. Ideally, the *states* of the interpreter should be chosen to eschew unnecessary details.

The essence of a denotational semantics is to map a language into some space of mathematically tractable objects. For simple programming languages these objects are mathematical functions from states to states. Denotational descriptions present a series of mappings from program constructs into these functions. A key feature is the notion that the mapping should be *homomorphic*: the function denoted by a program segment should be composed from the denotations of its components.

The previous two approaches both make the notion of state explicit and can thus be categorised as *model-based*. In contrast, property-oriented descriptions attempt to fix semantics without an explicit state.[4] An axiomatic semantics contains axioms and rules of inference that define a set of *judgements*. In Floyd-Hoare semantics of procedural languages, the judgements are triples in which

---

[3] Encouraging exceptions include the Turing programming language [HMRC87], Standard ML [HMT87], and SPARK-Ada [CG90]. Furthermore, formal semantics played an important role in the development of full Ada [BO80]. Formal description was also utilised in the standards for Modula-2 [Woo93] and PL/I [ANS76].

[4] *Algebraic semantics* can also be viewed as property-oriented and is briefly discussed in Sect. 7.1.

the middle component is a text in the language being described; the first and third components are predicates. The interpretation of such a triple is that if the first predicate (the pre condition) is satisfied and the text is executed to termination, then after execution the post condition will be true.

Here the notion of state is only implicit in the meta-variables used within the assertions. Axiomatic semantics is particularly concerned with proving properties of programs and, if an axiomatic specification of a language allows the proving of any true property (and no false property) of a program construct, then the construct is considered fully specified [Pag81]. If every part of the language is specified in this way, then the specification constitutes a semantics of the language. In practice, it turns out to be difficult to fully specify large-scale programming languages purely by axioms.

1.3 Applicative Languages

The majority of this paper is concerned with *imperative* programming languages (as characterised in Sect. 2). There are, however, some interesting semantic description techniques that can be carried over from handling *applicative* languages. Two common challenges are that the languages whose semantics are to be given have an unbounded number of admissible texts and that comprehensibility of the semantic description is a major objective.

One class of applicative programming language is functional programming languages and these – at least if they are *purely* functional – avoid some of the challenges that have to be faced with the semantics of languages that feature assignment-like constructs. Assignments require some model of storage, usually considered as an abstract meta-notion *state*; avoiding assignment allows programs in functional languages to be reasoned about as though they are conventional recursive functions. There might, of course, be a performance penalty in using purely functional languages, but that discussion is beyond the scope of the present paper.

It is important to remember that all programming languages provide a repertoire of basic operators and, crucially, put in the hands of programmers ways to express functions that extend this repertoire. Thus a programmer might write a program that computes factorial using only basic arithmetic operators; more ambitiously, a program for inverting matrices can be written in a language that has no such operator.

A first-order predicate language is a simple and traditional applicative language and discussing how its semantics can be recorded facilitates deriving messages that are taken forward to the subsequent sections of this paper. Starting with purely propositional expressions, a semantic function could be written that recurses through the structure of the expressions,[5] building up the meaning of the expression as a whole by combining the meaning of its parts. Ultimately, this function must rely on an association of the propositional identifiers with

---

[5] This task would be made easier with the use of an abstract syntax, a concept discussed later in this paper.

truth values. As with predicate calculus, there must be a way to determine the meaning of any predicates or functions. It is important to observe that these two sorts of associations remain fixed and can be stored in some form of static *environment*.

There are, of course, other ways of tackling the semantics of logical languages. In an equivalence-based strategy, some operators can be defined in terms of others (e.g. $p \Rightarrow q$ can be defined as $\neg p \vee q$). No matter the strategy used, there must still be a minimum set of basic operators (e.g. the Sheffer stroke).

Classical axiomatisations (such as that in [Men64, Sect. 1.4]) are unintuitive but natural deduction rules like those presented in [Pra65] provide both a semantics and some intuition as to how to reason about expressions in logical languages.

The responses to be carried forward to the review of semantic description techniques for imperative languages are then:

- Environments—what information is stored about identifiers; in what form; and how distinction is made between different denotations e.g. identifier-value and function-definition pairs.
- Fundamental bases of meaning—saying one has, for example, a *Boolean Algebra* doesn't fix (all of) the semantics because multiple models of such algebras exist.
- Understandability of description—as with deduction systems, semantic descriptions should be evaluated for intuition and usability for reasoning.

1.4   A Core Imperative Language

A basic challenge to be faced, even before addressing the semantics of a language, is to delimit the admissible utterances of the language. Although normally presented in two dimensional layout, it is still common to think of programs as strings of characters. Some version of Backus-Naur Form notation is adequate to define the set of (context-free) strings of most programming languages: this is known as *concrete syntax*. However, following Christopher Strachey's advice to "know what you need to say before deciding how to write it down", semantic descriptions can be based instead on an *abstract syntax*. This approach follows John McCarthy's proposal [McC63] although VDM notation is employed below.[6] The advantages of using an abstract syntax over concrete may be less apparent for a small language like the one considered here but for large languages, especially those with multiple syntactic forms of the same semantic construct, the benefits become more apparent. Use of abstract syntax shows concern with the *structure* of the language (rather than its form). The higher level of abstraction meshes nicely with more abstract semantic approaches; however, following tradition, examples of axiomatic semantics below are built around concrete syntax.

---

[6] The use of VDM notation should present the reader with no difficulty: it has been widely used for decades and is the subject of an ISO standard; one useful reference is [Jon90].

Figure 1 contains the abstract syntax of the simple core of the language discussed in this paper. Later sections in the paper add to this core to illustrate more complex language concepts and the challenges inherent in modelling these features.

$$Program :: types : Id \xrightarrow{m} ScalarType$$
$$body : Stmt$$

$$ScalarType = \text{INT} \mid \text{BOOL}$$

$$Stmt = Assign \mid If \mid While \mid Compound \mid \cdots$$

$$Assign :: lhs : Id$$
$$rhs : Expr$$

$$If :: test : Expr$$
$$then : Stmt$$
$$else : Stmt$$

$$While :: test : Expr$$
$$body : Stmt$$

$$Compound :: Stmt^*$$

Fig. 1. Abstract syntax of a core language

Even before getting to the semantic approaches *per se*, it is worth noting that there are differences as to how context-dependent checks (e.g. required consistency between uses and declarations of names) are recorded. These can be handled within semantics (i.e. dynamically), but it is normally more fruitful to handle these issues statically. Such static checks are called *context conditions* after van Wijngaarden *et al.* in the ALGOL 68 Report [vWMPK69]. Various methods for defining these kinds of checks have been developed by van Wijngaarden (two-level grammars), Knuth (attribute grammars [Knu68]), and researchers at the IBM Hursley Laboratory (dynamic syntax [HJ73]); a more thorough study would include [GP99] or [Pie02] on *type theory*. Full exploration of this topic is beyond the scope of the current paper.

Context conditions in the VDM style are generally written as predicates that determine whether an object of the abstract syntax is *well-formed* with respect to some type information. For the language whose abstract syntax is given in Fig. 1, these predicates would have the signature *wf-Construct : Construct × TypeMap* $\rightarrow \mathbb{B}$ and use an abstract *TypeMap* object of the type $Id \xrightarrow{m} ScalarType$ (a finite, constructed, function) that maps identifiers to their types.[7] In this simple case, the *TypeMap* is a direct copy of that in the *Program*. These functions generally check that the types assigned to variables match the variable declaration and

---

[7] The use of the type name *ScalarType* prepares the way for modelling compound types such as arrays below.

that inappropriate types are not used in expressions (for example, in an *If* statement, the *test* part must be of type BOOL). For constructs that contain sub-components, each such component must also be well formed.

2   Imperative (Deterministic) Languages

The identifying feature of an imperative programming language is that it provides statements that change things. What is affected differs between languages: changes might be updating a database or moving the position of part of a robot. Here the discussion focusses on the challenge of modelling assignments to variables but the same principles apply to other kinds of command as long as a suitable abstract model can be created for the target of the changes.

Assignments to variables destroy *referential transparency*: the value associated with an identifier changes during execution; values previous to an assignment are destroyed. Furthermore, the order in which statements are executed becomes important. An imperative program achieves its effect by executing a sequence of assignments; language features such as conditionals and loops merely orchestrate their execution.

As in applicative languages, programs make it possible to compute results that are not directly available as operators of the language. It therefore follows that a subsidiary challenge is to provide tractable ways of reasoning about the meaning of imperative programs whose specifications include operators that are not basic to the language and which achieve their effect using destructive assignments.

2.1   Operational Approach

John McCarthy was one of the first to present an operational approach to defining the semantics of programming languages. In his definition of 'Micro-ALGOL' [McC66], he described the approach as "defining a function ... giving the state ... that results from applying the program ... to the [initial state]". McCarthy was also careful to point out in his earlier paper on the topic [McC63] that this is an *abstract function*, because the language in which it is expressed is more abstract than either the language being described or, say, machine assembler code. This approach to semantics is now commonly referred to as an *abstract interpreter* because it interprets the various constructs of the language under discussion.

The core idea of operational semantics remains the same as when McCarthy first proposed it: meaning is given to a language with an abstract interpreter defined in terms of changes to abstract states. The capital Greek letter Σ is commonly used for the set of such states and, in simple cases, particular states directly associate identifiers with values such as Booleans or integers:

$$\Sigma = Id \xrightarrow{\ m\ } ScalarValue$$

$$ScalarValue = \mathbb{B}|\mathbb{Z}$$

As observed above, the key property of an imperative language is that assignments can change the state. An interpretation function for statements would take as parameters an (abstract) program and a state; its result is a final state. Historically, McCarthy [McC66] and even the early Vienna operational descriptions (such as the VDL descriptions of PL/I [Lab66]) did write such interpretation functions. In the current paper, the *Structural Operational Semantics* (SOS) style of [Plo81] is used uniformly since this notation copes with non-determinism (cf. Section 4.1) and can thus be used for all of the operational descriptions discussed.

SOS rules like the one below for assignment can be read like a classic interpretation function, when considered in a clockwise manner from bottom left, and this often feels more natural when looking at deterministic languages. However, it is important to remember that SOS rules are in fact *inference rules*: above the line is a series of premises which must all be true for the rule to apply; below the line is the conclusion. Each rule indicates a relation between the state before computation and the state afterwards, given that a series of conditions holds; it records a way of judging whether a particular computation is valid. This distinction becomes important when considering non-deterministic languages, as in Sect. 4.1.

The basic judgements are relations (thus their signatures use powersets) between pairs of program text and pre-state, and post-computation state. The relation for *statements* is:

$$\xrightarrow{st}: \mathcal{P}((Stmt \times \Sigma) \times \Sigma)$$

The precise way in which each statement in a program is interpreted obviously depends on the type of statement so one way to present a description would be to write an interpretation function by cases. However, it is more convenient to use pattern matching[8] and this approach is used in both operational semantics and denotational semantics:

$$\frac{(rhs, \sigma) \xrightarrow{ex} v}{(mk\text{-}Assign(lhs, rhs), \sigma) \xrightarrow{st} \sigma \dagger \{lhs \mapsto v)\}}$$

(The judgements for *ex*pression evaluation ($\xrightarrow{ex}$) are described below.)

Conditional statements are interpreted by cases as follows:

$$\frac{(test, \sigma) \xrightarrow{ex} \textbf{true} \qquad (then, \sigma) \xrightarrow{st} \sigma'}{(mk\text{-}If(test, then, else), \sigma) \xrightarrow{st} \sigma'} \qquad \frac{(test, \sigma) \xrightarrow{ex} \textbf{false} \qquad (else, \sigma) \xrightarrow{st} \sigma'}{(mk\text{-}If(test, then, else), \sigma) \xrightarrow{st} \sigma'}$$

Interpreting iterative statements is slightly more involved:

$$\frac{(test, \sigma) \xrightarrow{ex} \textbf{true} \qquad (body, \sigma) \xrightarrow{st} \sigma' \qquad (mk\text{-}While(test, body), \sigma') \xrightarrow{st} \sigma''}{(mk\text{-}While(test, body), \sigma) \xrightarrow{st} \sigma''} \qquad \frac{(test, \sigma) \xrightarrow{ex} \textbf{false}}{(mk\text{-}While(test, body), \sigma) \xrightarrow{st} \sigma}$$

---

[8] Each VDM record type has an associated constructor function equivalent to a type constructed by this function—thus $mk\text{-}Assign : Id \times Expr \to Assign$ can be used to distinguish the appropriate subset of *Stmt* in a pattern matching context.

Notice that the state used in the third premise is the one produced from an interpretation of the body—thus a convergence towards termination may occur. The issue of non-terminating loops is addressed below.

The basic notion of state used above plays the same role as the environment in a functional language and an evaluation function can be defined to determine the values of expressions.

$$eval : Expr \times \Sigma \rightarrow ScalarValue$$

The *eval* function above can be rewritten as a relation:[9]

$$\xrightarrow{ex} : \mathcal{P}((Expr \times \Sigma) \times ScVal)$$

which can be split by the cases in its syntactic classes

$$\frac{e \in Id}{(e, \sigma) \xrightarrow{ex} \sigma(e)}$$

$$\frac{(e1, \sigma) \xrightarrow{ex} v1 \quad (e2, \sigma) \xrightarrow{ex} v2}{(mk\text{-}Expr(e1, \text{PLUS}, e2), \sigma) \xrightarrow{ex} v1 + v2}$$

Other cases should be obvious.

This seemingly simple description actually fixes an important property of the language: the process of evaluating an expression is shown not to change the state (i.e. the values of variables)—the same σ is used throughout. Although the key feature of functions is not addressed until Sect. 3, it is important to note that functions with side effects would destroy this assumption.

Note that the rule for evaluation of variables does not require a variable to be initialised and, of course, this could cause errors. In order to avoid this problem, all variables can be automatically initialised in the rule for program interpretation. These have been omitted for brevity. An alternative would be to modify the evaluation rule for $e \in Id$ with an additional premise such as $e \in \mathbf{dom}\,\sigma$.

If a program body is a single statement, this is most usefully a *Compound* (cf. Fig. 1); its interpretation is defined by the interpretation of each of the statements in (left to right) order. The rule for interpretation of *Compound* statements is as follows.

$$\frac{(s, \sigma) \xrightarrow{st} \sigma' \quad (mk\text{-}Compound(rest), \sigma') \xrightarrow{st} \sigma''}{(mk\text{-}Compound([s] \curvearrowright rest), \sigma) \xrightarrow{st} \sigma''}$$

Here the state produced by the interpretation of the first statement, s, in the list is the state (σ') in which to interpret the rest of the statement list, *rest*. As this description is recursive, a base case is required and here this is reached once the list of statements becomes empty. The rule is applied by pattern matching against the input and at this point simply results in an unchanged state.

---

[9] Technically, the relations $\xrightarrow{st} / \xrightarrow{ex}$ are the least relations satisfying the rules.

$$\overline{(mk\text{-}Compound([\,]), \sigma) \xrightarrow{\;st\;} \sigma}$$

The SOS rules given so far embody the so-called *big step* operational semantics, as it directly defines the final state. This approach is also referred to as *natural semantics* by Kahn [Kah87] and Nielson and Nielson [NN92]. *Small step* operational semantics has to define the granularity at which interference can occur in concurrency and thus shows the steps between smaller portions of program text and state—the overall interpretation of a program is then the transitive closure of the step relation. Big step tends to feel more intuitive in its handling of multiple statements (and especially constructs like blocks); however, it is worth mentioning the existence of small step concepts because these are used later when concurrency comes into play in Sect. 4.

The core language could be extended to consider some form of external storage such as files with the addition of *Read/Write* statements; this would be accomplished simply by extending Σ to include a collection of (named) files.

2.2   Denotational Approach

For simple languages, the difference between the operational and denotational approaches is less marked than when language aspects such as jumps, non-determinacy or the passing of functions as arguments have to be modelled. One important point is that both approaches are built around an explicit notion of state. The technical distinction between operational and denotational approaches is, however, important and the point can be made by contrasting with the earlier *abstract interpreter* phrase: denotational semantics is more like a compiler in that it maps the source language into another language. For the simple language that is defined operationally in Sect. 2.1, the mapping (M) would be into functions from states to states $(\Sigma \to \Sigma)$. This state is the same as defined in the previous section.[10] Thus:

$$M : Stmt \to (\Sigma \to \Sigma)$$

and the convention of surrounding the (abstract) text parameters by ⟦⟧ is followed.

A language is needed to define the functional denotations and Church's Lambda notation is the standard as it provides an easy way to write un-named functions.[11] As a simple example, the assignment statement is mapped to a function which takes a state and returns that state modified with a mapping from the identifier to the evaluation of the right-hand-side expression in the previous state.

$$M \llbracket mk\text{-}Assign(lhs, rhs) \rrbracket = \lambda \sigma \cdot \sigma \dagger \{ lhs \mapsto eval(rhs, \sigma) \}$$

---

[10] An Oxford denotational semantics would insist that Σ was also a general function type; here the finite, constructed, mappings of VDM are used for Σ because this is not a significant issue in the comparison.

[11] Familiarity with this notation is assumed; a good learning resource is [AGM92].

Much is made in the literature on denotational semantics about the mapping to denotations being *homomorphic* in the sense that the structure of the commands in the object language matches the structure of the denotations. So for compound statements:[12]

$$M[\![mk\text{-}Compound([\,])]\!] = \lambda\sigma \cdot \sigma$$
$$M[\![mk\text{-}Compound([s] \frown rest)]\!] = M[\![mk\text{-}Compound(rest)]\!] \circ M[\![s]\!]$$

Here it can be seen that the sequence concatenation on the left matches the function composition on the right and thus the structure is preserved. The homomorphic property is that the denotation of the compound is built (only) from the denotations of its constituent statements.

Note that the loss of referential transparency requires the state notion. This is now so familiar that it is taken for granted but assignments themselves complicate the denotational ideal of the homomorphic mapping.

It is not difficult to see that there is a clear connection between operational and denotational descriptions (postponing for the moment issues of non-termination):[13]

$$interpret : Stmt \times \Sigma \to \Sigma$$
$$M : Stmt \to \Sigma \to \Sigma$$

M is the Curried form of *interpret*—they are essentially a $\lambda\sigma$ apart:

$$M[\![s]\!] = \lambda\sigma \cdot interpret(s, \sigma)$$

But Sect. 2.4 makes clear that the surface difference has a significant impact on reasoning about language descriptions.

The semantics of conditional statements is:

$$M[\![mk\text{-}If(test, then, else)]\!] =$$
$$\lambda\sigma \cdot \textbf{if } M[\![test]\!](\sigma) = \textbf{true then } M[\![then]\!](\sigma) \textbf{ else } M[\![else]\!](\sigma)$$

and again is similar to the operational semantics given in the previous section.

However, the denotational definition of *While*:

$$M[\![mk\text{-}While(test, body)]\!] =$$
$$\lambda\sigma \cdot \textbf{if } M[\![test]\!](\sigma) = \textbf{true}$$
$$\textbf{then } M[\![mk - While(test, body)]\!] \circ M[\![body]\!]$$
$$\textbf{else } \lambda\sigma \cdot \sigma$$

includes $M[\![mk\text{-}While(test, body)]\!]$ which makes it clear that *fixed points* are required (and this could be made completely explicit by using the fixed point operator μ).[14]

---

[12] It would be more common to write a denotational description without the constructor (*mk-Compound*) but it has been made clear above that larger languages require an abstract syntax and choosing to keep the same treatment of syntactic objects in the sketched operational and denotational descriptions is useful.

[13] Here, McCarthy's original *interpret*-style description [McC66] is used to make the point more clearly than can be done with the SOS rule.

[14] In early versions of denotational semantics, Christopher Strachey used the Y combinator to denote the fixed point of a while loop (see for example [Wal67, p. 17]).

2.3   Axiomatic Approach

The widest use of *Hoare axioms* [Hoa69] is in the verification or development of programs. It was, however, precisely concerns about 'leaving things undefined' in language semantics that led Tony Hoare to propose *Hoare triples*.[15] Perhaps the strongest case for specifying a range of permissible results is in languages that allow concurrent execution and this topic is reviewed in Sect. 4.2. Here, the axiomatic method is explained with the simple sequential language that has been introduced above.

In a deviation from the approach used in the paper so far, concrete syntax will be used in the sections concerned with axiomatic semantics. This is purely by convention: while there is no reason *not* to use abstract syntax, doing so would be unique amongst all other works on axiomatic semantics. The reason for the lack of use of abstract syntax is probably connected to the small scale (and relative syntactic paucity) of the languages to which axiomatic semantics is normally applied.

A so-called *Hoare triple* consists of a pre condition, program text and a post condition. These are now almost universally written as $\{P\}\ S\ \{Q\}$.[16] In the most widely adopted style, the pre and post conditions are predicates of single states. Note that in contrast with operational and denotational semantics, these states are not explicitly defined. The triple $\{P\}\ S\ \{Q\}$ records a judgement that if S is executed in a state that satisfies the predicate P, then (providing S terminates) the resulting state will satisfy the predicate Q.

Given this interpretation, inference rules can be provided for each language construct:

$$\text{Sequence}\ \frac{\{P\}\ S1\ \{Q\} \quad \{Q\}\ S2\ \{R\}}{\{P\}\ S1\ ;\ S2\ \{R\}}$$

$$\text{If}\ \frac{\{P \vee b\}\ Th\ \{Q\} \quad \{P \vee \neg b\}\ El\ \{Q\}}{\{P\}\ \textbf{if}\ b\ \textbf{then}\ Th\ \textbf{else}\ El\ \textbf{fi}\ \{Q\}}$$

$$\text{While}\ \frac{\{P \vee b\}\ S\ \{P\}}{\{P\}\ \textbf{while}\ b\ \textbf{do}\ S\ \textbf{od}\ \{\neg b \vee P\}}$$

The predicate P in the rule for **while** is a *loop invariant* and this concept is a key contribution to the way users think about programs even if they are not reasoning completely formally. As noted above, programming constructs can be used to extend what can be expressed in a language. It remains true however that if for example a loop is used to compute factorial, the proof needs axioms about factorial in addition to the inference rule for while statements.

---

[15] The background to [Hoa69] includes Bob Floyd's [Flo67] and is traced in [Jon03]; since that publication, earlier drafts have been found of Hoare's attempts to build on his comment, made at a conference in 1964 [Ste66, pp. 142–143], that "What is required is a method of describing a class of implementation ...".

[16] In Hoare's original paper [Hoa69], he actually wrote $P\ \{S\}\ Q$ but placing the braces around the assertions emphasises their role as being non-executable.

The caveat above about termination is important: the *While* rule does not on its own establish that the loop will terminate. This property of correctness assuming termination is often (badly) termed *partial correctness*. Dijkstra [Dij76] proposed the addition of *variant functions* to reason about termination and these were in fact employed without that nomenclature in both [Tur49] and [Flo67]. A more pleasing approach is indicated below when the switch to relational post conditions is discussed.

In practice, users are unlikely to give a post condition in exactly the form $\neg b \vee P$. Either the inference rules need to be complemented with weakening rules such as:

$$\text{consequence} \; \frac{\begin{array}{c} P' \Rightarrow P \\ \{P\} \, S \, \{Q\} \\ Q \Rightarrow Q' \end{array}}{\{P'\} \, S \, \{Q'\}}$$

or, perhaps more usefully, the other rules should be changed to reflect the potential for weakening—for example:

$$\text{While}' \; \frac{\begin{array}{c} \{P'\} \, S \, \{P\} \\ P \vee b \Rightarrow P' \\ P \vee \neg b \Rightarrow Q \end{array}}{\{P\} \; \textbf{while} \; b \; \textbf{do} \; S \; \textbf{od} \; \{Q\}}$$

Having considered the sort of statement that controls the order in which basic statements are executed, the axiomatic description of assignment statements must be addressed. The now standard[17] *backwards rule* can be written

$$\text{assign} \; \frac{}{\{P_e^x\} \, x := e \, \{P\}}$$

where P_e^x means substitution of e for x (with appropriate renaming to avoid unwanted capture).

The deceptively simple—and therefore appealing—rule is not without its problems. For example Krzysztof Apt in [Apt81] discusses the careful adjustments required if the left-hand-side of the assignment is a reference to an element of an array. Without wishing to undervalue what might be thought of as a lucky notational success, it must be observed that the aforementioned lack of referential transparency with variables in programs should prompt care when copying their names into predicates.

Another reservation about the assignment rule arises when languages allow multiple identifiers to refer to the same location (see Sect. 3.3); sticking to the

---

[17] Floyd in [Flo67] used a forward assignment axiom that needs an existential quantifier in its post condition; having discussed the developments with several people (including King whose Effigy system [Kin69] used the backward rule) it would appear to be the case that Bob Floyd spotted the simpler rule after his paper was published and that David Cooper took the information from Carnegie Tech (where he had been for over a year) to Tony Hoare in Belfast when Cooper gave a seminar there.

assignment rule above would appear to imply that *call-by-reference* is modelled by some form of copy rule.[18]

In [Hoa69], Tony Hoare indicates that the axiomatic approach obviates the need for an explicit model of state. This connects with the well-known *frame problem* in the sense that it would be convenient if the only thing affected by an assignment to x is the value of the variable with that name. This is, of course, not the case in the presence of call-by-reference parameter passing.

It was realised early on[19] that writing relatively large collections of axioms could lead to inconsistencies. The standard way out of this danger is to provide a model for which axioms can be shown to hold. Under Tony Hoare's supervision, this is exactly what Peter Lauer undertook in his thesis [Lau71]; a later—but better-known—reference is [Don76]. Essentially, it is necessary to show that if $\{P\}\ S\ \{Q\}$ can be deduced from the axioms, then this agrees with the operational semantics as follows:

$$P(\sigma) \vee ((S,\sigma) \xrightarrow{st} \sigma') \Rightarrow Q(\sigma')$$

If termination is considered, it is also necessary to show:

$$P(\sigma) \Rightarrow \exists\sigma'(S,\sigma) \xrightarrow{st} \sigma'$$

The *sequence* axiom above shows clearly why it is attractive to use post conditions that are predicates of a single state. It should, however, be obvious that this is not really a good idea! What a program is intended to realise is a final state that relates in some meaningful way to its initial state. VDM has used relational post conditions since before [Jon80]—Aczel showed in an unpublished note [Acz82] how to present rules for such relational specifications in a convenient way—and these rules of inference are used in subsequent VDM publications. A particular advantage of explicitly using relations is that Dijkstra's *variant functions* are avoided simply by saying that the specification of the body of a loop should be a well-founded relation.

Hoare's 1969 paper is one of the most influential references in theoretical computer science. It can be seen as the root of developments including Edsger Dijkstra's *weakest pre conditions* [DS90] and work on *refinement calculus* [Mor94, BvW98]. Furthermore, this whole line of thought led, after [Hoa71b], to the use of Floyd/Hoare axioms in the development process (rather than *post facto* proof). Further discussion of these developments is available in [Jon03].

2.4 Reasoning

There are two distinct needs to reason based on a (formal) semantics. On the one hand, a programmer might want to prove that a program satisfies its specification; on the other, the designer of a compiler might want to justify the design

---

[18] Various other extensions by Hoare include [CH72, Hoa72a, Hoa71a]; useful summaries are [Apt81, Apt84].

[19] Specifically at the April 1969 IFIP WG 2.2 meeting in Vienna at which Hoare first presented his axiomatic method [Wal69]. See [JA16] for more comments on this meeting.

of a compiling algorithm. (In both cases, the more important issue is how to use the semantics as the basis for a stepwise development but that does not affect the distinction.) Here, both tasks are first explained in terms of operational semantics.

In proving the correctness of a program, its specification should take the form of a pre condition and a post condition. The first of these describes any assumptions on the state before execution of the program; the second defines the acceptability of the state produced after the program as a relation to the initial state. The post condition is a predicate of *two* states (before and after) because all but the most trivial specifications relate values in the post-state to those in the pre-state (as with defining the result of a function with respect to its arguments):

$$pre : \Sigma \rightarrow \mathbb{B}$$
$$post : \Sigma \times \Sigma \rightarrow \mathbb{B}$$

This specification is related to the implementation by formulating the related *Proof Obligation* for the program S:

$$\forall \sigma \in \Sigma \cdot pre(\sigma) \;\Rightarrow\; post(\sigma, interpret(S, \sigma))$$

Discharging this proof obligation indicates that the program S satisfies the specification given.

In the task of proving correctness of translation, the proposed algorithm might have the signature:

$$translate : Stmt \rightarrow MachineCode$$

and the machine code might be given semantics by:[20]

$$mc\text{-}interpret : MachineCode \times \Sigma \rightarrow \Sigma$$

This allows us to formulate the proof obligation as follows:

$$\forall S \in Stmt, \sigma \in \Sigma \cdot mc\text{-}interpret(translate(S), \sigma) = interpret(S, \sigma)$$

Although it is possible to reason about the earlier program correctness task using either an operational[21] or a denotational language description, that is exactly the task for which axiomatic semantics was envisioned.[22]

In contrast, the task of reasoning about the correctness of a language translator appears to be best handled with one of the *model oriented* (i.e. operational or denotational) description methods. The choice between operational and denotational semantics as a basis for such proofs depends on a number of factors. The higher level of abstraction in noting that denotations are functions (for now, from states to states) certainly makes it easy to establish some properties

---

[20] This has been deliberately simplified by ignoring the fact that the abstract states (Σ) of the language description need to be reified to representations on the object-time storage organisation.

[21] This approach is explored in John Hughes' thesis [Hug11] and [HJ08].

[22] As observed in Sect. 2.3, such proofs also require axioms of any new operators.

of a language (e.g. the equivalence of a while loop to its unwrapping with a conditional around the original loop).

For translation algorithms that closely follow the phrase structure of the source language, denotational semantics is probably most appropriate because it is easy to reason about the functional semantic objects. Robert Milne and Christopher Strachey tackle implementation correctness in both the "Adams Essay" [MS74] and the two-volume book [MS76] published after Strachey's death; members of the IBM Lab Vienna addressed compiler correctness using denotational semantics as well. Unfortunately, as the latter were concerned with the large (and Baroque) language PL/I, most of the publications are only available as lengthy technical reports (e.g. [BBH+74, Wei75, Izb75, BIJW75, Jon76]).

Unfortunately, many compiling techniques are not obviously algebraic in form: optimisations such as register allocation or *strength reduction*[23] cut right across the phrase structure of the language and cause problems for descriptions reliant on homomorphic denotations. In such cases, it might well be easier to base the argument on an operational description—publications on using operational descriptions to reason about compiling include [MP67, Pai67, Luc68, Jon69, JL71].

One point of comparison that is worth clarifying is that operational semantics can be made to appear as compositional as denotational semantics. It is true that early attempts to provide operational semantics of large languages (e.g. the VDL descriptions of PL/I [WAB+68]) often fell into the trap of putting things in the state that were unchanged by simple statements—McCarthy referred to this as the *grand state* mistake. Furthermore, seeking a homomorphic mapping (to functional denotations[24]) encourages someone writing a denotational semantics to consider exactly what must be in the state. But a small state SOS description can closely follow the phrase structure of the language being described. The main penalty for using, for example, an SOS description is that proofs have to use induction over the steps of computation rather than, say, Scott induction [Win93, p. 166].

One significant point in the comparison of denotational and operational descriptions concerns termination. The program

while $x \neq 0$ **do** $x := x - 1$ **od**

will, for a negative initial value of x, simply iterate indefinitely. Reading a big step (or *natural*) operational semantics as inference rules means that the hypotheses cannot be discharged for such values. In contrast, the least fixed point of the denotation of this program is exactly the partial function that takes states with positive values for x to states where $x = 0$.

The greatest payoff for the level of abstraction in denotational semantics is in proving deeper properties of a defined language.

---

[23] Within a loop, a relatively expensive operation such as multiplication can be replaced by addition if one of the operands is the control variable of the loop.

[24] Finding neat functional denotations is not always possible. The topic of abnormal exits such as **goto** statements is postponed to Sect. 6 but forces considerable contortions of the space of denotations.

2.5   Section Summary

The main challenge presented by simple imperative languages is the need to store and update values associated with variables when assignments are made. The response given by both operational and denotational semantics is to model the storage of the computer with an abstract state. There is no fundamental difference between the states used in denotational and operational semantics. Axiomatic semantics avoids an overt state by using value replacement, but the collection of meta-variables used in assertions does essentially imply a state.

3   ALGOL-Like Blocks, Functions, Procedures

For the simple language presented above, the differences between the semantic description styles seem minor. But that language lacks many features that make real languages convenient for programmers. The challenge of describing language features like named procedures and environmentally-separated blocks adds significant complexity to the task of language description and begins to show interesting differences in the response by each semantic school.

The need to model the local entities of different blocks and sharing of locations presents particular challenges, especially in the presence of more complicated data structures such as arrays. Procedures add additional problems when different parameter mechanisms are considered and so-called *higher-order* procedures (whose parameters or results are procedures themselves) are particularly problematic in some approaches. This section discusses these challenges and the solutions in the different approaches.

It is interesting to observe how similar the treatment is in denotational and operational approaches—and to note the key difference on procedure denotations. Axiomatic semantics ends up taking a different tack by avoiding environments and instead using name substitution.

3.1   Local Naming

In first-order predicate calculus:

$$\forall x \in X \cdot (\ldots \forall x \in Y \cdot (\ldots) \ldots \exists x \in Z \cdot (\ldots))$$

the three bindings of x are distinct: they occupy separate *name spaces*. The need for separate name spaces in programming languages is even stronger because program texts are likely to be long.

Most programming languages offer ways of localising a name space so that the same identifier can denote a different variable in nested *blocks*.

$$Stmt = \cdots \mid Block$$

$$
\begin{aligned}
Block \; :: \; &types \; : \; Id \xrightarrow{m} ScalarType \\
&body \; : \; Stmt \\
&\cdots
\end{aligned}
$$

In the simple storage model of Sect. 2, identifiers are mapped to denotations (so far only values) and there is no need so far to change the underlying state notion. The only delicate point is that – at block exit – the semantics must recover the denotations of those identifiers that referred to a different variable in the inner block.

Context conditions must also be reconsidered now that the same identifier may denote different values and types throughout computation. This can be achieved by requiring that usage of names in a well-formed block matches the closest embracing declaration. A well-formed program now need only require that every constituent block is well-formed.

3.2   Functions, Procedures and (Simple) Parameters

The pragmatics of functions and procedures is that they can be used to factor out portions of program text that can be called from many places.[25] From a user point of view, procedure calls are statements that get executed in the order dictated by their position in a list of statements whereas functions occur in expressions.[26] Functions and procedures require similar modelling techniques in terms of the semantic objects required and are therefore treated together in the remainder of this section.

$Block$ :: $\cdots$
         $body$: $Stmt$

$Stmt = \cdots \mid ProcCall$

Context conditions of procedures are similar to those for blocks, but additionally require that the evaluated types of parameters in a procedure call match those declared in the procedure definition. This means that the $TypeMap$ object must also store information on procedure definitions.

Functions and procedures have fixed denotations so they do not belong in the store which contains values that can be changed (by assignment) within statements. This can be handled by introducing an $environment$ to contain the denotations:

---

[25] Although compiling techniques are not the main topic of this paper, it is worth observing that implementing general recursion and parameter passing required the invention of ingenious techniques—see [RR62]; there is a very detailed reconstruction of the development of the idea of the $Display$ mechanism in [vdH17].

[26] It is worth noting that functions which can cause side effects considerably complicate expression evaluation. At a minimum, they remove the possibility of saying that $eval : Expr \times \Sigma \rightarrow Value$ because of the potential state change inherent if functions with side effects are allowed within $Expr$. Something that causes language descriptions more trouble is that, unless the order of evaluation of expressions is strictly defined (which is rare because languages tend to leave compilers the freedom to optimise register use), evaluating expressions containing functions with side effects results in non-determinism. This general topic is resumed in Sect. 4.

$$Env = Id \xrightarrow{m} Den$$

$$Den = FunDen | ProcDen | \cdots$$

The basic model is not difficult; that having been said, the features that have been devised in various languages to make procedures more useful are myriad and necessitate extension of the role of the environment. The passing of parameters of simple values (e.g. $\mathbb{N}, \mathbb{B}$) is straightforward: these are simply given new identifiers within the local environment of the function or procedure. However, more complex parameter passing mechanisms require more consideration.

3.3　Sharing

Thus far, it has been assumed that identifiers denote simple distinct values such as numbers or Booleans. However, for reasons of efficiency, it is sometimes useful to have more than one identifier referring to the same entity. Because of potential name clashes, making precise the semantics of such sharing is non-trivial. Classically, logicians (e.g. in describing the Lambda calculus) have used a *copy rule* with "suitable changes of names to avoid clashes" to describe such concepts. For programming languages, the text of the procedure can be modified to copy in the names, references or values of arguments, with appropriate renaming to avoid name clashing. The ALGOL report [BBG+60] uses an informal description of this approach to attempt to fix the semantics; it can also be formalised, as in the operational description of ALGOL 60 [ACJ72].

Many programming tasks require composite entities such as arrays which gives rise to the notion of *left hand values* for elements of arrays. These considerations are the main reasons for allowing different ways of passing arguments to functions or procedures. Surprisingly many alternative parameter passing mechanisms have been devised and each has its use:

- Call *by value* is the most obvious and is appropriate for simple types—the argument (which might be an expression) is evaluated and this value is copied into the body of the function or procedure. Typically this is achieved by creating a new memory allocation for the value and therefore modifications to this variable are not seen in the calling scope.
- Copying of data can be reduced by using *by location* (or *by reference*) parameter passing, in which a pointer to the storage location of the argument is passed instead of its value. This enables the function to modify the value of the argument variable in a way that will affect the calling context.
- The full *by name* parameter mechanism of ALGOL 60 is even more challenging semantically: the denotations of arguments are evaluated anew each time the respective parameter name is encountered within the body of the function, thereby potentially triggering multiple instances of side-effects. (This specialises to *by location* mode when the argument (or *actual parameter* in ALGOL speak) is a simple identifier.)

– Call by *value/result* offers a useful compromise; by copying the value of each argument into a new location and then returning the (potentially modified) values to their original locations; it facilitates the return of multiple values from procedures/functions but avoids the problem of the same location being referred to by different identifiers.[27]

In model-oriented methods, all of the above can be modelled with:[28]

$$Env = Id \xrightarrow{m} Den$$

$$Den = \cdots \,|\, Loc$$

$$Loc = ScalarLoc \,|\, ArrayLoc$$

$$ArrayLoc = \mathbb{N}^* \xrightarrow{m} ScalarLoc$$

$$\Sigma = ScalarLoc \xrightarrow{m} ScalarValue$$

In SOS it is clear that the environment is not changed by simple statements such as assignments as *env* is not in the range of the $\xrightarrow{st}$ relation.

$$\frac{(rhs, env, \sigma) \xrightarrow{ex} v}{(mk - Assign(lhs, rhs), env, \sigma) \xrightarrow{st} \sigma \dagger \{env(lhs) \mapsto v\}}$$

The task of creating and passing locations is handled in the semantics of blocks and calling.

Similarly, in denotational semantics, the fact that environments are not changed by simple statements is apparent from the *Curried*:

$$M : Stmt \to Env \to \Sigma \to \Sigma$$

It is interesting the extent to which the description of semantic objects and a few type definitions (i.e. no actual rules or formulae) can suggest (to an experienced reader) the main points about a language. The rest of this paper is written at this level of abstraction.

The passing of parameters in environment-based semantics is not difficult—the semantic function, relation or mapping is extended to include an environment as a parameter and this environment is modified at evaluation time. The parameter passing mechanism chosen affects the level at which the environment or its sub-contents are modified.

It is, however, important to clarify how the context of a procedure or function is captured in model-oriented approaches. In an operational approach, one part of *ProcDen/FunDen* is its text. But this is not enough: if functions/procedures can be declared in any block and called from any deeper block, then there must be a way of fixing the *environment* in which they are to be executed, so that

---

[27] Unless the same argument is passed to different parameters—but this is an easy static check.

[28] Records are similar to arrays but have fields that are not necessarily of the same type; modelling records and combinations of arrays/records is straightforward.

there is a proper evaluation of any parameter identifier that is passed in, and no clashes with local names used within the text of the procedure. To address this, an environment is usually part of the interpreting function or relation for procedures and functions. This approach is essentially identical to the *static chain* method for address resolution, in which each scope contains some meta-information linking it to its direct lexical parent.

In denotational approaches, *FunDen/ProcDen* are functions in the standard mathematical sense, with the appropriate environment bound in forming a *closure*.[29] Environments are therefore also parameters to the meaning function, as seen above.

3.4   Handling Parameters and Sharing in the Axiomatic Approach

Using *by location* parameter passing means that multiple identifiers refer to the same *location* and, at a minimum, this undermines the axiom of assignment in Hoare triples. So the axiomatic approach, tending to ignore the concepts of both state and environment, uses quite a different strategy to model-oriented techniques: a form of repeated name substitution is used, essentially a modification of the copy rule described above.

The basic case for the invocation of a procedure is one where there are no parameters and no side effects; calling a procedure is essentially adding the body of the procedure to the main program body. The following simple rule (adapted from [Pag81]) applies:

$$\boxed{Invocation}\ \frac{\{P\}\ S\ \{Q\}\qquad N.body = S}{\{P\}\ \mathbf{call}\ \overleftarrow{N}\ \{Q\}}$$

Adding parameters requires that variables in P and Q referring to the parameters of N be replaced by the arguments (or argument expressions, or evaluated argument expressions, depending on calling mechanism). Such substitution must be conflict avoiding, but this is just generally assumed to be taking place rather than explicitly mechanised in axiomatic descriptions.

$$\boxed{Invocation'}\ \frac{\{P\}\ S\ \{Q\}\qquad N.body = S\qquad N.params = [N_1, \dots, N_n]}{\{P_{E_1,\dots,E_n}^{N_1,\dots,N_n}\}\ \mathbf{call}\ \overleftarrow{N}\,(E_1, \dots, E_n)\ \{Q_{E_1,\dots,E_n}^{N_1,\dots,N_n}\}}$$

Procedures with side effects can also be handled, and a way is provided in the (incomplete) axiomatic 'definition' of Pascal. This approach expands the notion of parameters to include all variables used globally within N and considers these to be 'implicit' parameters. They are then handled in the same way as 'explicit'

---

[29] As is the case with axiomatic semantics in Sect. 2.3, strictly, the function itself is not produced: the semantics maps to a Lambda expression that could be proved equivalent to the mathematical function using properties about the function.

parameters: functions are assumed to exist which map the initial values of both explicit and implicit parameters onto their final values and these are used in the assertion substitutions as in the rule *Invocation'* above.

Arrays (even without sharing) need careful handling in axiomatic semantics, as also discussed by [Apt81]. Allowing expressions as the subscripts in subscripted variables can lead to problems, particularly when these expressions reference the same array. One way to address this is to replace the whole array with a new one modified at the index to which assignment has been made, but this is not a particularly elegant solution.

3.5   Higher-Order Functions and Procedures

The pragmatics of allowing parameters to be procedures and functions is to facilitate higher-order programs. Not only is this concept beloved by functional language users, it is also a prime tool for abstraction in programming. For example, the simple *map list* idea

$$map\text{-}list : (A \rightarrow B) \times A^* \rightarrow B^*$$

provides a generic function that yields a sequence in which every element is the result of applying the function in the first argument to the corresponding element of the second argument; this is a small example of how high levels of re-use and abstraction can be achieved. There are, of course, far more exotic cases that introduce new ways of achieving recursion: see, for example, Knuth's "man and boy" example [Knu64] that was written as a challenge for ALGOL 60 compilers.

This topic is placed in a separate sub-section because it causes one of the most telling differences between operational and denotational approaches. The clue to the source of the problem is that, once functions can take functions as arguments, the possibility arises that a function can be applied to itself. (This also introduces a minor issue around types that is reviewed at the end of this sub-section.)

The fact that, in operational semantics approaches, the denotation of a procedure is a pair (containing the text of the procedure and its statically containing environment) means that no new concepts are needed to model the passing of procedures or functions.

In denotational approaches, however, the denotation of procedures are actual functions (as indicated in Sect. 3.3). During the development of denotational semantics, this gave rise to a serious mathematical problem: since the cardinality of the function space $X \rightarrow X$ must be greater than that of X, there is a paradox with functions that can take themselves as arguments. There was thus a point in time where Strachey's idea of *denotational* (or at that time *mathematical*) semantics claimed that semantics could be given by mapping programs to mathematical functions (expressed in the Lambda calculus), but the approach was built on sand in the sense that no one could offer a model of the untyped Lambda calculus.

This problem was resolved with Dana Scott's 1969 invention of domains with suitably restricted functions. This was a major intellectual achievement and has been widely described; perhaps the most accessible text remains [Sto77] but Scott's own [Sco80] provides a clear description of the context of his models of the untyped Lambda calculus.

The challenge of modelling self-applying functions gives rise to the largest divergence so far between operational and denotational approaches. It is interesting to look more carefully at what is going on here. The *homomorphic* rule says that the denotation of a construct should be built up from the denotations of its constituent parts. But the name of a procedure can only be given a denotation by storing it in an environment.

There is, in fact, another issue to be resolved for functions that can take themselves as arguments; that issue concerns defining their type. Consider first a binary tree structure built up with records:

$$BinTree ::\quad left\ :\ [BinTree]$$
$$value\ :\ \mathbb{N}$$
$$right\ :\ [BinTree]$$

The name of the type *BinTree* is used to express the recursive embeddings and the marking of the fields as optional ensures that instances can be finite.

In order to declare a function type that can take itself as argument, there must be a way of naming a function type. In fact, ALGOL 60 ducked this problem: the language is almost strongly typed except for function and array types. Both PL/I and Pascal offer such separate naming of function (entry) types. It is worth noting that separating function types is necessary for mutually recursive procedures because they cannot be given in an order such that each definition precedes use.

3.6 Section Summary

Blocks and procedures bring new challenges to semantic descriptions, particularly with the concerns of name sharing and local entities. Denotational and operational semantics solve this problem by separating out an environment from the state, but very cautious name substitution is needed in axiomatic semantics, particularly when advanced parameter mechanisms are used. Procedures become another kind of denotable value in model based semantics, but this requires careful foundation for denotational semantics when higher-order functions are allowed.

4 Modelling Non-deterministic Languages

There are two essentially different reasons that non-determinism figures in programming languages:[30]

---

[30] A separate need to have a formal treatment of non-deterministic specifications arises when considering *program development*—see Sect. 4.2.

– the originator of a language might wish to allow freedom to the designers of implementations to make optimisations such as common sub-expression elimination;

– a language might encompass features that result in non-deterministic execution—the most telling example is concurrency where differing progress of threads can yield a range of results for executing a program.

It is clear that the specification (or description) of a language must fix the full—and exact—range of acceptable outcomes. This matters both to programmers writing programs in the language and language implementers. The challenge is leaving some aspects of the language incompletely defined, but properly constrained. This problem is further complicated by questions of *granularity* of interleaving: a semantic description must be capable of describing granularity at least as fine as that handled by the language. The difficulty of these points is a significant challenge for the semantic description: having a sufficiently rich notation to allow communication of these aspects while remaining readable. These challenges existed as soon as languages such as PL/I were addressed; the various responses are interestingly different in appearance but do have a common core.

4.1 Operational Response

The pragmatics of concurrent programming languages should be obvious: both low-level systems programming and high-level applications need to express algorithms that accommodate differing run-time progress. In model-oriented semantic approaches, there appears to be no alternative to recording the text of the threads that remain to be executed and adjoining it to the shared state (Σ) that is being updated. Such pairings of states and remaining thread texts are referred to as *configurations*.

In order to capture the possible mergings of the threads, an operational semantics must show the non-deterministic choice between the threads. Precisely how this is done fixes the granularity of merging.[31] A first thought might be to record a function that maps a configuration to the set of its possible successor configurations but this becomes notationally messy. It is, of course, equivalent to think of this as a relation between configurations and it transpires that this is notationally much cleaner. There are many ways to define such a relation. The approach utilised in the early operational semantics VDL documents [Lab66, LW69], offered a way of describing such non-determinacy by using *control trees* that contain a structured version of the program text that still had to be executed—but these control trees were made part of the (grand) state.[32] Plotkin's SOS [Plo81] provides much clearer descriptions because the

---

[31] Many attempts to provide ways of reasoning about concurrent programs (see Sect. 4.2) make the assumption that assignment statements are atomic; for brevity, this simplification is followed here; but it must be realised that this level of granularity is unrealistic for real implementations of languages due to the possibility of values of variables being changed by parallel threads even during expression evaluation.

[32] For a fuller discussion see [JA16, Sect. 3].

non-determinacy is factored out of the rules themselves; it moves to the selection of a semantic rule (the remaining text and state are kept separate).

With the following definition of *Parallel* consisting of two threads

$$Parallel = (\,Thread \times Thread\,)$$

$$Thread = Assign^*$$

a large-step approach is inappropriate: an interpreting rule like $\xrightarrow{st}$ from Sect. 2.1 would interpret an entire sequence of assignments as one. This limits the language to executing the *Parallel* as though each *Thread* were atomic. What is needed is a set of rules which each peel off and execute one of the remaining statements in any non-empty thread. For this we use the relation for parallel interpretation, $\xrightarrow{par}$. A *small step* semantics interprets the next assignment in either the left or right thread:

$$\xrightarrow{par}: \mathcal{P}((\,Parallel \times \Sigma) \times (\,Parallel \times \Sigma))$$

$$\frac{(s,\sigma) \xrightarrow{st} \sigma'}{(([s] \frown restl, r), \sigma) \xrightarrow{par} ((restl, r), \sigma')}$$

$$\frac{(s,\sigma) \xrightarrow{st} \sigma'}{((l, [s] \frown restr), \sigma) \xrightarrow{par} ((l, restr), \sigma')}$$

Using this approach, assignments may be interleaved in any order, as the choice of which thread to interpret next is lifted to the choice of rule instantiation.

Extensions for other language features can be made in a similar style to this; for example, a small step model of a *while* loop unwraps the loop with a conditional surrounding it.

Note that so far the assumption is that assignment statements represent the level of atomicity in the language. Allowing interference to take place at the expression evaluation level is possible and makes two things clear:

- The way that SOS factors out the non-deterministic choice of rules that match the current configuration is extremely helpful in preventing the issue of concurrency from polluting a whole definition.[33]
- A further observation is that, in SOS descriptions, the non-determinacy with expressions looks different from that with statements: with expressions, the non-determinacy is resolved when a variable is accessed (or a function returns a value) and the effect is to place a value in the evaluation tree; with statements, the effect is reflected in a state change and the executed statement is discarded from the resulting configuration.

---

[33] But there is a sense in which the configurations are just a way of presenting the *control trees* that were much criticised in VDL operational descriptions (The danger with these control trees in a grand state semantics was that it was hard to determine where they could or could not be updated.).

Moving to a level of granularity larger than assignments, a programmer may wish to make *multiple* statements executable only as an atomic block.

$Stmt = \cdots \mid Atomic$

$Atomic \;::\; Assign^*$

$$\frac{(sl, \sigma) \xrightarrow{st} \sigma'}{([mk\text{-}Atomic(sl)] \curvearrowright rest, \sigma) \xrightarrow{st} (rest, \sigma')}$$

Atomicity is, of course, a key issue in the database world and it is interesting to note the similarities to—and differences from—the programming language universe. It would not be difficult to add data types to a programming language that provide ways to declare and manipulate relations similar to those in the standard relational model (see [Dat82]). As discussed at a Schloss Dagstuhl event on atomicity [JLRW05, Sect. 2.4.2], this then highlights the point that database systems strive to prevent data races, where possible, by system-induced locking (and, where pre-planning fails, to detect races and handle the recovery) whereas programmers using typical programming languages are held responsible to plan and control locking.

4.2   Axiomatic Response

As indicated in Sect. 2.3, the axiomatic approach copes with general non-determinism naturally. This observation that it is important to leave aspects of a language undefined was made by Tony Hoare in [Ste66, pp. 142–143] and—via multiple drafts—led him to his famous *axiomatic basis* paper [Hoa69].[34] Moreover, it became clear in using methods such as VDM that specifications that allow a range of implementations are a powerful way of structuring design decisions (see for example [Jon90, Abr10]).

Unfortunately the specific case of non-determinacy being caused by concurrent execution presents severe challenges for the axiomatic approach. The source of the difficulty is precisely the *interference* that has to be modelled explicitly in the operational descriptions of the previous sub-section. Before facing the fact that post conditions alone are insufficient to specify components that suffer interference, it is interesting to trace an early attempt to finesse that difficulty and its more recent manifestation in (Concurrent) Separation Logic.

Hoare singled out the case of disjoint concurrency in [Hoa72b] and made the observation that the post conditions of two parallel threads could be conjoined providing there were no shared variables. Hoare's 1972 paper covered normal (stack) variables in which case the disjointness is simply a check of the *alphabets* of the threads. John Reynolds introduced *Separation Logic* [Rey78, Rey89] to support reasoning about *heap variables* (i.e. data structures that contain pointers and whose topology can be changed by updating said pointers). Reasoning

---

[34] Of course, the soundness notion at the end of Sect. 2.3 needs to be enriched but this is straightforward.

about parallel threads that share a heap can be very delicate. An interesting collaborative attack (see [BO16]) led to *Concurrent Separation Logic* [O'H07] which has spawned many variants—see [Par10]. The essential idea is akin to Hoare's observation: what one wants to do is to conjoin the post conditions of parallel threads but this is only valid if the interference is avoided. What separation logics facilitate is concise statements of the disjoint ownership of heap addresses.[35] More recently, [JY15] notes that certain cases of heap separation can be viewed as reifications of abstract descriptions of separate entities.

In [O'H07], it is suggested that separation logic should be used to reason about race-free programs and *Rely/Guarantee* (R/G) conditions should be used for *racey* programs.[36] The initial publications on R/G go back to [Jon81]— more recently the same underlying concept has been expressed in a refinement calculus [Mor94,BvW98] style in [HJC14,JHC15]. This, in particular, makes algebraic properties such as the distribution of rely and guarantee conditions over sequential and parallel program operators much clearer.

The basic R/G idea is that acceptable interference should be documented with rely conditions in the same way that sequential Floyd/Hoare logic records acceptable starting states with pre conditions. Also, just as post conditions express obligations on the running code, guarantee conditions record the upper limit of interference that a component can inflict on its environment. Specifications of components using R/G conditions can then be used as a basis for design justification. In a step where the sub-components are also specified using R/G conditions, clear proof obligations exist to justify development steps for parallel operators. Unsurprisingly, these proof obligations are more complicated than those for sequential Floyd/Hoare logic but the essential property of *compositionality* is preserved.

Just as at the end of Sect. 2.3 the soundness of these inference rules needs to be proved. It is possible to extend the operational semantics to carry an interference relation and then to interpose it at points appropriate to the granularity of the language; this approach is used in [CJ06,Col08]. Alternatively, *Aczel traces* (see [Acz83] or the more accessible [dR01]) can provide a space of denotations and [CHM16] does this in a way that conducts proofs at a significantly higher level of abstraction.

Another method for modelling concurrency is that of *process calculi* or *process algebras*, which include ACP [BK84], CSP [Hoa85], CCS [Mil89] and π-calculus [SW01]. CSP is particularly relevant due to its influence on the programming

---

[35] This led Jones to make a suggestion at the MFPS meeting in 2005 where O'Hearn presented concurrent separation logic that it might better be thought of as *ownership logic*.

[36] Although this seemingly simple dichotomy ignores the way in which non-interference at an abstract level can be used to establish race freedom in a representation—a nice example is Simpson's *Four-Slot* implementation of Asynchronous Communication Mechanisms in [JP11]; this paper also introduced the idea of a notation for *possible values* which is, in turn, explored in [JH16].

language occam, used extensively by Inmos [INM88]. Although work on these approaches grew out of considerations of language semantics, they are no longer strictly within the scope of this paper.

4.3 Denotational Response

The key to the utility of a denotational semantic description is the choice of a space of denotations which admit tractable reasoning. Denotations for the language of threads above could be either relations over states or functions from states to sets of states. In either case, there is a need to mark (potential) non-termination. It is important to note that the problem of interference remains: just as an operational semantics must indicate the granularity of thread switching by the way in which configurations are changed and rematched, the relations must be composed appropriately.

Thus far, there is a lot of similarity between denotational and operational presentations of the semantics for non-determinacy resulting from concurrent threads. The combination of non-determinism with higher order functions (cf. Sect. 3.5) however poses extra difficulties for the denotational approach. Here *Power Domains* [Plo76, Smy76] are required to preserve the mathematical properties that overcome the cardinality paradoxes related to higher-order language constructs. Again operational semantics is inherently simpler because procedures and functions are modelled simply by their texts.

4.4 Section Summary

The challenges of parallelism bring some variance in the response from the various semantics. In operational semantics, the non-determinism is lifted to the rule level and the real power of SOS to merely constrain acceptable solutions (rather than generate a unique solution) is displayed. In some ways this is similar to certain axiomatic responses, where interference and interaction is constrained by logical propositions. Denotational semantics runs into foundational technicality since the traditional function can no longer be used as a base for denotations. Instead, contortions of the semantic domains such as power domains are required.

5 Applying the Ideas to a Concurrent Object-Based Language

This section outlines the semantics of a concurrent object-orient language known as COOL,[37] designed to be small enough to model in a small document but realistic in its handling of the issues identified above.

---

[37] COOL was inspired by – and is similar to – POOL [AR92]. COOL is used in teaching a course on language semantics at Newcastle University.

SIMULA 67 [DMN68] was designed as a language in which simulation programs could be constructed; this provides a wonderful intuition for *Object-Oriented* (OO) programming languages: objects are blocks that can be instantiated as required,[38] block descriptions are the class definitions, local variables are the instance variables and procedures are methods. The scope of method names is of course external to the class to enable objects to call methods defined for other objects.[39]

Key issues in the design of a concurrent language are how to generate and synchronise concurrent threads. Although it gives an unconventional OO language, the aims of this section can be achieved by limiting (instances of) objects to running one method at a time and generating concurrency by arranging that many objects can be active. This ensures that instance variables are free from *data races* and, crucially, that the level of interference is in the hands of the programmer because only by sharing references (to objects) is interference possible.

The move from the unconstrained concurrency of threads in Sect. 4 to a simple OO-language can be summarised as follows:

- The language in Sect. 4 has dangerous data races because of the single shared state.
- In COOL each object (instance) has a local state and can run as a thread.
- Such extreme separation needs to be tempered by providing some communication between the threads. This is easy to achieve by allowing methods to be called in objects. Parameter passing is by value; object references can be passed thus opening up both (controlled) sharing and passing of the ability to invoke methods.
- Any object can create an object (that is an instance of a class) and receives the unique *Reference* of the new object. The relevant statement might be called *New*.
- The only way in which objects can begin execution is by having their methods called by other objects (the exception is for the initial object which begins execution at program start). Objects retain references to their client objects and should eventually cease execution and return values.
- Thus far, there is no obvious source of the claimed concurrency but there are many ways to create parallel threads:
  - A class could have a designated initial method that begins to execute in any newly created object of that class: instantiating multiple objects results in concurrent execution. Similarly, a program could have a set of designated objects which all begin execution when the program starts (this latter approach is presented in the language description below).

---

[38] When Ole-Johan Dahl made this comment to Jones, the whole OO area became clearer.

[39] The desire to add some notion of object orientation to languages such as C did not necessarily result in languages with clear semantics. SmallTalk [GR83], however, is a principled OO language and Bertrand Meyer's Eiffel language [Mey88] adopts the pre/post specification idea to provide *contracts*.

- ABCL [Yon90] included a *FutureCall* statement that essentially forks the called method—the join occurs when the client object executes a *Wait* statement.
  - An alternative explored in [San99] is to have a *Release* statement that prematurely releases the client object before the server method is complete. Using this strategy, the client can resume execution while the server continues to execute. This can be further enriched by a *Delegate* statement, which passes responsibility to another object for executing and returning to the client when complete.
- A language built around objects that lacks inheritance is sometimes referred to as *object-based* but inheritance can be added to the features above by viewing it as a way of instantiating nested blocks.

An operational semantics for such a language can be built around the following semantic objects.

The basic threads per object are keyed by *References*:

$$ObjectStore = Reference \xrightarrow{m} ObjectInformation$$

This keeps a record of the states of all the objects that exist at a given time in the execution of the program.

Each *ObjectInformation* contains the information needed to determine the current state and activity of the object:[40]

$$ObjectInformation :: \quad class \; : \; Id$$
$$\sigma \; : \; Store$$
$$mode \; : \; \text{READY}|Run|Wait$$

The local *Store* of an object simply contains the current values of its variables:

$$Store = Id \xrightarrow{m} Value$$

$$Value = [Reference]|\mathbb{Z}|\mathbb{B}$$

where the set *Reference* is infinite and **nil** $\notin$ *Reference*.

Modes of objects indicate their current activity status. Objects which are READY are not currently doing anything; method calls may be made to such objects. The other modes indicate some form of activity.

$$Run :: \quad remainder \; : \; Statement^*$$
$$client \; : \; Reference$$

Objects in *Run* mode are currently executing. It is important to retain the list of statements which they have yet to execute, *remainder*, (compare with the configurations of Sect. 4.1) and the reference of the object which initiated their execution, *client*, which will be awaiting the eventual return of a value (or a special token indicating there is no return value).

$$Wait :: \quad lhs \; : \; Id$$
$$remainder \; : \; Statement^*$$
$$client \; : \; Reference$$

---

[40] The texts of object classes are stored in a separate *ClassStore*, discussion of which is postponed to the consideration of the *Program* type.

Objects waiting for a value to be returned must keep track of the (local) variable to which this value should be saved (*lhs*), the list of statements to which they will resume executing (*remainder*) and the *client* by which they were originally called.

Programs are defined as a specification of objects and some initialisation.

$$Program \ :: \qquad\qquad cs \ : \ ClassStore$$
$$startingclasses \ : \ Id^*$$
$$startingmethods \ : \ Id^*$$

The *startingclasses* sequence indicates which classes within the *ClassStore* should be initialised at program commencement and *startingmethods* indicates which methods within these classes should be executed.

ClassStore is the global directory of all classes in the program: the *ObjectStore* is the store of dynamic information on the extant objects; the *ClassStore* holds the static information on all possible objects.

$$ClassStore = Id \xrightarrow{m} ClassInformation$$

$$ClassInformation \ :: \ variables \ : \ Id \xrightarrow{m} Type$$
$$methods \ : \ Id \xrightarrow{m} MethodInfo$$

The information here defines the variables declared in the class and their types (there are no dynamic declarations in this language) and the methods available to be called in the language. More detail need not be given on *MethodInfo* but it contains parameter information and statements to be executed for each method.

Thus the main semantic relation has the type:

$$\xrightarrow{st} \colon \mathcal{P}((\,ClassStore \times ObjectStore) \times ObjectStore)$$

Once the program has commenced, the *ClassStore* and *ObjectStore* maps are globally available to the semantics during execution. However, individual objects have access to only the *ClassStore* object (to enable them to call methods in other objects) and of course their own internal store.

A full definition of COOL is available on the web[41] but it is a part of the message of Sect. 7 that it is possible to understand many design decisions of a programming language solely from its *semantic objects*.

6   Abnormal Ordering

Many programming languages contain features that bring about a non-sequential order of execution of statements. The most obvious example is the **goto** statement (attacked by Dijkstra in [Dij68] and defended by Knuth in [Knu74]) but it is certainly not the sole source of difficulty: (loop) breaks, exception mechanisms and even returns from functions or procedures present similar challenges. Expressed in denotational terms, the difficulty is that the *homomorphic rule* cannot directly apply when the meaning of a construct depends on something that is not present in the construct. Put another way, the obvious idea that the

---

[41] http://homepages.cs.ncl.ac.uk/cliff.jones/COOL-WWW-version.pdf.

semantics of the sequential composition of two statements should be the composition of the semantics of those two statements cannot apply when the first statement appoints as its successor a statement elsewhere.

One response from operational semantics that shows rather clearly what has to happen can be seen in VDL descriptions. In early Vienna Lab operational semantics, an explicit *control tree* recorded the text that was still to be executed; abnormal sequencing was modelled by surgery on this control tree.[42]

Within the denotational camp, there are two rather different responses to the challenges of abnormal ordering. Most researchers (and certainly those strongly connected to Oxford) use *Continuations*. The core idea is to recover some semblance of the homomorphic rule by making the denotation of a label represent the effect of starting execution at that label. In order to develop such denotations it is necessary to pass to every semantic function a denotation that corresponds to the execution of the remainder of the program. This makes the semantics higher order than one might expect and arguably more complicated than these specific constructs require.

In contrast, VDM denotational descriptions (and the Isabelle formulations of semantics in [NK13]) effectively extend the denotations from $\Sigma \rightarrow \Sigma$ to have ranges that can represent abnormal results. The potential messiness caused by the fact that something more complicated than functional composition is now needed for sequential composition can be hidden by *combinators*.[43]

Incorporating the exit ideas into SOS descriptions is something that has not been published. It would be easy to do this explicitly with extra cases for all language constructs but this would result in the heaviness visible in [ACJ72]— much lengthier than what VDM achieves with combinators. Since the latter could be read operationally, it should be possible to find a way of adding something like the combinators to SOS rules.

An axiomatic approach to jumps is proposed in [CH72], although the authors do acknowledge that jumps may be better avoided where possible and indeed most axiomatic semantic descriptions skip the topic entirely. The essential idea is adapted from earlier (operational) work by Landin [Lan65a, Lan65b], which treated jumps like procedures whose body is the sequence of statements following the label up until the end of its enclosing block. Rather than returning control to the calling context, however, it is resumed from the end of the block enclosing the label. Clint and Hoare's approach is largely the same, although they prefer to restrict the declaration of labels (and their 'bodies') to the beginning of blocks. The rules do allow for labels to be declared anywhere within the block, with some slight added complexity. However, only one label may be declared per block, and further restrictions prevent jumping into compound and conditional statements.

---

[42] It is interesting to note that [McC66] had an explicit program counter that could be seen as a hint of what had to be done with control trees when a massive language like PL/I (complete with concurrency) had to be described.

[43] In [Mos11], Mosses makes the interesting link between VDM's use of such combinators and Eugenio Moggi's *monads* [Mog89]. The differences between the VDM exit scheme and continuations are teased apart by proofs of equivalence in [Jon78, Jon82].

It is interesting to note that this approach bears some obvious similarities to the continuations used in denotational semantics. Although notationally very different, the idea of a label representing computation left to be performed is at the core of both ideas.[44] There is also a clear comparison to the configurations used in the operational semantics of Sect. 4.1 in which the *text* of the computation yet to be executed is stored.

7 Closing Remarks

This section mentions some current research (Sect. 7.1), related references (Sect. 7.2) and offers some general conclusions.

7.1 Algebraic Semantics

Work on this topic is too recent to present a full evaluation; here only some pointers and superficial comments are offered. For sequential programs, a search for "Laws of Programming" was started in [HHJ+87]; Hoare [HvS12, HMSW11] and others [Hay16, HCM+16] build on Kozen's *Kleene algebra with tests* [Koz97] to record algebraic laws that abstract from any detailed model of concurrent programming languages. As with *Boolean algebras*, the algebraic laws normally admit more than one model: saying, for example, that the sequence operator of semicolon is associative but non-commutative does not preclude a semantics in which statements are executed right to left.

The clear advantage of recording algebraic laws about programming constructs is the same as in classical algebra: if proofs can be conducted at that level of abstraction they are likely to be much easier and more general than any attempt to reason about a model-oriented language description. A specific example is the use made in [Hay16] of an *interchange law* to justify the equivalent of the most important Rely/Guarantee parallel introduction rule. Furthermore, Hayes and colleagues have gone on to present a *Synchronous Program Algebra* that also covers synchronous event-based concurrent languages [HCM+16]. It is interesting that there are echoes here of the *program schema* research [Pat67, LPP70] that was one of the earliest avenues of programming language research.

7.2 Related References

Frank de Boer has provided a proof system for POOL [dB91] which he shows to be consistent and complete with respect to an operational semantics. The assertion language works on three levels and is not first order—although it is not a higher order logic in the sense that, say, HOL is. There are also some restrictions of the POOL language.

---

[44] Indeed, in de Bakker's book *Mathematical Theory of Program Correctness*, a book showing the use of all kinds of semantics in program proof, de Bruin gives a similar axiomatic rule but notes that it is hard to see clearly the correctness of this rule or use the rule in proofs [dBDBZ80]. Instead, a denotational-style continuations semantics is presented and proofs are built around that.

Another paper by the current authors [AJ18] looks at four complete formal descriptions of ALGOL 60, making technical comparisons as well as providing a historical context for the development of the semantic styles in general and the creation of the descriptions in particular.

Although not within the scope of this paper, which focuses on programming languages, other kinds of formal language have benefited from the application of semantic methods. Hardware description languages have been treated formally to good effect: see [Gor95] and [BJQ2000] for semantics of Verilog and the collection of papers [KB12] for VHDL. Semantic descriptions have also been written for specification languages, such as CLEAR [BG80] and Z [Spi88].

7.3 Conclusions

A number of the most important challenges presented by programming languages to formal description are discussed in this paper.

- The challenge of associating identifiers with variable values is solved in operational and denotational semantics with a notion of state that is essentially the same in both cases. In axiomatic semantics an explicit state is apparently avoided, but the meta-variables used in assertions in essence form an implicit state.
- In axiomatic semantics, phrase structuring in programming languages, such as that used in blocks and procedures, is handled by copying text and careful name substitution to avoid clashes. In model-oriented approaches, an abstract environment associates identifiers with locations. This is once again similar in both denotational and operational semantics.
- One area in which the semantic approaches differ significantly is handling non-determinism and concurrency. In SOS, a relation is defined economically by factoring out the non-determinism in the way in which rules match configurations. In axiomatic approaches a number of options have been explored including separation logic, temporal logic and rely/guarantee. Denotational semantics requires complex refactoring of its domain spaces.
- The description of an illustrative concurrent object-oriented language indicates that it may be easiest to use an SOS approach to bring all these aspects together in a readable form.

Clearly, there are some genuine differences in the way that semantics are recorded in the main approaches but there are also some common modelling ideas that are obscured by superficial differences of presentation.

The complexity of formally recording the complete semantics of practical programming languages—larger and more feature-rich than the one demonstrated in this paper—seems unavoidable. Unfortunately, most programming languages are not even described formally *post facto*, let alone during the design process. Sadly, most programming languages are also not very good: they are hard to learn, too packed with features whose interactions prove awkward, or their behaviour is difficult to predict. One of the authors of the current paper has several times undertaken the task of writing a formal semantics for a language which had been designed without the benefit of a formal model. The experience bears out the argument that the payoff from formality comes from its early employment. John Reynolds often made comments such as "Formality should be the midwife of languages rather than the mortician". With more careful use of formalism at an appropriate point in the design phase, many unfortunate problems could be avoided. Although working out a formal semantics is a non-trivial task, it takes significantly less time than building a compiler and the former provides a better basis for thought experiments than the latter. Furthermore, a wider knowledge of formal semantic techniques could result in a staged approach:

- Working out and recording the *semantic domains* of a language is an extremely cost-effective way of sorting out the fundamental concepts of a language—see the discussion in Sect. 5 and note that the semantic domains for PL/I cover less than two pages of its 100 page description [BBH+74].
- Although denotational descriptions of concurrent languages are still a subject of research, SOS descriptions provide a convenient way to make sure that the more novel aspects of updating the state of a language have been properly thought out.
- Again, it might not be practical to create a complete algebraic characterisation of a language, but thinking about the question of equivalences that should hold ought yield a language that is easier to use.
- Programmers using a language have to reason about the effects of their programs—they might do this less formally than in a textbook but their reasoning is in any case dependant on rules of inference about the constructs of the language. A statement for which it is too difficult to provide such rules is an indication that the programmer's task has been made gratuitously difficult.

Acknowledgements. The authors are extremely grateful to Mike Dodds, Shmuel Tyszberowicz and Ian Hayes for constructive and detailed comments on drafts of this paper. Some of the material was also presented at HaPoC-2017 in Oxford and useful comments were made by participants. Funding for the authors' research comes from UK EPSRC both as a PhD studentship and the *Strata* Platform grant.

References

[Abr10] Abrial, J.-R.: The Event-B Book. Cambridge University Press, Cambridge (2010)

[ACJ72] Allen, C.D., Chapman, D.N., Jones, C.B.: A formal definition of ALGOL 60. Technical report 12.105, IBM Laboratory Hursley, August 1972

[Acz82] Aczel, P.: A note on program verification. Manuscript (private communication), Manchester, January 1982

[Acz83] Aczel, P.H.G.: On an inference rule for parallel composition. Private communication (1983)

[AGM92] Abramsky, S., Gabbay, D.M., Maibaum, S.E. (eds.) Handbook of Logic in Computer Science: Background: Computational Structures, vol. 2. Oxford University Press Inc., New York (1992)

[AJ18] Astarte, T.K., Jones, C.B.: Formal semantics of ALGOL 60: four descriptions in their historical context. In: De Mol, L., Primiero, G. (eds.) Reflections on Programming Systems - Historical and Philosophical Aspects, pp. 71–141. Springer Philosophical Studies Series (2018, in press)

[Ame89] America, P.H.M.: The practical importance of formal semantics. In: de Bakker, J.W. (ed.) 25 jaar semantiek. CWI (1989)

[ANS76] ANSI: Programming language PL/I. Technical report X3.53-1976, American National Standard (1976)

[Apt81] Apt, K.R.: Ten years of Hoare's logic: a survey–part I. ACM Trans. Program. Lang. Syst. **3**(4), 431–483 (1981)

[Apt84] Apt, K.R.: Ten years of Hoare's logic: a survey - part II: nondeterminism. Theor. Comput. Sci. **28**, 83–109 (1984)

[AR92] America, P., Rutten, J.: A layered semantics for a parallel object-oriented language. Form. Asp. Comput. **4**(4), 376–408 (1992)

[Ast19] Astarte, T.K.: Formalising meaning: a history of programming language semantics. Ph.D. thesis, Newcastle University (2019, forthcoming)

[BBG+60] Backus, J.W., et al.: Report on the algorithmic language ALGOL 60. Numerische Mathematik **2**(1), 106–136 (1960)

[BBH+74] Bekič, H., Bjørner, D., Henhapl, W., Jones, C.B., Lucas, P.: A formal definition of a PL/I subset. Technical report 25.139, IBM Laboratory Vienna, December 1974

[BG80] Burstall, R.M., Goguen, J.A.: The semantics of clear, a specification language. In: Bjøorner, D. (ed.) Abstract Software Specifications. LNCS, vol. 86, pp. 292–332. Springer, Heidelberg (1980). https://doi.org/10.1007/3-540-10007-5_41

[BIJW75] Bekič, H., Izbicki, H., Jones, C.B., Weissenböck, F.: Some experiments with using a formal language definition in compiler development. Laboratory note LN 25.3.107, IBM Laboratory Vienna, December 1975

[BJQ2000] Bowen, J.P., Jifeng, H., Qiwen, X.: An animatable operational semantics of the Verilog hardware description language. In: Formal Engineering Methods, pp. 199–207. IEEE (2000)

[BK84] Bergstra, J.A., Klop, J.W.: Process algebra for synchronous communication. Inf. Control **60**(1–3), 109–137 (1984)

[BO80] Bjørner, D., Nest, O.N. (eds.): Towards a Formal Description of Ada. LNCS, vol. 98. Springer, Heidelberg (1980). https://doi.org/10.1007/3-540-10283-3

[BO16] Brookes, S., O'Hearn, P.W.: Concurrent separation logic. ACM SIGLOG News **3**(3), 47–65 (2016)

[Bur66] Burstall, R.M.: Semantics of assignment. Mach. Intell. **2**, 3–20 (1966)

[BvW98] Back, R.-J., von Wright, J.: Refinement Calculus: A Systematic Introduction. Springer, New York (1998). https://doi.org/10.1007/978-1-4612-1674-2

[CG90] Carré, B., Garnsworthy, J.: Spark–an annotated Ada subset for safety-critical programming. In: Proceedings of the Conference on TRI-ADA 1990, TRI-Ada 1990, pp. 392–402. ACM (1990)

[CH72] Clint, M., Hoare, C.A.R.: Program proving: jumps and functions. Acta Informatica **1**(3), 214–224 (1972)

[CHM16] Colvin, R.J., Hayes, I.J., Meinicke, L.A.: Designing a semantic model for a wide-spectrum language with concurrency. Form. Asp. Comput. **29**(5), 1–22 (2016)

[CJ06] Coleman, J.W., Jones, C.B.: Guaranteeing the soundness of rely/guarantee rules. Technical report CS-TR-955, School of Computing Science, University of Newcastle, March 2006

[Col08] Coleman, J.W.: Constructing a tractable reasoning framework upon a fine-grained structural operational semantics. Ph.D. thesis, Newcastle University, January 2008

[Dat82] Date, C.J.: A formal definition of the relational model. ACM SIGMOD Rec. **13**(1), 18–29 (1982)

[dB91] Boer, F.S.: A proof system for the language POOL. In: de Bakker, J.W., de Roever, W.P., Rozenberg, G. (eds.) REX 1990. LNCS, vol. 489, pp. 124–150. Springer, Heidelberg (1991). https://doi.org/10.1007/BFb0019442

[dBDBZ80] de Bakker, J.W., De Bruin, A., Zucker, J.: Mathematical Theory of Program Correctness, vol. 980. Prentice-Hall International, London (1980)

[Dij68] Dijkstra, E.W.: Go to statement considered harmful. Commun. ACM **11**(3), 147–148 (1968)

[Dij76] Dijkstra, E.W.: A Discipline of Programming. Prentice-Hall, Englewood Cliffs (1976)

[DMN68] Dahl, O.-J., Myhrhaug, B., Nygaard, K.: SIMULA 67 common base language. Technical report S-2, Norwegian Computing Center, Oslo (1968)

[Don76] Donahue, J.E.: Complementary Definitions of Programming Language Semantics. LNCS, vol. 42. Springer, Heidelberg (1976). https://doi.org/10.1007/BFb0025364

[dR01] de Roever, W.P.: Concurrency Verification: Introduction to Compositional and Noncompositional Methods. Cambridge University Press, Cambridge (2001)

[DS90] Dijkstra, E.W., Scholten, C.S.: Predicate Calculus and Program Semantics. Springer, New York (1990). https://doi.org/10.1007/978-1-4612-3228-5

[Flo67] Floyd, R.W.: Assigning meanings to programs. In: Proceedings of Symposium in Applied Mathematics. Mathematical Aspects of Computer Science, vol. 19, pp. 19–32. American Mathematical Society (1967)

[Gor75] Gordon, M.: Operational reasoning and denotational semantics. Technical report STAN-CS-75-506, Computer Science Department, Stanford University, August 1975

[Gor95] Gordon, M.: The semantic challenge of Verilog HDL. In: Proceedings of theTenth Annual IEEE Symposium on Logic in Computer Science, LICS 1995, pp. 136–145. IEEE (1995)

[GP99] Gabbay, M., Pitts, A.: A new approach to abstract syntax involving binders. In: Proceedings of the 14th Annual IEEE Symposium on Logic in Computer Science, LICS 1999. IEEE Computer Society (1999)

[GR83] Goldberg, A., Robson, D.: Smalltalk-80: The Language and Its Implementation. Addison-Wesley, Boston (1983)

[Hay16] Hayes, I.J.: Generalised rely-guarantee concurrency: an algebraic foundation. Form. Asp. Comput. **28**(6), 1057–1078 (2016)

[HCM+16] Hayes, I.J., Colvin, R.J., Meinicke, L.A., Winter, K., Velykis, A.: An algebra of synchronous atomic steps. In: Fitzgerald, J., Heitmeyer, C., Gnesi, S., Philippou, A. (eds.) FM 2016. LNCS, vol. 9995, pp. 352–369. Springer, Cham (2016). https://doi.org/10.1007/978-3-319-48989-6_22

[HHJ+87] Hoare, C.A.R., et al.: Laws of programming. Commun. ACM **30**(8), 672–687 (1987). See Corrigenda in Commun. ACM **30**(9), 770

[HJ73] Hanford, K.V., Jones, C.B.: Dynamic syntax: a concept for the definition of the syntax of programming languages. In: Annual Review in Automatic Programming, vol. 7, pp. 115–140. Pergamon (1973)

[HJ08] Hughes, J.R.D., Jones, C.B.: Reasoning about programs via operational semantics: requirements for a support system. Autom. Softw. Eng. **15**(3–4), 299–312 (2008)

[HJC14] Hayes, I.J., Jones, C.B., Colvin, R.J.: Laws and semantics for rely-guarantee refinement. Technical report CS-TR-1425, Newcastle University, July 2014

[HMRC87] Holt, R.C., Matthews, P.A., Rosselet, J.A., Cordy, J.R.: The Turing Programming Language: Design and Definition. Prentice-Hall Inc., Upper Saddle River (1987)

[HMSW11] Hoare, C.A.R., Möller, B., Struth, G., Wehrman, I.: Concurrent Kleene Algebra and its foundations. J. Log. Algebr. Program. **80**(6), 266–296 (2011)

[HMT87] Harper, R., Milner, R., Tofte, M.: The semantics of standard ML: version 1, Laboratory for Foundations of Computer Science, Department of Computer Science, University of Edinburgh (1987). Hard copy

[Hoa69] Hoare, C.A.R.: An axiomatic basis for computer programming. Commun. ACM **12**(10), 576–580 (1969)

[Hoa71a] Hoare, C.A.R.: Procedures and parameters: an axiomatic approach. In: Engeler, E. (ed.) Symposium on Semantics of Algorithmic Languages. LNM, vol. 188, pp. 102–116. Springer, Berlin (1971)

[Hoa71b] Hoare, C.A.R.: Proof of a program: FIND. Commun. ACM **14**(1), 39–45 (1971)

[Hoa72a] Hoare, C.A.R.: A note on the FOR statement. BIT **12**(3), 334–341 (1972)

[Hoa72b] C.A.R. Hoare. Towards a theory of parallel programming. In Operating System Techniques, pages 61–71. Academic Press, 1972

[Hoa73] Hoare, C.A.R: Hints on programming language design. Invited Address at SIGACT/SIGPLAN Symposium on Principles of Programming Languages, Boston, October 1973

[Hoa85] Hoare, C.A.R.: Communicating Sequential Processes. Prentice-Hall, Upper Saddle River (1985)

[Hug11] Hughes, J.R.D.: Reasoning about programs using operational semantics and the role of a proof support tool. Ph.D. thesis, Newcastle University (2011)

[HvS12] Hoare, T., van Staden, S.: In praise of algebra. Form. Asp. Comput. **24**(4–6), 423–431 (2012)

[INM88] INMOS. occam 2: Reference Manual. Prentice Hall (1988)

[Izb75] Izbicki, H.: On a consistency proof of a chapter of a formal definition of a PL/I subset. Technical report TR 25.142, IBM Laboratory Vienna, February 1975

[JA16] Jones, C.B., Astarte, T.K.: An exegesis of four formal descriptions of ALGOL 60. Technical report CS-TR-1498 School of Computer Science, Newcastle University, September 2016. Forthcoming as a paper in the HaPoP 2016 Proceedings

[JH16] Jones, C.B., Hayes, I.J.: Possible values: exploring a concept for concurrency. J. Log. Algebraic Methods Program. **85**, 972–984 (2016)

[JHC15] Jones, C.B., Hayes, I.J., Colvin, R.J.: Balancing expressiveness in formal approaches to concurrency. Form. Asp. Comput. **27**(3), 465–497 (2015)

[JL71]   Jones, C.B., Lucas, P.: Proving correctness of implementation techniques. In: Engeler, E. (ed.) Symposium on Semantics of Algorithmic Languages. LNM, vol. 188, pp. 178–211. Springer, Heidelberg (1971). https://doi.org/10.1007/BFb0059698

[JLRW05] Jones, C.B., Lomet, D., Romanovsky, A., Weikum, G.: The atomic manifesto: a story in four quarks. ACM SIGMOD Rec. **34**(1), 63–69 (2005)

[Jon69]   Jones, C.B.: A proof of the correctness of some optimising techniques. Technical report LN 25.3.051, IBM Laboratory, Vienna, June 1969

[Jon76]   Jones, C.B.: Formal definition in compiler development. Technical report 25.145, IBM Laboratory Vienna, February 1976

[Jon78]   Jones, C.B.: Denotational semantics of goto: an exit formulation and its relation to continuations. In Bjørner and Jones [BJ78], pp. 278–304

[Jon80]   Jones, C.B.: Software Development: a Rigorous Approach. Prentice Hall International, Englewood Cliffs (1980)

[Jon81]   Jones, C.B.: Development methods for computer programs including a notion of interference. Ph.D. thesis, Oxford University, June 1981. Printed as: Programming Research Group, Technical Monograph 25

[Jon82]   Jones, C.B.: More on exception mechanisms. In: Bjørner and Jones [BJ82], Chap. 5, pp. 125–140

[Jon90]   Jones, C.B.: Systematic Software Development using VDM, 2nd edn. Prentice Hall International, Upper Saddle River (1990)

[Jon03]   Jones, C.B.: The early search for tractable ways of reasoning about programs. IEEE Ann. Hist. Comput. **25**(2), 26–49 (2003)

[JP11]   Jones, C.B., Pierce, K.G.: Elucidating concurrent algorithms via layers of abstraction and reification. Form. Asp. Comput. **23**(3), 289–306 (2011)

[JY15]   Jones, C.B., Yatapanage, N.: Reasoning about separation using abstraction and reification. In: Calinescu, R., Rumpe, B. (eds.) SEFM 2015. LNCS, vol. 9276, pp. 3–19. Springer, Cham (2015). https://doi.org/10.1007/978-3-319-22969-0_1

[Kah87]   Kahn, G.: Natural semantics. In: Brandenburg, F.J., Vidal-Naquet, G., Wirsing, M. (eds.) STACS 1987. LNCS, vol. 247, pp. 22–39. Springer, Heidelberg (1987). https://doi.org/10.1007/BFb0039592

[KB12]   Kloos, C.D., Breuer, P.: Formal Semantics for VHDL. Springer, Heidelberg (2012). https://doi.org/10.1007/978-1-4615-2237-9

[Kin69]   King, J.C.: A program verifier. Ph.D. thesis, Department of Computer Science, Carnegie-Mellon University (1969)

[Knu64]   Knuth, D.E.: Man or boy. ALGOL Bull. **17**(7) (1964)

[Knu68]   Knuth, D.E.: Semantics of context-free languages. Theory Comput. Syst. **2**(2), 127–145 (1968)

[Knu74]   Knuth, D.E.: Structured programming with GO TO statements. Technical report STAN-CS-74-416, Computer Science Dept, Stanford University, May 1974

[Koz97]   Kozen, D.: Kleene algebra with tests. ACM Trans. Program. Lang. Syst. **19**(3), 427–443 (1997)

[Lab66]   Vienna Laboratory: Formal definition of PL/I (Universal Language Document No. 3). Technical report 25.071, IBM Laboratory Vienna, December 1966

[Lan65a] Landin, P.J.: A correspondence between ALGOL 60 and Church's lambda-notation: part I. Commun. ACM **8**(2), 89–101 (1965)

[Lan65b] Landin, P.J.: A correspondence between ALGOL 60 and Church's lambda-notation: part II. Commun. ACM **8**(3), 158–167 (1965)

[Lau71] Lauer, P.E.: Consistent formal theories of the semantics of programming languages. Ph.D. thesis, Queen's University of Belfast (1971). Printed as TR 25.121, IBM Lab. Vienna

[LPP70] Luckham, D.C., Park, D.M.R., Paterson, M.S.: On formalised computer programs. J. Comput. Syst. Sci. **4**(3), 220–249 (1970)

[Luc68] Lucas, P.: Two constructive realisations of the block concept and their equivalence. Technical report TR 25.085, IBM Laboratory Vienna, June 1968

[LW69] Lucas, P., Walk, K.: On the formal description of PL/I. Annu. Rev. Autom. Program. **6**, 105–182 (1969)

[McC63] McCarthy, J.: Towards a mathematical science of computation. In: IFIP Congress, vol. 62, pp. 21–28 (1962)

[McC66] McCarthy, J.: A formal description of a subset of ALGOL. In: Formal Language Description Languages for Computer Programming, pp. 1–12. North-Holland (1966)

[Men64] Mendelson, E.: Introduction to Mathematical Logic. van Norstrand (1964)

[Mey88] Meyer, B.: Object-Oriented Software Construction. Prentice-Hall, Upper Saddle River (1988)

[Mil89] Milner, R.: Communication and Concurrency. Prentice Hall, Upper Saddle River (1989)

[Mog89] Moggi, E.: An abstract view of programming languages. Ph.D. thesis, Laboratory for the Foundation of Computer Science, Edinburgh University (1989)

[Mor94] Morgan, C.C.: Programming from Specifications, 2nd edn. Prentice Hall, Upper Saddle River (1994)

[Mos11] Mosses, P.D.: VDM semantics of programming languages: combinators and monads. Form. Asp. Comput. **23**(2), 221–238 (2011)

[MP67] McCarthy, J., Painter, J.: Correctness of a compiler for arithmetic expressions. Math. Asp. Comput. Sci. **19** (1967)

[MS74] Milne, R., Strachey, C.: A theory of programming language semantics. Privately circulated (1974). Submitted for the Adams Prize

[MS76] Milne, R., Strachey, C.: A Theory of Programming Language Semantics (Parts A and B). Chapman and Hall, Boca Raton (1976)

[NK13] Nipkow, T., Klein, G.: Concrete Semantics. A Proof Assistant Approach. Springer, Cham (2013)

[NN92] Nielson, H.R., Nielson, F.: Semantics with Applications: A Formal Introduction. Wiley, New York (1992)

[O'H07] O'Hearn, P.W.: Resources, concurrency and local reasoning. Theor. Comput. Sci. **375**(1–3), 271–307 (2007)

[Pag81] Pagan, F.G.: Formal Specification of Programming Languages. Prentice-Hall, Upper Saddle River (1981)

[Pai67] Painter, J.A.: Semantic correctness of a compiler for an ALGOL-like language. Technical report AI Memo 44, Computer Science Department, Stanford University, March 1967

[Par10] Parkinson, M.: The next 700 separation logics. In: Leavens, G.T., O'Hearn, P., Rajamani, S.K. (eds.) VSTTE 2010. LNCS, vol. 6217, pp. 169–182. Springer, Heidelberg (2010). https://doi.org/10.1007/978-3-642-15057-9_12

[Pat67] Paterson, M.S.: Equivalence problems in a model of computation. Ph.D. thesis, University of Cambridge (1967)

[Pie02] Pierce, B.C.: Types and Programming Languages. MIT Press, Cambridge (2002)

[Plo76] Plotkin, G.D.: A powerdomain construction. SIAM J. Comput. **5**, 452–487 (1976)

[Plo81] Plotkin, G.D.: A structural approach to operational semantics. Technical report DAIMI FN-19, Aarhus University (1981)

[Pra65] Prawitz, D.: Natural Deduction: A Proof-Theoretical Study. Dover Publications, New York (1965)

[Rey78] Reynolds, J.C.: Syntactic control of interference. In: Proceedings of Fifth POPL, pp. 39–46. ACM (1978)

[Rey89] Reynolds, J.C.: Syntactic control of interference part 2. In: Ausiello, G., Dezani-Ciancaglini, M., Della Rocca, S.R. (eds.) ICALP 1989. LNCS, vol. 372, pp. 704–722. Springer, Heidelberg (1989). https://doi.org/10.1007/BFb0035793

[RR62] Randell, B., Russell, L.J.: Discussions on ALGOL translation at Mathematisch Centrum. English Electric Report W/AT, 841 (1962)

[San99] Sangiorgi, D.: Typed pi-calculus at work: a correctness proof of Jones's parallelisation transformation on concurrent objects. TAPOS **5**(1), 25–33 (1999)

[Sco80] Scott, D.: Lambda calculus: some models, some philosophy. Stud. Log. Found. Math. **101**, 223–265 (1980)

[Smy76] Smyth, M.B.: Powerdomains. Technical report, Department of Computer Science, University of Warwick, May 1976

[Spi88] Spivey, J.M.: Understanding Z—A Specification Language and its Formal Semantics. Cambridge Tracts in Computer Science 3. Cambridge University Press (1988)

[Ste66] Steel, T.B.: Formal Language Description Languages for Computer Programming. North-Holland, London (1966)

[Sto77] Stoy, J.E.: Denotational Semantics: The Scott-Strachey Approach to Programming Language Theory. MIT Press, Cambridge (1977)

[SW01] Sangiorgi, D., Walker, D.: The π-Calculus: A Theory of Mobile Processes. Cambridge University Press, Cambridge (2001)

[Tur49] Turing, A.M.: Checking a large routine. In: Report of a Conference on High Speed Automatic Calculating Machines, pp. 67–69. University Mathematical Laboratory, Cambridge, June 1949

[Tur09] Turner, R.: The meaning of programming languages. Am. Philos. Assoc. Newsl. Philos. Comput. **9**(1), 2–6 (2009)

[vdH17] van den Hove, G.: New insights from old programs: the structure of the first ALGOL 60 system. Ph.D. thesis, University of Amsterdam (2017)

[vWMPK69] van Wijngaarden, A., Mailloux, B.J., Peck, J.E.L., Koster, C.H.A.: Report on the algorithmic language ALGOL 68. Mathematisch Centrum, Amsterdam, October 1969. Second printing, MR 101

[WAB+68] Walk, K., et al.: Abstract syntax and interpretation of PL/I. Technical report 25.082, IBM Laboratory Vienna, ULD Version II, June 1968

[Wal67] Walk, K.: Minutes of the 1st meeting of IFIP WG 2.2 on Formal Language Description Languages. Kept in the van Wijngaarden archive: Held in Porto Conte. Alghero, Sardinia (1967)

[Wal69] Walk, K.: Minutes of the 3rd Meeting of IFIP WG 2.2 on Formal Language Description Languages, April 1969. Held in Vienna, Austria

[Wei75] Weissenböck. F.: A formal interface specification. Technical report TR 25.141, IBM Laboratory Vienna, February 1975

[Win93] Winskel, G.: The Formal Semantics of Programming Languages. The MIT Press (1993). ISBN 0-262-23169-7

[Woo93] Woodman, M.: A taste of the Modula-2 standard. ACM SIGPLAN Not. **28**(9), 15–24 (1993)

[Yon90] Yonezawa, A. (ed.): ABCL: An Object-Oriented Concurrent System. MIT Press, Cambridge (1990). ISBN 0-262-24029-7

Author Index

Printed in the United States
By Bookmasters

Printed in the United States
By Bookmasters